Contents

ILLUSTRATIONS

Dramatis Personae

SARA BAARTMAN, known in Europe as the Hottentot Venus, also as Saartje, Sartjee, and as Sarah Bartmann

DAVID FOURIE, settler, Sara's first master

CORNELIUS MULLER, settler, Sara's second master

RIDER BAARTMAN, Sara's brother

PIETER CESARS, Hendrik's brother, Elzer's employee, and the man who brought Sara to Cape Town

JAN MICHAEL ELZER, the wealthy butcher, Sara's first master in Cape Town

HENDRIK CESARS, husband of Anna Catharina Staal and one of two men who brought Sara to England

ANNA CATHARINA STAAL, wife of Hendrik Cesars

HENDRIK VAN JONG, Sara's Dutch partner

JOHANNES JACOBUS VOS, president of the Burgher Senate, to whom Hendrik Cesars was indebted

ALEXANDER DUNLOP, ship's surgeon in his Royal Britannic Navy, and doctor at the Cape Slave Lodge, one of two men who brought Sara to England

WILLIAM BULLOCK, owner of the Liverpool Museum, also known as the London Museum and the Egyptian Museum

"SAINT" ZACHARY MACAULAY, leading abolitionist, who led the investigation into her status in England

"SAINT" THOMAS BABINGTON, leading abolitionist

STEPHEN GASELEE (also spelled "Gaslee"), Dunlop's attorney, knighted in 1815, Justice of Common Pleas 1824–37, served as a model for "Mr. Justice Stareleigh" in Dickens's *The Pickwick Papers*

DUKE OF QUEENSBERRY ("OLD Q"), famous London rake who had Sara brought for a viewing at his house in Piccadilly

HENRY TAYLOR, the man who brought Sara to Paris

REAUX, the animal trainer and store owner in Paris and likely member of a theatrical troupe in Cape Town, and Sara's last owner

GEORGES CUVIER, scientist and founder of comparative anatomy

SARA BAARTMAN
AND THE
HOTTENTOT VENUS

INTRODUCTION

❧✦❧

S ara Baartman and the Hottentot Venus have had mysterious careers. Sara Baartman was born on the South African frontier in the 1770s. She lived nearly three decades in South Africa. She then spent some five years in Europe before dying in Paris at the end of 1815. Sara Baartman loved, and was loved, and for many years before she went to Europe she was a mother and a working woman in the Cape. Yet she has come down to us in history captured by the icon of the Hottentot Venus, a supposedly paradoxical freak of race and sexuality, both alluring and primitive, the very embodiment of desire and the importance of conquering the instincts. Writings on Sara Baartman have subsumed the life of this beautiful woman almost totally in those brief, if momentous, years she spent in Europe displayed as the Hottentot Venus. A short period at the end of her life has come to stand for all that passed before.[1]

In Cape Town, and then in England and in Paris, Sara Baartman as the Hottentot Venus fancied and troubled the minds of people who, in their often quotidian ways, helped fashion the modern world. It was, by all accounts, an extraordinary epoch. During her lifetime American colonists declared their independence and quashed Native American cultures. In Saint Domingue, slaves revolted and created Haiti, a new society free of the plantation master but still full of sorrow. Across Europe revolutions came and went, in France by the stamp of feet and the guillotine's percussive thump. Napoleon's armies marched and perished. The masses moved in and out of the factories of Manchester, Liverpool, Birmingham, or worked on the docks of the great city of London. The Luddites rioted against the factory system. Gas lighting came to Soho. King George III went insane. The Romantics imagined the beauties of nature, the emotions and the transcendental, the monstrous and the exotic. Scientists measured and classified the world.

Where, Europeans wondered, did the Hottentot Venus fit in the order of things? What makes us human? What is intellect, feeling, love? Many believed the Hottentot Venus was more ape than human, or that she represented a fifth category of human, a *Homo sapiens monstrous*, a kind of Frankenstein's monster scarcely capable of emotion and intelligence yet also a reminder of the primitive living deep within the self.

That fiction became a constant presence throughout much of Europe during the nineteenth and twentieth centuries. On Baartman's death in December 1815, Georges Cuvier, then Europe's most revered scientist and the father of comparative anatomy, eagerly dissected her body for his investigations and remade her in a plaster cast as the Hottentot Venus. Sara Baartman disappeared from history as the identity she had performed onstage and in Europe's halls was entombed in science and figured ever more prominently in the Western imagining of women, race, and sexuality: the primitive woman with extraordinarily large buttocks and, so many were told, remarkable sexual organs. A huge illustration of the Hottentot Venus greeted the tens of thousands of visitors who crowded into the Universal Exhibition in Paris in 1889, and her plaster cast was made available to the more than thirty-one million people attending the International Exhibition of 1937, just before the outbreak of the Second World War when ideas about the supposed inferiority of the races nearly destroyed Europe. Dickens and Darwin, Hugo, Freud, Picasso, Eliot, H. G. Wells, James Joyce, and many others knew or wrote of the Hottentot Venus, as did the most important writers on the so-called inferiority of the darker races. "Every one, the basest creatures, every Hottentot," Wells wrote, "every stunted creature that ever breathed poison in a slum, knows that the instinctive constitution of man is at fault here and that fear is shameful and must be subdued." The Hottentot figured in Gobineau's famous *Essay on the Inequality of the Human Races* (1855), one of the foundational texts in the rise of modern racism and translated and published throughout Europe and America. The *Essay* was especially influential in the American South and in Germany in the decades that led to spectacle lynching and to the Holocaust. As the venerable *Edinburgh Review* put it in 1863, "There is no vast difference between the intelligence of a Bosjesman and that of an oran-ùtan, and that the difference is far greater between Descartes or Homer and the Hottentot than between the stupid Hottentot and the ape."[2]

The Hottentot Venus confirmed to Europeans the inferiority of the Hottentot and people with dark skins. It also confirmed the inequality and unfitness of all women, for women were closer to nature, and the Hottentot Venus was closest of all. "Hottentot women," Robert Knox wrote in his *Races of Man*, "offer certain peculiarities more strongly marked than in any other race"—by which the Scottish anatomist, infamous for stealing corpses, meant women's buttocks and genitals. The sexual body determined character, being even. Politicians and bureaucrats devised laws throughout Europe to control the biological deviance of prostitutes and their Hottentot sexuality that preyed on men. Well into the twentieth century, doctors in Europe and America excised women's genitals to make them less pronounced, less like those of the Hottentot Venus, to better control their presumed sexual cravings and brute drives.[3]

In the 1940s and 1950s, Percival Kirby, a Scottish musicologist working in South Africa, wrote a series of articles on the Hottentot Venus. Most everyone had forgotten about the Hottentot Venus, even if her ghost continued shaping people's perception of black women's sexuality. Feminism helped her resurrection. In the 1980s the Hottentot Venus returned, as a symbol not of sexual excess and racial inferiority but of all the terrible things the West has done to others. Scholars started reading Kirby. His investigations became the basis for poems, plays, sculptures, and other representations that now powerfully depicted the terrible display of the Hottentot Venus in Europe as the moniker of everything wrong with Western civilization: Enlightenment science, racism, the abuse and exploitation of women, the travesties of colonialism, and the exoticization of non-Western peoples—the so-called "Other."

Sara Baartman also reappeared in South Africa. In 1994, apartheid ended. South Africans began demanding the return of Baartman's remains for proper burial in the place of her birth. The French refused: they claimed her body was theirs. Baartman's history became the grist of domestic and international politics. Baartman emerged as South Africa's "mother and her life as the Hottentot Venus a reminder of the injustices black South Africans have endured over the past three and a half centuries." For the French, retaining the body meant defending the power and enlightenment of French science. But science so clearly tied to race could not win: Sara Baartman was reburied in a state funeral in South Africa on National Women's Day in August 2002.

In the 1990s, Sara Baartman thus began appearing from history's shadows. But who *was* this person who became the Hottentot Venus? Until very recently when the question has been posed, if it has been posed at all, the answer has focused on the five years Baartman lived in Europe and performed as the Hottentot Venus. Various publics around the world took the European representations of Sara Baartman and turned them on their head to expose modernity's darker side. Scholars used Kirby's work as gospel, assuming that nothing could be found out about Sara Baartman's life in South Africa: her colonial history either remained of no interest or was presumed inaccessible.[4]

As historians working on topics such as colonialism, race, gender and sexuality, we wondered if a different approach to Sara Baartman's life might be possible. What if we looked at the totality of her life and resisted the temptation of reading her history backward as a story of inevitable victimization? How might the past look then?

We began work on Sara Baartman's life in 2003, fascinated by the tremendous, perhaps impossible, burden that seemed to be placed on this African woman who lived in the late eighteenth and early nineteenth centuries. We began innocently, perhaps naively, wanting to discover the person behind the Hottentot Venus, where necessary to set the record straight, to tell the story of a woman who grew up in South Africa and who was killed in Europe by a figment of other people's imagination.

The journey took us to three continents and research in five countries in more than a dozen archives and libraries. We tried to track down every possibly relevant record in the period especially from about 1750 to 1816, and then from the 1990s to the present. We conducted genealogical research to identify some of the possible relatives of Sara Baartman. Discussions with people brought us from the outskirts of Port Elizabeth to the small town of Graaff Reinet to the desolate and impoverished community of Lavender Hill near Cape Town. We spoke as well to various interested parties. Some people refused to speak with us. Others requested anonymity. What seemed like a puzzle, the search for pieces of evidence to complete a picture, became more like a mystery full of twists and turns with

one issue leading inexplicably to another and some questions left unan-
swered and perhaps unanswerable.[5]

All the while the very act of writing raised perplexing issues. We learned
that biography was a genre more suited to the life of the Hottentot Venus
than to the fragments recorded for posterity about Sara Baartman, even as
we still found out far more about the person than people had thought the
records would reveal. Fixing Sara Baartman within the conventional genre
of biography raises fundamental questions about how we know what we
know and how we write about people whose lives traversed so many geographies and different cultural worlds. Sara Baartman's life confounds conventional narrative biography in at least two senses. She was in many senses
one of the "defeated and the lost" whose history, as one philosopher put
it, "cries out for vengeance and calls for narrative."[6] Yet the closer we get
to the defeated and the lost, the more fragmentary the evidentiary record
becomes. This is the case not simply with Sara Baartman but with the
great swath of humanity, the billions of people who bequeath posterity
the simple lineaments of their lives. Sara gave only one interview during
her life, in London, and it was given in Dutch, under the watchful eyes
of officers of a court, and then translated and handed down to history as
a paraphrase. Two other interviews in Paris are probably fictive. These are
not the materials most biographers have to work with. Sara Baartman left,
then, mere fragments of history.

Biography also promises "to satisfy the lingering desire for a solid world
peopled by knowable characters"[7] by arranging the life of a person absent
its strangeness, as if culture was but the patina etched by history upon a
universal unchanging self. Biography, however, emerged at a particular
time and place in Europe's imagining of the self; indeed, biographical
writing was being crafted in Sara Baartman's lifetime. It emerged along
with the idea of the possessive individual, that person who has agency,
autonomy, a vision of self. This idea of the person, of the self, is not so
easily transferred to anytime and anyplace and to worlds where there is no
clearly possessive subject, no "me," "myself."[8]

And live she did. Should history write only of people at the moment of
their fame, or of people with sufficient privilege to preserve in the present
the lineaments of their lives? We think not. We are drawn to Sara Baartman's life and to the strange legacies of the Hottentot Venus. Therein one

can find many fascinating, if disturbing, stories. But her story—or perhaps their stories—also is a cautionary tale about silence and the limits of history, and about what happens when someone, or something, comes to stand for too much, when the past can bear no more.

Europeans created the Hottentot Venus as the living missing link separating beast from man, the drives from the intellect, the anxious space between our animal and human selves. Sara entered Europe's psyche, modernity's psyche, not as a woman, a living, breathing person with emotions and memories and longings, but as a metaphor, a figment, a person reduced to a simulacrum. That figment subsumed the person. We will always know more about the phantom that haunts the Western imagination, a phantom so complete that it has nearly become a living, breathing person, than we do about the life of Sara Baartman, the human being who was ultimately destroyed by an illusion.

These paradoxes and silences give us pause. Ghosts haunt these pages. The thousands of people hunted down and murdered on South Africa's eastern frontier appear as partial and veiled images, fragments or traces really. So also those forced into servitude. Sara survived an era of extraordinary violence when all across the world native peoples died out and colonial societies were made and remade and the modern world was born. In South Africa, for the survivors of genocide and colonial violence, the many dead abandoned without proper burial became ghosts visiting in the dry winds of the African veld. Sara lived in a world shattered by violence.

To many South Africans during the 1990s, as the country made its miraculous if painful transition to democracy, Sara remained a mournful spirit exiled from her land of birth; only a proper burial in South Africa might allow her spirit to become an ancestor. And yet she remains imprisoned still, literally behind bars that surround her grave site, but also ensnared by diverse people's expectations, by histories that remain traumatic. In large parts of Africa ancestors are revered but also allowed to finally die, to pass on, ultimately to be forgotten. This book is about discovery, about what really might have happened, and about the extraordinary power of people's imaginations. It also is about letting go, another burial of sorts.

I

WINDS OF THE CAMDEBOO

Sara Baartman, the story goes, was born in 1789 in the Gamtoos River valley where she is buried today. Baartman was taken as a young child out of the wilds of Africa to Cape Town and then, as a young woman, to England and France, where she died before her time. In fact, Sara Baartman, or, as she was known in the Cape and in London, Saartje Baartman, was born a decade earlier, in the 1770s. And she was born not in the Gamtoos River valley, but some fifty miles to the north. Many misunderstandings of Sara's life have flowed from these simple mistakes, and from the assumption that historical research in South Africa would yield little knowledge.[1]

Sara spent her early years in the Camdeboo, the "Green Valley" in the Khoekhoe language she spoke as a child. The Camdeboo is a five-thousand-square-mile ancient valley that bridges the great arid Karroo to the west and, to the east, the wetter lands nourished by the rivers flowing down from the Winter Mountains. In times immemorial it was an exuberant swampland populated by bewildering creatures, the fossilized remains of which have attracted scientists for nearly three centuries; the fact that Sara came from an ancient land would heighten the curiosity of European scientists who imagined in her body the early biological history of our species. Over many thousands of years the swampland turned to veld, or prairie, the skeletons of gargantuan crocodiles and the few springs that broke through the surface the only reminders of the valley's swamp beginnings. Today the region is almost entirely scrubland.[2]

When Sara's parents were children around the middle of the eighteenth century, vast numbers of animals still lived in the valley, rhinoceroses, elephants, lions, leopards, and jackals. There were huge herds of wildebeests, eland with long, curved horns like scythes, and animals like the quagga, a kind of cross between a horse and a zebra whose final numbers died in faraway lands like Amsterdam and King Louis XIV's menagerie at Versailles. These animals numbered not in the thousands but in the tens of thousands. In the springbok migrations, what farmers called the *trek-bokke*, the "traveling buck," the animals moved into the Camdeboo in the hundreds of thousands, perhaps even in the millions. The entire valley turned brown and white as the animals ate the veld to the ground. The vast oceanic herd might take three or four days to pass through the valley, the sound of their stamping hooves beating into the mountains.

"Khoekhoe" means "men of men."[3] Most lived as pastoralists. In the seventeenth century and into the early eighteenth century the Inqua chiefdom controlled much of the Camdeboo. They occasionally fought the Sonaqua, hunter-gatherers who preyed on their stock from mountain strongholds. Sara Baartman's descendants lived among the Gonaqua, who inhabited the far eastern edge of the Camdeboo and southward along the Sundays River valley. The meaning of the word "Gonaqua" has disappeared, nor do we know when people first began using the word to describe themselves. At the beginning of the eighteenth century the Gonaqua numbered perhaps twelve to sixteen thousand people. The land was especially bountiful in the area near Sara's natal home near the Reed and Bird rivers. A dribble of small streams descending the Tooth Mountains offered people and livestock easy access to clean water. Gonaqua moved their stock up and down the valleys in search of nourishing grasses. Some lived in more or less permanent settlements near rivers or around the few springs that pierced the earth like the one that became Baartman's Fonteyn.

Immediately to the east of Gonaqua lands lay the Xhosa, who spoke a different (Bantu) language and who, in addition to keeping cattle, farmed small plots of land. By 1700 contact between the two groups had been taking place for well over a century, occasionally violently but most often peacefully. Xhosa men occasionally took Gonaqua women as their wives. Some Gonaqua entered Xhosa chiefdoms, and both groups traded goods such as beads. There were subtle shifts in language as well. But Gonaqua never adopted agriculture, practiced circumcision, or employed a strict system of patrilineal reckoning. And, unlike the Xhosa, their women milked the cows.

Communities ranged from a single extended family to more than two hundred people. The clan that would earn the surname "Baartman" likely

FIGURE 1.1. "Female Hottentot with Child." Hand-colored aquatint, c. 1822. E. F. Steeb. Image provided by Iziko Museums of Cape Town.

numbered around thirty or forty people; this we know from the records of men contracted to labor for white farmers.[4] The clan had a leader, but while Khoekhoe occasionally had politically weak chiefs, they had no need for elaborate genealogies or the heroic stories of kings and princes. Authority was rarely heritable and depended, instead, on prowess and good fortune. Men herded sheep and cattle and hunted. Women gathered tubers, berries, and insects and helped with the animals. At night they made sure they protected their stock from lions and leopards.

Sara grew up on a colonist's farm, over the years her extended family drawn into the orbit of colonial servitude. Sara earned her Dutch name "Saartjie" as a child on a farm during a time of breathtaking violence. Her first name is the Cape Dutch form for "Sara" that marked her as a colonist's servant. "Saartjie," the diminutive, was also often a sign of affection. Encoded in her first name were the tensions of affection and exploitation. Her surname literally means "bearded man" in Dutch. It also means uncivilized, uncouth, barbarous, savage. Saartje Baartman—the savage servant.

Her parents likely lived on land claimed by a settler. In 1763, the Cape government granted David Fourie a (very) roughly six-thousand-acre swath of Camdeboo pastureland. It was located about fifteen miles east of the small town of Jansenville and sixty miles from the Indian Ocean, and close to the old wagon road that connected the coast with the prosperous farming town of Graaff Reinet. Fourie called his farm Baartman's Fonteyn, the "savage's fountain" or spring. Fourie likely laid claim to the spring precisely because it sustained the Gonaqua's flocks of cattle and sheep. Savage's Spring both acknowledged the Gonaqua's presence and then denied them a right to it by the very act of naming his farm. Baartman's Fonteyn lay near the Reed (Riet) River beneath the Tooth Mountains. Farmers called this area the Zwartland, the Black Land, the Land of the Blacks. Northeast of the farm lay the Bruintjieshoogte, the "Brown People's Heights," where colonists took the lands of the Gonaqua, pillaged communities, and raised sheep and cattle for the East Indies trade. The farm has long since disappeared. The only unremembered traces we have today are registered in some of those who today share the Baartman surname.[5]

Sara had a Gonaqua childhood, though one touched, increasingly so, by the farmer Fourie and the world he brought to the Camdeboo. When she was born in the 1770s, women would have buried the placenta and salved her skin with a balm of buchu root and animal fat. Sara's parents gave her a name that disappeared amid the violence of the late eighteenth century. The record is silent as to whether in adulthood Sara remembered the names she had lived by in the Eastern Cape. Given her precise knowledge of Khoekhoe culture, Sara likely did, and equally likely she kept such knowledge to herself, knowing that all around her were people who would not, perhaps could not, understand. The name tied her to the world outside the hut, to the animals, plants, to the fortunes and sorrows of her birth, and especially to the winds of the Camdeboo. For every person had her own breath of air that continued after one's body lay safe beneath a rock cairn, the breeze that carries away a child's first writhing gulp and crying exhale.[6]

The modern Western world is so accustomed to the concept of the fixed person and self, the person tied to the body, that it is difficult to imagine other possibilities. Sara would have had an array of names connected to the conditions of her birth, daily life, kin, clan, duties, and rights. The Gonaqua had no clearly marked word for either "I" or "me" or, for that

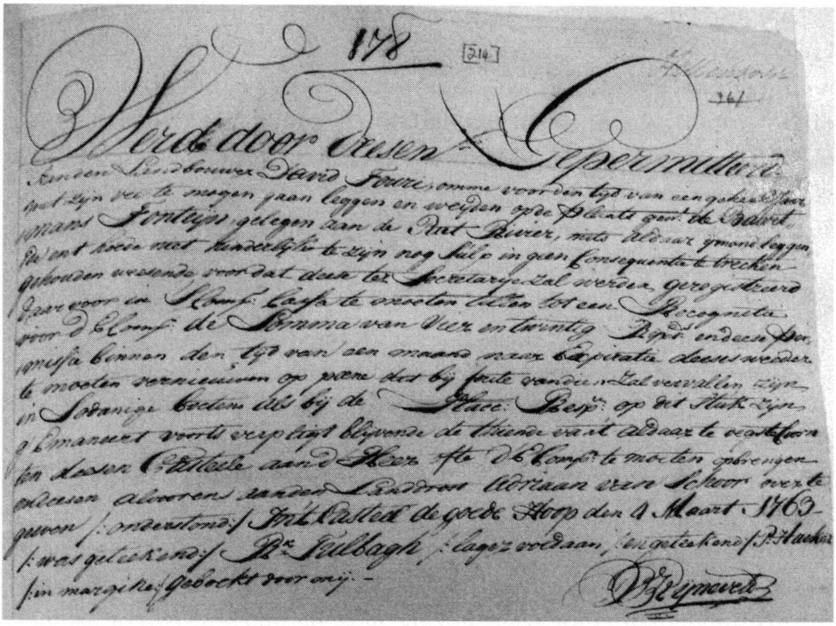
178

Word door deesen Gepermitteerd
aan den Landbouwer David Fourie, omme voor den tyd van een geheel Jaar
met zyn vee te mogen gaan leggen en weyden op de plaats genaamd de Baartmans Fonteyn

't Casteel de Goede Hoop den 4 Maart 1763

FIGURE 1.2. The title deed registering the farm Baartman's Fonteyn to David Fouri, 4 March 1763. Reproduced with permission of the Cape Archives.

matter, "you." There might be dozens of words that referred to one of these pronouns. "You" and "we" seem hopelessly connected. Yet some of the words for "I" also mean "you" and, as well, the flesh of the eland though which a person's blood flows.

The Gonaqua gazed upon the stars and moon and danced to the eland, turning their arms into horns and their feet into hooves stamping the ground. They danced because all the animals were once men and women in the time of the First People. The great antelope was both ancestor and oneself. As a young child Sara would have watched as kith and kin danced to the eland, became the antelope, and she listened to the stories of her parents and elders. One story concerned death. The Moon, Khoekhoe said, carries the soul away, the spirits of the dead held in its bone-white palm. Once we lived forever beneath the southern skies. Moon promised that we would rise from the places where we fell, to live and to walk with the animals on the veld. But Hare, Moon's messenger, lied. Moon became mad, and in his anger we lost our immortality.

Sara learned as well how Tortoise could defeat the selfish, undeserving
Hyena that preyed on the weak, how wise Tortoise brought rain from the
mountains and good fortune to those who remembered its lessons. Stories
of the tortoise were in part masculine stories speaking of a woman's body,
of the temptations of sex, and of the responsibilities of elders to teach the
young the ways of the world. Years later Sara received a tortoise necklace
after her first menstruation as she began to learn about sexuality and the
obligations of men and women, the respect accorded each. Sara brought
the tortoiseshell necklace to Europe, her last, her only, physical connection
to a world she had lost.[7]

Much of what we know of the Gonaqua comes from various travelers'
reports and from the official records of the Dutch East India Company
that ruled the Cape from 1652 until 1795. The Gonaqua attracted the
attention of various Enlightenment explorers interested in collecting flora
and fauna and describing the noble savage before his apocalyptic fall at
the hands of Western civilization. The great scientist Carolus Linnaeus, to
whom we owe the biological classification of "genus" and who produced
the first modern attempt at organizing all of nature, sent two of his most
brilliant students to the Cape. Carl Peter Thunberg made it past the Gamtoos and into Gonaqua country in the early years of the 1770s. There he
visited a Khoekhoe leader who "paid us a visit in the evening, and encamped with part of his people not far from us." Gonaqua "had fine cattle," and from whom Thunberg "got milk. . . . in plenty." He visited a few
of the very large communities

> consisting of a great many round huts, disposed in a circular form. The
> people crowded forward in shoals to our waggon, and our tobacco seemed
> to have the same effect on them as the magnet has on iron. The number
> of grown persons, appeared to me to amount to at least two or three hun-
> dred.. . . . To the chief of them we presented some looking-glasses, and were
> highly diverted at seeing the many pranks these simple people played with
> them. . . . they even looked at the back of the glass, to see whether the same
> figure presented itself as they saw in the glass.[8]

Linnaeus's other student, Anders Sparrman, headed to the Cape in
1771, where the young explorer joined Captain Cook on the second voyage of the *Resolution* and its voyages across the southern oceans to New
Zealand and Tahiti. Arriving in England in July 1775, the twenty-seven-

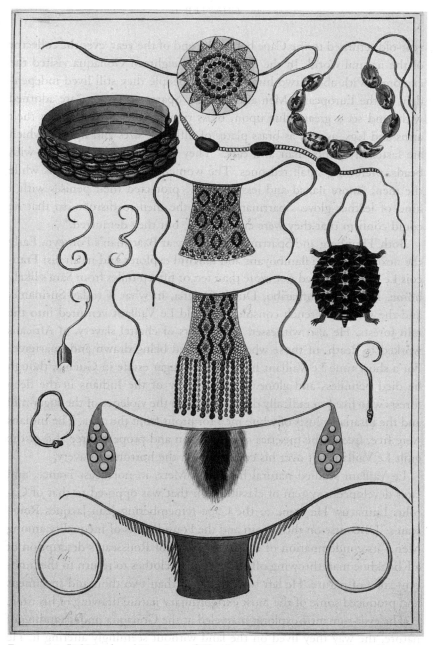

FIGURE 1.3. "16 Numbered Drawings of Clothing and Ornaments . . . " From *François le Vaillant, Traveller in South Africa, and His Collection of 165 Water-colour Paintings 1781–1784.* 2 v. illus. (part col.), vol. 1. Cape Town, Library of Parliament, 1973, plate 67. Permission of Library of Parliament. Accession number 34340.

year-old returned to the Cape before the end of the year, ever the collector of the natural world. In the Eastern Cape eighteen Gonaqua visited the explorer. With about two hundred other people they still lived independent of the Europeans. Men and women, Sparrman wrote, "are adorned with, and set a great value upon, brass rings, which they wear on their arms and legs, as well as brass plates of different sizes and figures, which are fastened in their hair and ears." They also adorned themselves with beads, preferring small red ones. The women wore leather aprons while the men, "more naked and less covered," protected their penises with a kind of leather glove. Sparrman begged the men to disrobe, so that he could confirm that they were circumcised, but they demurred.[9]

Both Thunberg and Sparrman traveled near Baartman's Fonteyn. Early the next decade the flamboyant and fanciful explorer and naturalist François Le Vaillant passed not more than ten or fifteen miles from Sara's likely home. Born in Paramaribo, Dutch Guiana, in what is today Suriname, and the son of a French consul, as a child Le Vaillant ventured into the rain forests. He also witnessed the horrors of chattel slavery, of Africans worked to death, of those who had resisted being drawn and quartered. For a short time Le Vaillant had owned a sugar estate in Guiana, though he died penniless and alone. He also knew of the Indians in the deep forests who lived so radically differently from the violence of the sugar mill and the insatiable lusts of white men for profit from the cane. The Indians were free, free of the miseries of civilization and property, free also of the guilt Le Vaillant felt over his complicity in the horrors of slavery.

Le Vaillant studied natural history at Metz, in northeast France, and later developed a system of classification that was opposed to that of Carolus Linnaeus. He came to the Cape remembering Jean-Jacques Rousseau's "Discourse on the Origin and the Foundations of Inequality among Men," its condemnation of civilization, and of Rousseau's description of a Khoekhoe man throwing off his European clothes to return to the innocent state of nature. He left with no fewer than two thousand specimens and produced some of the most extraordinary nature drawing of his time.

The ever-romantic explorer marveled at the Gonaqua understanding of nature, the way they lived on the land without seemingly altering it. He praised their men, their hunting prowess, and the "reciprocal offerings of friendship" that made one whole. Le Vaillant glorified their women whom he considered beautiful and chaste. He fell in love with a woman whose name he could not understand but whom he called Narina, the "gentle Narina" named after a Khoekhoe flower. The two spent many days together, the young woman and the thirty-year-old eccentric with his beard and ostrich plume hat, the two running across the Camdeboo, sharing food, exchanging glances. Narina accepted the explorer's presents and stopped painting her body with ochre and charcoal, which, "she knew. . . . was disagreeable to me." When they departed, Le Vaillant "bereaved myself of all my trinkets to adorn her," but no presents could console his beautiful Narina, who he said had sunk into a deep melancholia.[10]

These reports shed no direct light on Sara or on the farm Baartman's Fonteyn. What they do indicate is the fascination Europeans had for the Khoekhoe, particularly the Gonaqua. By the end of the eighteenth century more had been written about the "Hottentots" than any other ethnic group south of the Sahara Desert. They had become the subject of acute fascination by some of Europe's finest thinkers. Linnaeus had classified Hottentots within the category of *Homo sapiens monstrous* that included wolf-boys, wild girls, and the like, believing that male Hottentots had but one testicle. The philosophes Rousseau, Voltaire, and Diderot invoked the Hottentot in what was then the single most important philosophical topic of the day, the science of man and the history of civilization.

There was always a tension within European reportage. Seventeenth-century observers typically portrayed Khoekhoe as a dirty, even vile people. In the more romantic imagination in the second half of the eighteenth century, Gonaqua often earned the reputation for being kind and generous, and their women fair and beautiful. Whatever was repugnant and debased owed to contact with the West.

Herein lay what would become a fundamental and enduring debate between the importance of nature and culture in the history of humanity. Sara Baartman would figure prominently within this debate, one that continues today in discussions of the relative power of nature and nurture. In the nineteenth century, however, as biology became the regnant discipline, scientists became interested less in the cultural life of the Khoekhoe than with their bodies, and particularly the female body and its reproductive organs. Biology, as it were, trumped history and culture. The Venus Hottentot became the essence of primitiveness, and then of the primitiveness of female sexuality. In the triumphs of science there was little room for history in the short term or for the messy complexities of the past.

NARINA, JEUNE GONAQUOISE. *Tom.1.er Pag.370.*

FIGURE 1.4. "Narina, jeune Gonaquoise." From François le Vaillant, *Voyage de F. Le Vaillant dans l'intérieur de l'Afrique, par le Cap de Bonne-Espérance.* Paris: Chez Déterville, 1796, plate 11.

That messiness in large part is located in South Africa's colonial history. In the eighteenth century Gonaqua offered to the Dutch East India Company, which then ruled the Cape, the prospect of being trading partners, exchanging African livestock for European brass and other items. The Asian trade and the emergence of Cape Town as a major port linking the Atlantic and Indian oceans created a demand for foodstuffs to sustain the growing port city and the sailors voyaging to the Indies, the Coromandel Coast, Brazil, the Netherlands, the farthest reaches of the explored world. Ever the monopolist, the company was committed to trade, not settlement, in peaceful cooperation with native peoples whenever it served the world's first multinational corporation best. It recognized some as chiefs, or "captains," as people with whom it might be able to acquire cattle and sheep in exchange for various trading goods. Officials gave these captains an absurdly heavy and awkward staff, a *palangbanger,* a word taken from the Dutch colonial experience in Southeast Asia, that had at its head had "a fearful great brass head bearing the Company's arms."[11] Khoekhoe captains jealously guarded their *palangbangers,* lugging the staffs around and displaying them to the few European visitors who passed by or using them when trading cattle to company servants.

Through the middle of the eighteenth century most of the Europeans who came among the Gonaqua were intrepid hunters who occasionally strayed among them in pursuit of elephant tusk, shooting the beast again and again until the great animal collapsed, then lumbering back to Cape Town with their prize. The hunters brought back stories of Khoekhoe rich in sheep and cattle. Soon more traders began visiting in search of Khoekhoe stock. Few ventured very far past the Gamtoos River, and those who did left almost as soon as they had arrived, returning over the western hills with ivory tusks strapped to their horses or bringing cattle and sheep back to Cape Town.

The second half of the century was remarkably different, particularly the years around Sara's birth and childhood. By the time Le Vaillant visited the Gonaqua, smallpox had "made its baleful appearance" and "swept off half their people."[12] West of the Gamtoos, Sparrman met a Khoekhoe man who "had, a few months before, reigned over above a hundred" people, but now had become shepherd of a white man's flocks. "We saw," Sparrman continued, numbers of fugitive Hottentots of both sexes who were no longer pursued, "partly on account of their age and infirmities, and partly because it was not worth any colonist's while to lay hold them, as they would be liable to be demanded back by their former masters. One of these that I passed on the road, a very old man, died (as I was told) the day after of weakness and fatigue."[13]

The Hottentots, Thunberg wrote,

> were constantly obliged to give way, and retire farther into the country. The Dutch always took possession at first of the best and most fertile parts of the land, in the wider valleys, leaving to the Hottentots, for a little while longer, the inferior tracts, between the mountains, in the narrower vales, till, at length, the poor savages were driven even out of these, and obliged to entirely quit their beloved native land.[14]

Because Sara was born in the 1770s, and not at the end of the 1780s, she experienced this very transformation. She lived on Baartman's Fonteyn, a large expanse of grazing land where in all likelihood Khoekhoe "kraals and [Boer] habitations were mixed."[15] David Fourie claimed the land, but his control remained at best tenuous. She lived in a world no longer African, but not clearly colonial either. Europeans began settling among the Gonaqua after the middle of the eighteenth century, descendants of the original free burghers (*vrijburghers*), religious refugees, and rough men who jumped ship to seek their fortunes on land. Fourie descended from the French Huguenots who settled in the rolling mountains near Cape Town in the late 1680s during Europe's Counter-Reformation and the persecution of Protestants throughout much of France in the century following the Council of Trent. In the Cape's congenial Mediterranean climate, the Fouries reproduced prolifically and by the early part of the eighteenth century they could be found across a stretch of land nearly four hundred miles into the interior. The Fouries arrived in Africa poor, and for at least a century few if any prospered. David's penury forced him into a late marriage; he was twenty-nine when, in 1751, he took the hand of Louisa Erasmus, who would bear no fewer than ten children.[16]

David Fourie came to the Camdeboo and into the Gonaqua world a middle-aged man of forty-one with most of his life well past. The Fouries arrived in a wagon with wheels greased with fat, and near the spring they built a crude one-room home of earthen floors with three- or four-foot-high walls. Strips of meat hung from the rafters amid the smells of butter, milk, and sweat. They had long dreamed of a decent house with rooms

FIGURE 1.5. "Camp at Camdeboo, Where the Two Black Brothers Dwelt." From *François le Vaillant: Traveller in South Africa, and His Collection of 165 Water-colour Paintings.* 2 v. illus. (part col.), vol. 1. Cape Town, Library of Parliament, 1973, plate 14. Permission of the Cape Archives.

set off in two wings and large herds of cattle and sheep they could trade for Belgium linen, cotton from India, blue porcelain from China, coffee, tobacco, and sugar, but David Fourie and his family never amounted to much.

The Gonaqua living near the spring made room for David Fourie and his family, helping the settlers, tending their livestock, hunting, teaching Fourie the lay of the land. Mostly they would have kept to themselves, watching over their own animals and trying to live much as they always had except for an apprehension that their world was changing in ways they could neither clearly identify nor control.

The Baartmans met Khoekhoe coming to the Camdeboo disfigured by disease and with stories of violence and death at the hands of settlers. The horrors they described became real in the 1770s, the very decade when Sara was born on the farm and the Khoekhoe began serving their new master. The settlers formed commandos (posses), sometimes two or three hundred strong, capturing large flocks of sheep and herds of cattle. They also hunted people. In September 1775, a commando including Fourie men killed nearly 200 people and captured more than thirty "little ones" in ten days of violence. A single raid killed 122 and captured 21 children. The commando camped just miles from the farm. Stories of the massacres likely spread among the Baartmans at the farm.[17]

David joined a commando of six other farmers in late August 1779 as the planets danced their way westward and the moon sat bright and fat in the evening sky. At daybreak they drank their coffee, stuffed cheap tobacco in their pipes, broke camp, and mounted their horses with the morning's mist lifting from the veld. Eight days later the farmers had slaughtered twenty-six people and captured five before heading back to their homes in the Camdeboo, Fourie mortally wounded. He brought back a "hottentot child." The men bound the captive, securing a rope from the child's wrists to Fourie's saddle. The small, young child straggled alongside him, alone and hungry and terrified. By the time the two of them reached the farm, Fourie was slumped in his saddle. Louisa attended to her husband's injury, but Fourie surrendered to his wound.[18]

One is tempted to imagine that this young child was Sara Baartman. A captive tale would add drama and would dovetail with the desire to imagine Sara Baartman's early life as one in which she is ripped from a pristine and innocent African world. The captive tale is a narrative structure that is widespread in Western literature and popular culture. A Parisian newspaper article written near the time of Sara's death, where Sara is betrothed to a prince only to be captured and her people slaughtered, also participated in this fiction. And wouldn't it be comforting in a way to have such a clear and dramatic tale of dispossession and exploitation drive the story of Saartje Baartman. And yet, it seems that her life unfolded more prosaically, in the myriad small horrors of a frontier colonialism.

For nearly a generation the Baartmans must have lived worrying that their relationship with David Fourie might sour, or that the violence overrunning the Camdeboo would finally reach their kraal. Fourie's death in 1779 shattered life at Baartman's Fonteyn. Louisa was now a widow with children who were leaving home, poor and surrounded by people whose world she did not understand. She struggled for a while but, in the 1780s, unable to cope with the harshness of frontier life, Louisa abandoned the farm and liquidated its meager assets, including the Africans who lived on the farm.

The Baartman clan dispersed toward the end of the decade. Baartmans spread across the valley's farms. An orphan boy went to Johannes Scheepers to labor as a house servant. A large section of the clan was contracted to serve Johannes Hendrick Lubbe, a thirty-five-year-old colonist who held a farm to the north of Baartman's Fonteyn at the fork of the Renoster and Riet rivers. This information, fragments really, provides additional evidence that the Baartmans were located not in the Gamtoos but farther north. More important, these fragments are also redolent of the world within which Sara lived as a young child. A few of the Baartmans had Christian names—Isaac, Abraham, Jacob. This suggests that these were members of the second generation of people associated with European colonists. Two names reach to a world that was swiftly disappearing: Windvogel, the bird wind, but now with his new surname Baartman, and at the top of the list "Koning baartman." He would have been the clan leader, now reduced to being a servant, but called "king" in bureaucratic Dutch that inscribed his name in the indenture records of the Graaff Reinet district.[19]

In around 1779, Sara went with her immediate family to farms owned by a Cornelius Muller. A few years later they moved again with Muller to his farm, the Kraal of War near the Gamtoos River and a main wagon trail heading west to Cape Town. The move split Sara's family from the other Baartmans who remained in the Camdeboo, though many likely fled southward at century's end.[20]

Born in 1748, Cornelius grew up dirt poor on two farms in the Long Valley between the Zwartberg and Langkloof mountains on land taken from the Attaqua and other native Khoekhoe and Bushmen. As a young child Cornelius witnessed smallpox spread like a veld fire, killing large numbers of Khoekhoe. Cornelius could travel to Pieter Hendrik Ferreira's farm, Envy, passing "a great number of tombs, consisting of small heaps of stones." These were the graves of Khoekhoe who had "died of ulcers, in great numbers." They had succumbed to "the small pox which had made this extraordinary devastation."[21]

Cornelius's mother, Adriana, spent much of the time from her marriage to the early 1760s pregnant, producing no fewer than eleven children; Cornelius was the third child and the second son, born when his father was twenty-eight.[22] The Mullers were a kind of average family on the far-flung frontier, poor in property and prolific in progeny, with children scurrying about the homestead and Michiel keeping an eye on his eighty head of cattle and two hundred sheep.[23] Cornelius married in 1770, just two years after his father's untimely death. At about the same time the

Dutch government in Cape Town granted him no fewer than two farms in Hessequaland, a strip of territory between the Langeberg Mountains and the Indian Ocean. He took as his wife Susanna Elizabeth Ferreira, born in 1754, the daughter of a family famous for their exploits along the frontier.[24]

The eldest and always the most successful of the Mullers, Hillegert, settled in the east in the valleys of the Camdeboo beneath the Snow Mountains, where colonists could fine excellent veld for their stock. Here he became rich in slaves and sheep. When he returned to the Gamtoos region around 1793, Hillegert owned nearly twenty slaves and more than a thousand sheep, making him one of the wealthiest sheep farmers in the region.[25] Cornelius was never as successful as his older brother. In the late 1770s, with the demands of a growing family, the lure of wealth and the promise of richer grasses, and the growing successes of his older brother, Muller and his brood, now grown to five with the infant Andriana in swaddling and at Susanna's breast, climbed onto their ox-drawn wagon and moved east all the way to near the Coega River, where he had a loan farm for thirteen years until 1791. The family subsequently moved back across the Gamtoos to their farm the Kraal of War.

At the Kraal of War, Sara became a young woman. Her father worked the livestock, his wife and children performing domestic labor. Baartman senior occasionally ventured west, a four-month or even six-month trek helping to bring his master's livestock to Cape Town and returning with cloth and coffee and gunpowder. Sara learned Dutch, the settlers' language, as well as their manners and mannerisms. She heard stories from her father of faraway Cape Town. Where her parents would have once worn skins karosses, the beaten hides draped to protect the groin and across the breasts of women who had born children, Sara likely combined the kaross with old, ragged, spun clothes discarded by the farmer.

Sara also knew Gonaqua ways. She may have still seen men stalking their prey with bow and poisoned arrows, praying for forgiveness to spirits before the vanquished beast, or watched women mix sheep fat and ochre to color the body red and soothe the skin or to render on their bodies delicate lines of black and red like the eland. She may have heard stories that Gonaqua had told for generations, of the eland and the moon and of the meanings of the bit of tortoiseshell hung round her neck.

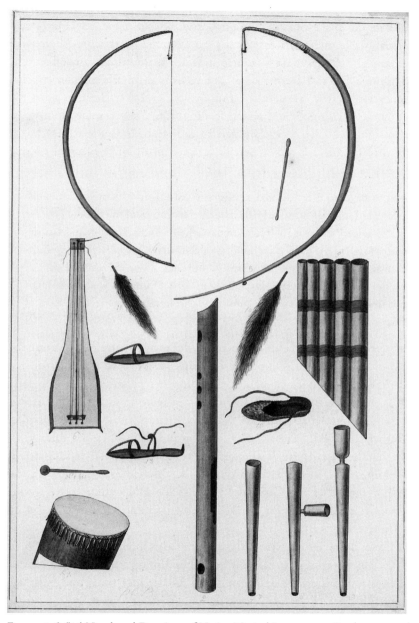

FIGURE 1.6. "14 Numbered Drawings of Native Musical Instruments, Implements and Shoes." From *François le Vaillant, Traveller in South Africa, and His Collection of 165 Water-colour Paintings 1781–1784*. Cape Town, Library of Parliament, 1973, plate 66. Permission of Library of Parliament. Accession number 34340.

But in the space of a childhood the world had changed rapidly and irrevocably. Neither song, dance, nor story offered protection. There were too many ghosts now. Sara was surrounded by extraordinary violence, "annihilation," "extermination" even. The records at times depict an epochal violence and terror: a recently captured boy bound by iron rings to the Boer's house; a woman and child bleeding from a merciless whipping; or a man who had tried to escape tied to the ground, beaten to death, his body thrown into a river. "There is scarcely an instance of cruelty," one explorer put it,

> said to have been committed against the slaves in the West-India islands, that could not find a parallel from the Dutch farmers of the remote districts of the colony towards the Hottentots in their service. Beating and cutting with thongs of the hide of the sea-cow or rhinoceros, are only gentle punishments, though these sort of whips. . . . are most horrid instruments. . . . Firing small shot into the legs and thighs of a Hottentot is a punishment not unknown to some of the monsters who inhabit the neighborhood of Camtoos river.[26]

In the late 1780s, Sara's life became definitively unmoored from the world of the Gonaqua. On one of the trips westward to Cape Town, her father died in an attack by bandits. Her mother passed away in the early 1790s, probably in her later thirties or early forties. Muller's life was also winding down. Cornelius Muller's dreams of living better than his father vanished. With Muller in debt and facing penury, one of his few valuable assets lay in his servants. The demand for laborers, particularly domestic servants, had grown considerably in Cape Town with the British conquest of the Cape in 1795. Muller could obtain some goods and money in exchange for a human being, making a profit and spiting his Khoekhoe servants.

A Cape Town trader passed through the area in the spring of 1795 or 1796, when sheep and cattle cared for their young and succulent grasses peeked through the veld. Spring was also the time for travel and business. Muller sold Sara to Pieter Cesars, the employee of a wealthy Cape merchant. He sold Sara as chattel; she was a slave in all but name (the Dutch would not allow people indigenous to an area to be enslaved). Sara walked away from the Kraal of War with the trader, rags for clothes, the tortoise-shell hanging from her neck.

Sara left in the mid-1790s, not in 1807; she was a young woman of about twenty. She would live in Cape Town for more than a decade before embarking for London. In the Eastern Cape, Sara had seen unspeakable acts of violence, bodies torn limb from limb. She had grown up in an apocalypse when the winds of the Camdeboo howled down through the valley. We know she treasured the tortoiseshell, she kept it all her life. And she would remember the stories her father had told her of the lands toward Cape Town, where the moon set carrying souls on its westward journey.

A few years after Sara arrived in the port city, servants rebelled against their masters, and the entire region convulsed in violence and hatred and fire and gunshot in the great Hottentot Rebellion of 1799–1802. Some of the Baartmans took up arms against their colonial usurpers. After the end of the war, in 1803 and just a few years before Cornelius died, three of his "wandering Hottentot" servants deserted his service and fled to the newly established mission station at Bethelsdorp, where they sought refuge under the cloaks of the London Missionary Society. There the eccentric missionaries Van der Kemp and Read preached an egalitarian and radical Christianity that conceived of a multiracial colonial world with a place for all at God's table.

Muller could do little to get his servants to return beyond appealing to the local authorities. In a great breach to Muller's sense of racial etiquette, one of them had insulted him in the presence of the other servants. Rider Baartman, perhaps Sara's brother, was the brave soul. Emboldened by the revolutionary rhetoric of missionaries, Rider Baartman told Muller to his face that he was "rogue, a bandit and a thief." Affronted, shaking with anger from such contempt shown by his servants, Muller stormed back to his house. There he wrote to the commander at Fort Frederik demanding that his servants be returned, complaining that he had been "heavily affected by" Rider Baartman's verbal harangue, and planning to give the servants a good thrashing when and if the Boer ever got his hands on them.

Rider Baartman fought with Cornelius Muller over the fate of his siblings. He knew that the farmer was capable of the worst kinds of violence, murderous beatings, and of breaking families apart and selling them to Cape Town traders. Muller had succeeded in splitting Sara from the other Baartmans, but he failed in meting out retribution to Rider Baartman. Rider Baartman had spoken the truth about Cornelius Muller and more.[27]

In later years Rider moved north to the Graaff Reinet along with other Gonaqua, many of them passing lands that once had been theirs. In 1830, he was convicted of theft and sentenced, by a jury of white farmers, to a year in jail with hard labor. Sara's other brother and at least two of her sisters escaped to the Bethelsdorp mission station. There they had children, and their children had children, and soon there were Baartmans spread over the region. Some lived at the Theopolis mission station: Veldman, Betje, and Kaatje.[28] Others moved north in 1828 to the Kat River settlement. Two Baartmans gave faithful service to the British military in the 1800s. And one, in 1851, became a rebel in a new war against persecution and white supremacy at Africa's southern tip.

The Baartman name lives on in twenty-first-century South Africa. Most make do working in the Eastern Cape. No longer servants or subject to the whims of masters or to the racial oppressions of nearly two centuries of prejudice, the Baartmans are now citizens of a democratic state. Memories of those distant years, of the farm Baartman's Fonteyn, of the child Sara Baartman, of the daily struggles of life in early colonial South Africa, have long since faded into silence and into the winds of the Camdeboo.

2

CAPE OF STORMS

Sara Baartman left the frontier with Pieter Cesars, the itinerant trader who had traveled very far from his home beneath Cape Town's Table Mountain. She departed at the very moment the Gonaqua disappeared as an independent people. "The prediction of Vaillant . . . has turned out but too true," wrote a traveler and government official who explored the Cape in 1797 and 1798. "The name of Ghonaqua . . . is just on the eve of oblivion."[1]

Cesars had come to the Eastern Cape at the behest of his employer, Jan Michiel Elzer, a wealthy and powerful Cape Town butcher. Elzer had ordered Pieter to exchange wares for sheep and cattle. The trade in human beings entered this commercial mix. The high demand for female servants in the Western Cape, particularly in Cape Town, could be met as a result of the violence and breakup of Khoekhoe communities along the eastern frontier. Perhaps Elzer encouraged (discreetly given its illegality) Pieter to acquire servants, or the itinerant acted on his own initiative. We do not know how many servants Cesars acquired or if any were Sara's relatives.[2] What we do know is that they lumbered forward . . . people, animals, and no doubt an ox-drawn wagon with its wooden spokes and wheels creaking across the path westward to the Cape of Storms.[3]

Sara Baartman would have passed farms owned by the Ferreira clan, who lived near Muller's Kraal of War at the eastern mouth of the Lang-kloof, the Long Valley. They were among the earliest European colonists in the Eastern Cape, and most everyone—black and white alike—knew a Ferreira or had heard of their exploits. Certainly Sara would have, for Pieter Ferreria had a farm not too far from Baartman's Fonteyn. The Ferreiras were consummate pioneers, men and women who learned the Khoekhoe language and knew how to make a living on the frontier.

Legendary hunters, their men could bring down an antelope at nearly a hundred yards.

The Ferreiras killed men and women with similar ease. Strong, square men of Portuguese descent weakened only by congenital holes in their hearts, they shot, whipped, tortured, and otherwise humiliated hundreds of Africans. The government banished one of the Ferreiras whose brutality they feared might foment rebellion. Another Ferreira bound her servant in chains and gouged the woman's eyeballs out with a spoon. The Ferreira clan is there still: Sara's grave stares down on Ferreira descendants who grow navel and Valencia oranges for national and international markets.[4]

Sara's father had moved livestock along the route Sara traveled in the mid-1790s. When she was younger, her father had returned to the kraal with stories of his journey through valleys where San and Khoekhoe bandits plundered livestock caravans heading to Cape Town. He might have spoken of the buildings lying close together in straight rows, of the high flat mountain, of the tall wooden ships in the harbor with white sails strained like beaten wings against the strong Cape wind. But Sara came to the Cape alone, her father having died in a bandit raid, her mother while working on a white man's farm.[5]

The Langkloof led to the rugged, dry karoo of scattered farms and flocks of fat-tailed sheep. Spring softened this harsh and dry land and was the best time to move people and animals westward. In their threadbare cottons and shoes of animal hide, Sara and the other servants might have traveled in the wagon. More often they would have walked, herding the sheep and cattle tramping along innocent of their fate before the butcher's knife.

The trip to Cape Town took anywhere from two to three months, an entire season. The group moved slowly, making no more than ten or twelve miles on a good day. Whenever possible travelers stopped at established resting places where they might barter an animal for supplies. Servants slept in the open veld among the livestock. These were not comfortable nights. Lions and leopards knew that the caravans offered the possibility of an easy kill. The animals might track a caravan for days, staying safely outside of musket range until nightfall, when the great cats snuck up on the livestock and, occasionally, on the servants among them; sometimes even the settlers and traders huddling in their wagons fell victim to their attacks.

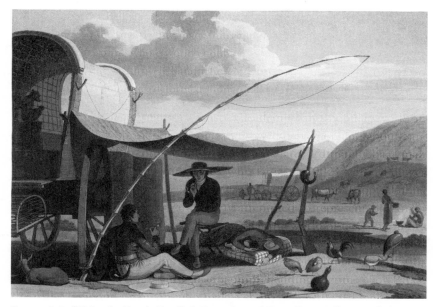

FIGURE 2.1. "Halt of a Boer's Family." From Samuel Daniell, *A Collection of Plates* . . . London, 1804. (c) British Library Board. All Rights Reserved. 458.h.14 part 2, 17.

Sara Baartman traveled from the wild eastern frontier into lands more securely settled by colonists. It was a journey away from a world she knew so well, a home even despite a life of sadness and disruption, with its familiar sights and colors and sounds and smells. With each day she became more of a colonial woman.

In the Long Valley Sara walked across a landscape of colonial settlement and violence and subjugation. The Inqua and Attaqua had disappeared. Survivors of disease and colonial violence either labored on white farms or had fled eastward or up into the mountains. Sara passed through a valley that had become a vast graveyard. Rock cairns marked people who had died in the great smallpox epidemic of the 1750s, "a great number of tombs, consisting of small heaps of stones."[6] Thousands of loose bones lay scattered where Boers had left dead Khoekhoe as carrion. This could be a terrifying sight, all these people denied a proper burial. The survivors could not put a name to the bones. The land no longer held the stories and souls of the Khoekhoe: it was alienated land, alienated from heart, from history.

Near the top of the valley, just north of what is today the town of George, the wagon road dropped a bit to the south before continuing its way west across the Gourits River. The group crossed a rickety bridge over a small stream that turned violent during the rainy winter season. Good, well-watered lands now beckoned. The terror of being attacked by lions and leopards no longer accompanied sleep. Rich soils replaced the rocky karoo outcrops. Swellendam village sat green and well fed with its church and one-roomed buildings. Craftsmen made a living repairing the wagons damaged by the long trip and merchants by selling their wares to needy visitors.

From Swellendam, travelers passed through the village of Caledon. From the high pass through the Hottentots Holland mountains, Sara Baartman would have seen the broad arc of False Bay, where captains fooled themselves with the promise of easy harbor and the ocean's waves beat to some eternal drum. In the distance, Table Mountain rose some three thousand feet out of the ocean. At its foot lay Cape Town.

Descending into the valley took much of the day. Wagons and oxen and livestock negotiated their way down the perilously steep pass that emptied travelers near the renowned estate of Vergelegen, or Situated Far Away, founded originally by Governor Willem van der Stel in 1700. Blessed with natural splendor, sometimes leading it to be called the Versailles of South Africa, Vergelegen also experienced the brutality of slavery. In the mid-1700s, its brutal and despotic owner, Michael Otto, beat his slaves, leaving them naked and tied to a tree beneath the fierce summer sun. So renowned was Otto's violence, among slave and master alike, that even the Dutch East India Company reprimanded him for torturing and not infrequently murdering his chattel.[7]

Travelers protected from such brutality regained their strength amid the most beautiful and fertile land in the entire Cape. Fields of wheat, vegetable plots, and vineyards stretched out as the valleys warmed to the late spring sun. Rows of oak trees, introduced a century earlier by the first colonists, lined the paths leading to the manor houses of the great estates: Vergelegen, Blaauwklippen (Blue Stones), Rust en Vrede (Rest and Peace). Visitors to the Cape reckoned the wine produced by these estates was second only to that of Great Constantia, the famous farm established in 1685 by Governor Simon van der Stel, whose slaves began the Cape's vinous economy.

FIGURE 2.2. "Hottentot Holland, and Somerset-West." From George French Angas, *The Kafirs Illustrated* . . . London: J. Hogarth, 1849. (c) British Library Board. All Rights Reserved. Cup.652.m.25 plate v.

The rich lands of the wine country near Stellenbosch, the second-oldest settlement in the Cape, appeared. Stellenbosch soil produced mostly rough tannic wines and stinging brandies for sailors. In this area of verdant luxury nurtured by the toil of thousands of slaves, Pieter Cesars may have sold one or more of the servants he had brought from the Eastern lands, perhaps Baartman's kith or kin. In 1810, Sara spoke of having four sisters and two brothers and indicated that they were still alive.[8] In any event, the Baartman name begins entering the local Western Cape archival record in the 1830s in records listing the contracts of "Hottentots" and Free Blacks, and later in baptisms.[9]

Straight ahead lay a wind-torn wasteland of sand and brush, the Tiger Valley, the Cape Flats, as if nature, wanting to contrast the beauty of the sea and the bounteousness of Stellenbosch, had conjured a desert, had thrown up one more obstacle, one more hardship, before travelers reached the delights and dangers of Cape Town. In the 1790s, a mere twenty or so farmers had small holdings on this dry expanse. A few of the farms grew some vegetables or even had a few lemon and orange trees, but these produced little, and their fruits tasted poorly and were destined mainly for the farmer's hungry bellies. In the winter, when snow fell on the Hottentots Holland, heavy rains inundated the Flats, giving the area the look of a lake with the scattered farmhouses so many tiny islands. In summer, as temperatures crept past ninety-five degrees Fahrenheit, terrific winds from the southeast blew across the Flats, swirling sand and dirt everywhere.

Far away lay Constantia, home to the oldest, grandest estates at the Cape founded by the early governors and worked by their slaves. From grapes brought from Germany came muscatel wines. Under the strong Cape sun and cool sea breezes, the grapes produced golden sweet, fragrant, and unctuous wines coveted throughout Europe and demanded by the likes of Napoleon, King Louis Philippe, and Frederick the Great. In *Sense and Sensibility*, Jane Austen recommended Vin de Constance to mend a broken heart.

The Flats finally gave way to greener, hillier land. The winds twisting about the mountains turned the silver trees on and off. As travelers rounded the Devil's Peak, a panorama unfolded with the city nestled at the bottom of Table Mountain, which held as if in its arms a wide reach of white sand and surf north along the great Atlantic Ocean. Robben Island lay three miles offshore, a prison and leper colony that would become infamous in the twentieth century for holding Nelson Mandela.

More prosaic concerns troubled travelers who stopped at one of the oxen posts, the last before entering Cape Town. A bit closer to town they passed the beer brewery at New Land and then, at Salt River, the remains of the military post that once had protected the Dutch from Khoekhoe attacks. Now, long after those wars had ended, the post had become a rudimentary store selling coffee, tea, and wine.

A few miles past Salt River, Sara Baartman entered Cape Town. She had made the entire journey with Pieter Cesar. Now she went to work as a domestic servant for Pieter's employer, Jan Michiel Elzer. A German Lutheran born in the 1740s near Baden at the edge of the Black Forest, Elzer came to the colony as a young man. In 1769, he married a burgher's daughter, Cornelia Theron. Elzer began his career filling meat contracts for the Dutch East India Company. With the rising demand for meat, Elzer ventured farther and farther away from the Western Cape and, through the 1770s and 1780s, all the way to the eastern frontier. His contract with the company was highly desirous, and the frontier trade made Elzer a wealthy man. He purchased slaves descended from Batavia and owned various plots of land and farms in Constantia and in the interior, and a house in Strand Street in the middle of Cape Town. As his wealth increased, Elzer could afford to stay at home, instead sending employees like Pieter Cesars, who returned with stock and who delved in the black market trade in Khoekhoe to serve as domestics cleaning houses, washing laundry, cooking food, and occasionally serving as nursemaids. It was in this capacity that Sara Baartman spent her first years in Cape Town.

Walking the last mile of her journey, Sara would have passed warehouses and wealthy burgher homes, the customhouse, and the new Lutheran church where Elzer and his family prayed. Table Mountain stood three thousand feet above the city's white plaster buildings. At sea, three-masted ships swayed to the Atlantic. Cesars and Baartman would have walked down Strand Street, formerly Sea Street and home to many of Cape Town's most prosperous burghers. Sara's life on the frontier had been one of considerable poverty and relative solitude. Neither the Fouries nor the Mullers owned much; the lives of many frontier Boers differed little from those of the Khoekhoe they despised and not infrequently hunted down. There were no grand houses on the eastern frontier, nor even a single town, and it might take a day's ride to get from one farm to another. Sara had lived in small communities, some no larger than ten or twenty people. With no possessions except for her clothes and the tortoiseshell necklace, Sara moved into a wealthy household on Strand Street, the widest and busiest of all of Cape Town's streets, in an exotic and cosmopolitan port city.[10]

It is easy to forget what an extraordinary experience this must have been. Sara had never seen ships at anchor, nor churches, nor people dressed in ways remarkably different from the Eastern Cape's simple cottons and quilts. She now lived just a few blocks from the company gardens and within earshot of the docks. From Strand Street merchandise voyaged deep into Africa and across the Atlantic and Indian oceans, quite literally tens of thousands of miles. Stock trains moved down to the nearby butchers. Wagons filled with goods lumbered on the street, the hubs and spokes stained with animal fat. The Cape's legendary winds created a miasma of smells, at one moment the aromas of coffee and teas and spices, the curries of Asian slaves, the flesh of slaughtered sheep and cattle, or the cold ocean's wet saltiness.[11]

Sara Baartman would have heard so much that was new: church bells, the imam calling the faithful to prayer, the cannons announcing the arrival

FIGURE 2.3. "A Panorama of Cape Town." By William John Burchell, c. 1815. Includes Papendorp in the left of the picture. Courtesy of Museum Africa. MA 167.

of a new ship. New sights called: vessels bound for India, the East Indies, Europe, and the Americas sat at anchor in the bay or docked alongside the dilapidated jetty rotted by sea worms. Some sights were harsh, like the gallows within view of the jetty or the stench of offal and human excrement. Others were as sweet as *koeksusters*, the fried braided pastries swimming in their syrupy bath made by Dutch settlers. And always there was Table Mountain. Following a heavy rain, waterfalls careened over the steep mountain's edge, the sun turning the mist into a dazzle of color. In clear weather the mountain seemed to go on forever. And when the clouds returned, they created a layer of grays and whites that hung off the mountain's edge like a tablecloth set for a grand banquet.

The world came to Strand Street. Disembarking sailors walked the short distance from the jetty and across Strand Street in search of women and wine, which Cape Town's residents hustled for profit. Sara would have heard Dutch and English but also French, Portuguese and German, Malagasy, Mbundu, KiSwahili, Malay, Gujarati, Arabic, and Chinese. What Sara did not hear, or heard only rarely, was her own language. She was very much a stranger in this new world of Cape Town. But not for long.

Climbing up Table Mountain to the stream to wash clothes, Sara would have labored alongside slaves from Indonesia, India, Madagascar, Angola, and Mozambique, and with people born into Cape slavery with roots in European culture as well. Working women from all over Cape Town converged on this spot, sometimes one hundred or more. Servants washed Indian calicoes, silks from the Orient, wools and linens from Europe. As the clothes dried, the washerwomen sat on the rocks and talked of the goings-on around town.[12]

Table Mountain witnessed societies dominate its valleys only to be defeated or to depart abruptly: the Khoisan, the Dutch, the British. In 1795, not long before Sara arrived at Elzer's door, a British fleet had sailed into Table Bay. The commander carried with him papers claiming English prerogative to the Cape dating back to 1620 and based on the visit of an English explorer. This was a ruse to prevent the French from taking the "Gibraltar of the Indian Ocean," the gateway to Asia's vast riches. The colony quickly fell after the Battle of Muizenberg a few miles from Cape Town. But it left French interest in the Cape that was to prove pivotal in the life of Sara Baartman.

Nearly two centuries of Dutch rule ended quietly as the twelve-hundred-strong British infantry took the old castle. Then, nearly as suddenly, the British departed in the late summer of 1803, just eight years after claiming the Cape as their birthright. The Treaty of Amiens slackened the conflict between England and a France now firmly under Napoleon Bonaparte, who had turned the Netherlands into little more than a vassal state for his political enjoyment. The treaty returned the Cape to Dutch (Batavian) rule, though with the proviso that the port would remain open to British ships. Napoleon's further exploits and European politics led to the British recapturing the Cape in 1806. This time they kept it.

In Cape Town most everyone was new. Sailors arrived from the far reaches of the world, the vast majority lower-class men roughly the same age as Sara herself. Most were new to maritime life, impressed through force and poverty, not keen on the sea, and very eager to exchange long months of cramped conditions and bad food for port city fun. More than five thousand British military men lived in Cape Town by the time Sara Baartman arrived, almost doubling the white population of the entire Cape district and transforming the local economy. Sara Baartman was in Cape Town precisely because of this economic transformation, for the port city's rapid and uneven growth created an unprecedented demand for women's labor.

In late spring, when Sara likely arrived in the Cape, the city reeled from busy sea traffic. Sailors usually had a month or six weeks of shore leave before setting sail again. Their presence created an instant demand for food, drink, lodging, clothing, and prostitutes. The sailors brought raucousness to the town as its inhabitants did their level best to make money off the transients. When the great ships left, people repaired relationships strained by revelries, profiteering, and exploitation. Life turned more slowly again. The winter's black nor'westers covered Table Mountain with damask clouds. Winds and rains beat the peninsula, muddying the roads, dirtying the hems of women's dresses and nearly sweeping people off their feet, and spitting sea salt into people's eyes and hair. Soon the city longed for those warmer months of excitement and the promise of income.

Cape Town survived on this tide of men, this economy of maritime masculinity. An unexpected decline in the number of ships arriving at the port depressed rents, cut into the profits of traders, and deprived many women of their only way of making money. But in the boom years of the late 1790s, traders and the rest of Cape Town's residents tried to take advantage of the swelling population. Quick money could be had, the quicker the better.

Many burghers kept lodging houses. The bars at the Tavern of the Two Seas seemed as numerous as the places to sleep; often one or two drinking houses could be found on each block. Sailors and Cape Town's workers drank and shared stories of home and exotic places like the Spice Islands, cavorted, gambled, and fought, or whiled away time teasing the baboons that came down the mountains scavenging for food. Many Cape Town men pimped women over whom they had control to the "Lords of six weeks," the soldiers and sailors who had some money in their pockets and who sought female company after the long voyages across the Atlantic and Indian oceans.

For a brief time in 1790, Burg Street, in the middle of the town near the company gardens and close to where Sara lived, became Venus Street, the better to direct sailors to Cape Town's red lights. In an administrative error the official placed the street sign at the home of one of Cape Town's ministers. After sailors kept knocking on his door requesting sex, the minister asked Cape Town's officials that the street be returned to its former name.

Sara was Elzer's domestic servant. It would have been simply impossible to live in the middle of Cape Town and not be aware of the commerce that flowed down its streets or of the drunkenness and sexual lasciviousness that spilled out of the city's taverns and brothels. Commercial sex was everywhere, and it was very hard for a black woman to avoid the attentions of transient men. The Dutch East India Company had long profited from and encouraged prostitution. At the Slave Lodge on Adderley Street a few blocks from Elzer's house, the company had at times ordered slave women to make themselves available for sex. The lodge's surgeon was familiar with venereal diseases and childbirth. For slave women, one of the few routes to manumission was by selling their bodies. With this money they paid for their freedom and for that of their children, and thus entered the Free Black community.[13]

The promise of freedom was offered more than it was delivered. The ebb and flow of men and the ravages of alcohol and prostitution created a vicious and vibrant urban economy. Particularly in the 1790s, masters began hiring out their chattel to secure additional income, or slaves hawked food and gave part of their profits to their owner. New economic opportunities may have become available to the servile class, but manumission rates remained particularly low for a port city; the commercial exuberance of the late eighteenth century widened the crevices of class and color.

Sara had spent much of her childhood betwixt and between communities, a Gonaqua girl and a colonial servant. She arrived from the farthest frontier a woman who spoke an indigenous language foreign even to those Capetonians whose ancestors had been vanquished in the wars of the seventeenth century or who had died in the huge smallpox epidemic during the early 1700s. Saartje Baartman, technically owned by no one, but orphaned, vulnerable, and beholden to others, also shared the particular vulnerabilities of being a colonized woman.

The insecurity of women took many forms: beatings, rape, moving from one master to another, being forced to sell one's body to obtain food or clothing and possibly even one's freedom. It was perhaps in this context that Sara first became pregnant.[14] Sara likely conceived the child, the first of three born in South Africa, while traveling down the Langkloof to Cape Town. We know nothing of Sara's earlier sexual history on the frontier. Given her age it is likely Sara was already sexually active by the time she left the Eastern Cape. Sexual violence within the colonial farming household was not uncommon, and Sara would have certainly known of, or had directly experienced, the predations of white frontiersmen.

Sara never identified the father of her first child—perhaps Pieter himself or a servant helping him bring livestock to town for slaughter or someone she encountered along the way. And we do not know the intimate conditions of this sexual encounter, whether someone took advantage of her in an act of violence, or if she forged a bond of affection during the long journey. Sara rarely discussed this child—its existence recorded only by Pieter's sister-in-law and in De Blainville's record of a conversation with Sara less than a year before her death in Paris. Perhaps Baartman's silence suggests an experience of trauma, experiences best forgotten.[15]

Had the child had been born in the Eastern lands, family would have helped Sara with the pregnancy and the birth, both occasions for celebration. Women would have buried the afterbirth in a hole in the hut. But in Cape Town as a new arrival, Sara was utterly alone. And masters often disliked their servants falling pregnant, since they believed it took them away from their work, and the presence of another mouth to feed meant less money in one's pocket. Slave women's children became slaves, but not so the children of the Khoekhoe, who masters sought to indenture them as soon as possible. Elzer did not have to worry long. The baby died.

We can imagine that the pregnancy and the child's death must have shaken Sara badly. Except for the periodic wildfires of smallpox, the Eastern Cape had a relatively safe disease environment, and what evidence we have points to relatively low rates of infant mortality. Cape Town, on the other hand, had extraordinarily high rates of infant death among the laboring classes.[16] Sara would not have expected her child to have perished. Sara's baby joined the other dead of slave and African descent in the burial ground for outcasts on the city's edge, now called Prestwich Place and the scene of great debate around how to honor the remains of the poor and the meaning of death, poverty, and identity in a post-apartheid South Africa. Two hundred years before that debate, and some four hundred miles away from kith and kin, Sara carried her firstborn from the wealth of Strand Street to a pauper's place of reckoning and disregard and delivered her baby to an unmarked grave.[17]

In the summer of 1799 Jan Michiel Elzer died, though unlike Sara's child the powerful and devout Lutheran butcher received a dutiful burial. Elzer was in his fifties and just shy of his thirtieth wedding anniversary. In the course of his successful life he had fathered a number of children and had become a respectful Cape Town burgher.[18] The death of a patriarch, especially one who had prospered like Elzer, awakened many anxieties. Widows brooded about their future, children fretted about their inheritance, and slaves and servants worried about whether or not they might be moved from one household to another or sold outright. Elzer's employees must have worried as well, including Pieter Cesars. Elzer had trusted him enough to send him to the farthest reaches of the colony. With his patron dead, Pieter faced an uncertain future.

It is difficult to reconstruct Sara's movements during these years, and we have done so by piecing together evidence from tax rolls, wills, and the legal testimony of different individuals, including Baartman. Around the beginning of 1800, Sara left the center of wealthy Cape Town for the gritty outskirts near the public bakery and the Military Hospital, where hundreds of sailors recuperated or lived out their final days. She moved to Pieter Cesars's small house in Papendorp in what is now Woodstock, Number 2 Lobster Road, at the bottom of the Devil's Peak east of the city.[19]

There was nothing beautiful or grand about Papendorp, no imposing buildings or wide streets bustling with sailors, merchants, and officials. Over the years an old farm had turned into a bric-a-brac community of a few hundred people, most poor with little or no property. Within eyesight of beautiful Cape Town but trapped by the mountain at its back and exposed to the South Atlantic, Papendorp was flogged by the Cape winds, which shook walls, tore off roofs, and deposited sand and dirt nearly everywhere.

Pieter Cesars, the man who had brought Sara to Cape Town a few years earlier, was in his thirties and had been married for more than a decade. It was to his household that Sara moved. In the winter of 1787, when the Dutch East India Company's alliance with the French had turned the port into a "Little Paris," Pieter had appeared before the *predikant* and betrothed Johanna Maria Barends "of the Cape," this last simple clause identifying the bride as descending from slaves. His brother Hendrik took as his wife Johanna (Anna) Catharina Staal. The same year Willem Cesars married Helena Christina "of the field," another surname that clearly marked slave ancestry. Pieter and Johanna Maria already had three children by the time they married in the Dutch Reformed Church. By 1800, the household numbered a total of nine people: the couple, four sons and three daughters, and, unlike his brother Hendrik, no servants. Between

1805 and 1807, the household declined precipitously. The daughters had grown up and left the household. Most devastating was the loss of his wife, Johanna, who may have died in or shortly after childbirth. Pieter had lost his employer and then his wife. He also had three or four sons to take care of, including an infant.

In Papendorp, Sara was particularly valuable to Pieter as a wet nurse. Having lost her own child, she likely now had to nurse Pieter's baby. She brought to her breast the child of the man who had purchased her five years earlier. Sara swept the Cape's dirt past the house's rickety door and saw the ships arriving or at anchor in Table Bay. Cape Town life continued with its spring and summer tides of sailors. Sara grew accustomed to life in the port city and learned anew the lessons of bondage and the pains visited upon women.

Sara's stay with Pieter did not last long. Around 1803, Sara moved the short distance from Pieter Cesars's house to a cottage coated with white plaster made more luminous in the Cape sun, the house of Hendrik Cesars and Anna Staal, Pieter's brother and sister-in-law. They lived under the Roode Bloem, the Red Flower, on about one-half acre of land. Their home, Welgelegen, or Happily Situated, had two plain windows and a simple door, and a single fireplace indoors. For the next seven years Sara would live on and off at Welgelegen and in the interstices between slavery and freedom, more a servant than a slave, sometimes a companion but always enthralled to others, free to come and go at one level, but never truly independent.

Cape Town society and especially the Papendorp community were small. The Free Black community in which Sara now lived numbered not much more than about seven hundred people in 1800; women outnumbered men by a ratio of 3:2.[20] Relations of blood and marriage and work created a world where people cared to know about one another's business. By the time she entered the household of Hendrik and Anna, Sara would have been able to trace the lines of marriage that connected one family to another, had nursed one Cesars child, and likely knew as well intimate details around sexuality and the domestic life of the Cesars clan.

Papendorp housed Cape Town's laboring classes who daily scattered in search of work. The perilous South Atlantic rich with *snoek* and *kob* called men with roots in Asian fishing communities. Papendorp's residents could see topsails piercing the sea's horizon. The docks could not accommodate

FIGURE 2.4. "House from Which the Female in Piccadilly Called the Hottentot Venus Was Taken Not 2 Miles from the Cape." John Campbell. "Three Sketches." Courtesy of Museum Africa. MA 1953 704c p107 (1).

the large number of vessels arriving in Table Bay, and many men helped shuttle cargo and people between ship and shore. Most ships laid at anchor in the bay immediately across from the Devil's Peak, their captains anxious that the Cape's storms and hurricane winds would ground or destroy their vessels. As soon as the anchor dug into the sand, small boats with steep bows appeared selling victuals for clothes and whatever else sailors had to offer. When they were not fishing, Papendorp's men sat on the beach, conical hats protecting them from the sun as their cracked hands wove nets and repaired boats. The imam called them to afternoon prayer, and the mosque on the hill offered them shade. Women worked as washer-women, hawkers, day servants, and prostitutes. Men passed the Naval Hospital and the pentagonal fort near the water's edge steeling themselves for a hard day's work on the docks and in the slaughterhouses. During grape-picking season men and women headed away from the city to nearby farms, where they nursed their backs with a tot of wine at the end of each long row of vines.

Welgelegen was one of Papendorp's better houses. But nowhere inside could be found the fine blue porcelain from China or the European furniture Sara had run her hands across while living on Strand Street. Life was hard in Papendorp. Poor nutrition and venereal disease, the "Venus sickness," led to ghastly rates of infant mortality, infertility, and shortened lives. In 1797, adult Free Black women had on average just over one child; free burgher women living only a mile away had six or seven or more children who survived to adulthood.[21] Sara's life with Elzer had been one of relative comfort. In Papendorp, she lived in a community toughened by economic insecurity and disease, but one that also offered relative freedom to a woman who had been constrained in the townhouse in Cape Town.

Sara now shared the tangled lives of South Africa's poor, whose histories and lives were marked by slavery. Both Hendrik and Anna were Free Blacks, descendants of slaves from East and South Asia. Hendrik likely was the second generation of Cesars to be born into freedom. We think that his great-grandfather came to South Africa from the great spice port city of Macassar in the Celebes Islands. This ancestor appears in the record books as Caesar, a classic name for those enslaved under the Dutch, who parodied the slaves' terrible status with a name that cruelly summoned greatness. Caesar lived in the Cape as the chattel of Governor Simon van der Stel, who ruled the colony for two decades from 1679 and founded South Africa's wine industry. In the 1680s Caesar toiled along with his wife, Susanna, and their children on the governor's wine estate, Great Constantia, tending to vines heavy with sweet muscatel grapes. Caesar's wife hailed from Ceylon. The couple entered the Dutch Reformed Church in the mid-1680s, Christian if still enslaved, beginning with Susanna in 1685 and Caesar the following year.[22]

In baptism the singular slave name "Caesar" began its journey to the family name "Cesars"; freedom in the early years of the eighteenth century secured the transformation. The Cesarses moved from Constantia and settled beneath Table Mountain just outside Cape Town in the very earliest years of South Africa's Free Black community. In all likelihood born in the 1760s and a solid decade older than Sara, Hendrik was born into Free Black status.[23] But he came of age in a time of rising discrimination. However free and Christian, neither Hendrik nor Anna ever managed to escape their slave pasts, since their slave ancestors had been liberated but not granted the status of a citizen. They may have hoped that baptism and marriage might secure a higher status within Cape colonial society. The move of the Cesars men to the marriage altar in the 1780s may well have indicated their anxieties with living in a more intolerant and racialized world. In that decade, the Dutch East India Company used sumptuary laws to mark Free Blacks from free burghers. Free Black women could no longer dress themselves in fine clothes like settler ladies. They could only be seen in public wearing chintz and striped cottons. If officials caught Free Blacks purchasing cloth from company slaves, they punished them like chattel, whipping them and sentencing them to ten years of work in chains. Every time he left Cape Town, Hendrik had to carry a pass, just like a slave.[24]

Burghers gossiped and poked fun at Free Black aspirations as surely as they made certain their impossibility. Crucially, Free Blacks had no access to the formal lines of credit. There were, in short, few possibilities for obtaining wealth at the competitive and economically mean-spirited Cape of Storms. Cesars and Staal married poor, better off than most other Free Blacks, but poor nonetheless. Ten years later they still had little more than their cottage under the Red Flower. But the arrival of the British in 1795 brought new opportunities. Cape Town's population swelled. The demand for labor skyrocketed, from domestic laborers to chandlers to caulkers who pressed oakum into the seams of ships to keep them afloat.

Into this burgeoning economy Hendrik borrowed heavily to purchase slaves and servants. He then could either resell them for a profit, rent them out as workers, or simply send them out into the town to make money. While Sara lived at Welgelegen the household changed markedly. In 1797 the couple had neither slaves nor servants. War in the Eastern lands yielded people easily trafficked west to Cape Town, so also a decline in the price for slaves. Between 1805 and 1807 upwards of five Khoekhoe entered the household, in addition to two slaves from Mozambique, Jonge and January.[25] By 1805, Hendrik and Anna felt they had done well enough to record a will in which they promised to manumit Jonge and to provide him with fifty *rixdollars*. This act of manumission was a feature of wills, and particularly a feature of the Free Black community, which had very high rates of manumission for their slaves.[26]

Sara thus entered a much different domestic world than she had experienced with Elzer, a world where the anxieties of getting ahead needled themselves into the most banal relationships between master and servant. There were also domestic frustrations and sorrows. Like Sara, Anna bore children who died. Where a decade of marriage should have produced three or four children, Anna had given Hendrik but a single boy. By 1800 the couple nestled their son into a small wooden coffin, perhaps joining Sara's baby at the other end of town, or in one of the graveyards in District Six. Anna's fortunes turned in the early years of the new century. She gave birth to a young daughter who survived, her namesake, Anna Catherina Cesars, born in Papendorp around 1802 or 1803.[27]

Sara may again have found herself as a wet nurse, bringing baby Anna to her breasts having just finished suckling Pieter's child.[28] Wet-nursing tied Sara, powerfully so, to the household and made it far more difficult for her to venture out in Cape Town with the rest of Papendorp's residents. With little more than her calico and striped cotton dresses and waiting to be summoned by her mistress to feed the infant, Sara likely settled under the sloping roof attached to the house. She slept on the floor or on a rudimentary mattress, the winds whistling round the building's corners and water breaching the shed during one of winter's black nor'westers.

Breast-feeding her master's child must have been lonely as each day most of Papendorp's tatterdemalion population moved into the city in search of work. On the other hand, the arrival of other Khoekhoe into the household meant that Sara was able to speak her native language again after a silence of more than five years. When she had lived in Cape Town in the 1790s, Sara was one of just a handful of Eastern Cape Khoekhoe women. By 1805, there were nearly four hundred Khoekhoe now living in the Papendorp area, many of them evidently newcomers from the Eastern Cape following the great Hottentot Rebellion of 1799–1802 when servants rebelled against their masters and the entire region convulsed in fire and gunshot, hatred and genocide.[29] Her parents were dead, but much of her family remained in the Eastern lands. Sara had left just a few years before the outbreak of the war; some of her kin had taken arms against the settlers. Sara was now able to press her tongue to her palate and to her lips and issue clicks that neither her masters nor the slaves could understand, to learn something of what had happened to the Gonaqua, and to impart to the those new to Papendorp knowledge about how to navigate life in the port city. Perhaps in the port city night they sang and danced to the eland.[30]

Sara's ties to the Eastern Cape and to her childhood, however, weakened with each year she spent in Cape Town. She was, increasingly so, a colonial subject, the pendulum of her life swinging toward people like Hendrik and Anna and to the maritime world of the port city with its distinctive sights and smells and motley people. By the time Sara moved to Happily Situated, she was neither a young girl nor an innocent native, each sustained narratives that swiftly turned to conventional wisdom. Sara was instead a woman and a Capetonian. Sara did not have deep roots in the city like Elzer or the Cesarses, but she also knew more about the city than most other city dwellers for whom the port remained a stopping place in a life that led elsewhere. Cape Town had become Sara's home.

For her part, Anna Staal cultivated a close relationship with Sara. As two women who had lost children they had much in common, as did many women at the Cape. They spent time together, the one working and caring for the young child, the other watching. Welgelegen was an intensely intimate setting. Anna and Hendrik observed Sara dressing herself, her movements about the Roode Bloem, Sara's work collecting her master's clothes to be washed up the mountain. The smells of the clothes Sara carried on her back three miles up Table Mountain to the Devil's Peak brought her life ever close to her master's and mistress's. Sara observed as well Hendrik's comings and goings, the ways he deployed his servants in the port economy, his frustrations with mounting debts, and his powerful desires to advance up the ladder of Cape colonial society.[31]

Up on the side of Table Mountain Sara beat the clothes clean, draping them across the fynbos to dry. Down toward the city people could see a mosaic of cloth forming on the mountainside. From the Devil's Peak Sara would have seen the churches and the company gardens, ships at anchor in Table Bay, her Papendorp home. A dirt road, little more than a path, lay near the stream where Sara worked. The road hugged the back of Table Mountain against slopes rising two or three hundred feet high and through some of the last stands of Cape Yellowwood. The road joined Cape Town to Hout (Wood) Bay some twelve miles away, a tiny hamlet and military outpost of not more than a few hundred people. Small numbers of troops regularly made the six- or seven-hour trek to the bay and the community that was in most respects very isolated from the hubbub of the port city.

Sara would create a temporary home beneath the cliffs overlooking Hout Bay. The departure of the British in 1803 severely depressed the Cape economy. The prices for imported goods skyrocketed, and the demand for Cape products stalled, then declined. Crucially, the number of sailors and naval seamen dropped precipitously. The Cesarses, falling into debt, could scarcely afford to feed their servants, and the sluggish economy made it difficult for Hendrik to rent them out to employers in the city. Sara ended her work as wet nurse, though she continued walking up to the Devil's Peak with her master's clothes.[32]

FIGURE 2.5. "Hout's Bay." Artist uncertain, perhaps Cecilia Ross, c. 1802. Courtesy of Museum Africa. MA 293.

During these economically depressed years of Batavian rule (1803–06), Sara traveled between Papendorp and Hout Bay. She walked these distances because of bondage and out of affection. Sara had met a man, Hendrik van Jong. Sara's Hendrik was a very poor European, the lowest of the low destined to serve in the armies and navies of Europe, a mere drummer in the Twenty-second Battalion of the Batavian infantry. Though they never solemnized their union before the *predikant*, for nearly two years they lived together in Hout Bay as husband and wife, "yet [Sara] being always in the employ of Hendrik Cesars." Each week or so Sara returned to her masters, washing clothes, spending a few nights in the shed, then passing through stands of yellowwood and silver trees as she walked back to the bay.[33]

For Sara, the relationship was the first in her adult life that was hers to hold. Van Jong received a pittance from the Batavian government. But for the two years Sara lived on and off with her lover near the seaside, poor but together, lugging some food and alcohol around the mountain. Life moved slowly beneath trees moistened by Atlantic breezes. There were barely any buildings, no shops, taverns, or brothels of the port city just ten miles away. The woods and the cascade of mountain helped protect the couple from the strong southeast winds. In winter they huddled together to beat off the cold.

At Hout Bay on the edge of the Atlantic Ocean, Sara conceived her second child. As the pregnancy developed into 1804, moving between Hout Bay and Papendorp became burdensome. We do not know where Sara gave birth to her second child, who may have assisted with the labor, or whether Sara endured the labor alone. But the child died, yet another baby dead. Soon Sara's drummer left, too, forced away by the vagaries of politics among the great powers. The calamities of war had returned as Napoleon's troops spread across Europe. The British navy again entered Table Bay in 1806, there to remain for well over a century. The ragtag Twenty-second Battalion disbanded during the winter. Hendrik van Jong returned to Holland once the South Atlantic weather had calmed. Sara likely bid him good-bye in the closing months of 1806.

Sara left Hout Bay and returned permanently to Papendorp, to her other Hendrik, the one who owned her as if a slave, who could order her to work. Back in the house, vulnerable again, Sara became pregnant by Jonge the Mozambican slave. With this baby, as with Baartman's first, we do not know the conditions of its genesis, whether in relationship or by rape. But like its siblings the infant perished. Sara seemed destined not to hold a child in her arms until it was too heavy to carry. A few years later in London Sara would speak only of her child conceived near the beach at Hout Bay with Hendrik. Although the child's name is unrecorded, Sara cared enough, loved enough, to speak of its birth, and its death, to strangers who inquired of her life in a foreign land that would soon become her home. At the same time, Sara withheld information about the other two children, both apparently conceived under conditions she would just as soon forget.[34]

Sara had spent a decade in Cape Town before the British took control of the Cape for a second and final time. Sara arrived in the port one of only a few Khoekhoe women from the Eastern Cape. By about 1805, other Khoekhoe had joined her in the Western Cape. Lonely at first, Sara was able to converse with people from home even as she was forging ties that inevitably led her away from the Gonaqua and the frontier. Sara had lived in three different households in two different areas of Cape Town. She had encountered a cosmopolitan population, people from Africa, the United States, Brazil, England, Europe, and Asia. Sara's most important emotional relationship had been with a European man, a relationship of enough importance to figure into the story she told, in London, 1810, of her own life. Clearly, then, Sara Baartman was a poor and exploited woman, but she most certainly was not an unknowledgeable girl recently brought to Cape Town.

The story of Sara's voyage to England began innocuously enough with the second British conquest. The recession that had malingered in the early part of the century ended. With the arrival of the British a massive military presence returned to Africa's southern tip. The volume of commercial traffic skyrocketed, over the next decade doubling each year. Ships arrived or hoisted sail for Europe, the Americas, India, and the East Indies, the four corners of the globe. Vast amounts of cloth, goods, and silver bullion traveled past the Cape of Storms. By 1810 the city had grown to more than fifteen thousand inhabitants crammed into fewer than fifteen hundred dwellings; the arrival of various fleets might swell the population by another five thousand or more. The city now had more single men than at any other time in its history, its streets bustling with excitement and seamen's bluster. With a few hard-earned coins in their pockets, sailors drank themselves into a stupor and looked for women.

They arrived hungry for pleasure and their minds brimming with fantasies. From the time of Captain James Cook, tales of the eroticism of native, slave, and Free Black women made their way through the maritime world. Sailors crowed of their sexual exploits and bragged of new ones to come once afoot in the city. Within the space of just a few feet, men could indulge their thirst for cheap wine and their fantasies of the legendary silkiness of Malay prostitutes or the other women who sold their bodies. Now they could quench their desires with that most sexed object of all—the Gonaqua woman from the frontier. In the late eighteenth century talk of Gonaqua women was just that, men's redolent sexual fascinations with a woman who combined innocence with lust and who had the most extraordinary organs of pleasure anywhere in the world. In 1806, there were Gonaqua women in Cape Town.

Hundreds of soldiers and sailors lived in the vicinity of Papendorp. Nearly within earshot of the house was the Naval Hospital, where upwards of six hundred sailors and soldiers recuperated at any given time. Poor ship nutrition was often responsible for landing in a hospital bed. The hospital conditions often worsened one's condition. "Multitudes . . . have been lost for want of air & wholesome accommodation . . . having been so close packd in their Hospital with scurvy—ulcers &c that it was certain death going into to it," wrote Lady Anne Barnard. A physician and head of the

FIGURE 2.6. "Military Hospital, Cape Town . . . nr Woodstock Pavillion." G. Duff,
c. 1860. Courtesy of Museum Africa. MA 1959 1824 p7.

hospital spent much of his time drunk amid the men dying in front of
him. The men lived and died "above the publick ovens where all the bread
is used in the place is baked & where the languishing creatures are baked
into the next world along with it."[35]

With the British a cornucopia of possibility opened up to men like
Hendrik, who had scraped together a life by trading and exploiting the
labor of his servants and slaves. In 1805 Hendrik had no fewer than four
Khoekhoe women working in his household, including a girl under fourteen years of age. Two years later he had just two females, one of whom
was Sara.[36] Hendrik likely got rid of two Khoekhoe, including the child,
as a direct response to the increasing labor demands that came with the
British conquest.

The couple, however, had borrowed heavily. Walking to Plein Street
near the company gardens in the city's center, Hendrik borrowed from
one of the wealthiest, most influential men of the Cape and perhaps the
single most powerful settler in the entire colony, Jacobus Johannes Vos:
graying merchant, moneylender, landlord, wine producer, and farmer
and, in 1806, none other than president of the Burgher Senate responsible
for administering Cape Town.[37] A few threads of history connected
Cesars and Vos. Both men had roots in Asia and in slavery. The Vos family

hailed from the East Indies, Jacobus's father arriving in the Cape in the middle of the eighteenth century. Like many other people who had moved into the settler ranks, the Vos family was marked by servitude. Jacobus Vos's maternal great-grandmother had been a slave from Bengal, born in the 1680s. Her marriage to a European man and the language recording the baptism of her children washed from their history the curse of Ham.

By the time Hendrik approached Jacobus, the wealthy burgher politician owned some sixty thousand vines, fifty slaves, and properties across Cape Town. Vos had a Cape Town store filled with sugar, spices, and dry goods. He had grown rich from his connections with the Dutch East India Company and seamlessly navigated the transition to British rule. Vos would have known Elzer; both sat at the pinnacle of Cape Town wealth and had prospered through contracts with the company. Vos lubricated his political and commercial connections at the Concordia Club, where he was a member, the posh "Temple of Concord and friendship" where controversial discussions were prohibited and whose members were required to donate twenty-five bottles of their best wine. Jacobus Johannes Vos was a very shrewd and very wealthy man.

And Hendrik was not. Vos profited from the status hierarchy at the Cape by loaning money to Free Blacks at interest rates twice that charged to settlers. As for Hendrik, his ambitions and pale skin did nothing to relieve him of the burden of being a Free Black, and so he depended on Vos for credit. By 1808, he had failed to make good for the loan a number of times. The fifty-year-old Vos, wealthy from profit and rotund from rich food but in failing health,[38] reminded Cesars of his obligations and demanded return of the principal and interest. Each time Hendrik pleaded for an extension, always promising that soon his pockets would be full of money and his debts cleared.

By 1808, and with Vos breathing down his neck, it seems Hendrik began to show Sara to the sick patients dreaming of the city's carnal delights and with a few shillings in their pockets. According to Anna, Sara showed herself to those "who wished to see her." But when the sailors in the hospital looked at Sara, they bound her in the ribbons of European desire to "know" the Hottentot Woman and in their own longings for sexual entertainment. She became a special kind of show, a Hottentot Venus.

For a price the sailors could view Sara, perhaps even touch her. We do not know if Sara exchanged sexual favors with the men. Many slave owners prostituted their female chattel. Masters received the great bulk of the money and laid claim to the bastard children that inevitably resulted from the sex trade. Hendrik, like many at the Cape "at the same time a huckster and a trader,"[39] would have made more money from sex than from simply offering Sara to the men's view. In all likelihood Sara became something of an early nineteenth-century exotic dancer and may have provided sex as well.

If Sara Baartman performing as the Hottentot Venus first emerged within Cape Town's military hospital among men who knew of and desired Gonaqua women, there was also another context that tied her to the exotic, the erotic, and exhibition, a connection that would return in the final years of her life. On Hottentot Square up near the Malay quarter, the *bo-kaap*, in 1800 the governor had inaugurated the African Theater.[40] By 1803 the theater was being run by Charles-Maurthurin Villet, a French émigré who produced comedies and vaudeville productions for an eager public. Villet was joined by a community of artists and other French refugees fleeing Napoleon's wrath who found the Cape a beautiful and distant haven from the turmoil of Europe.

Villet's interests incorporated more than theater. Born in Saint Domingue, Villet was a classic French traveler of the era, interested in exotic flora and fauna. He helped bring the exotic to the city's saturnalia, opening a shop of curiosities on Long Street next to a "retail shop" owned by Anna Catharina Staal's mother.[41] Villet's collection of preserved animals turned the shop into something like a museum that attracted residents and visitors to the Cape; he later donated his collection to what would become the South African Museum in Cape Town, a museum that later became infamous for displaying a diorama of San people alongside stuffed animals.

At the African Theater, Villet collected a number of exiles like himself, forming a troupe that performed "opera comique." People of note included Jean Reaux (also spelled Riaux), Charles Etienne Boniface, and Louis-Balthazar Meurant.[42] Reaux had fled France and had come to the Cape in 1805. He was a ballet master, part of Villet's circle, and presented his students' work at the African Theater. Reaux clearly had some revolutionary enthusiasm left. Along with other young men, he demonstrated outside the house of the mayor of Stellenbosch, an action that landed

FIGURE 2.7. "New Theatre, Hottentot Square." A collection of plates illustrative of African scenery and animals, with descriptive letterpress. Samuel Daniell. London, 1804. (c) British Library Board. All Rights Reserved. 458.h.14 part 1, 10.

him in jail. In January 1811, he unsuccessfully petitioned Governor Caledon not to send him away from the Cape, blaming his indiscretion in Stellenbosch on his youth and inebriation and saying he was a loyal supporter of England. Reaux argued that a return to France would "be his final ruin." The governor remained unmoved. The next month the ballet master asked that Reaux be given leave from prison in order to make money to settle his debts, and most particularly to acquire money so that he could pay for the manumission of a slave woman with whom he had formed a relationship. In May 1811, the month that Sara would leave London for the English provinces, Reaux's friends petitioned again, saying that they had lent Reaux sufficient money to pay off his debts. This made no difference to the governor, who ordered the Frenchman to leave or be imprisoned and sent to Britain.

Reaux owed money to his friend Johann Grieg Siems, who lived near Willem Cesars, Hendrik's brother. We have no evidence of Sara being displayed at the theater or at Villet's shop, but it is highly likely that Hendrik had a connection to the French community that had formed around the African Theater. Most tantalizing is the fact that the man responsible for showing the Hottentot Venus to the Parisian public, from 1814 to the time of Baartman's death at the end of 1815, kept a shop in Paris's artistic epicenter and shared the exact same surname as the troubled Cape Frenchman Jean Reaux. Were they one and the same person, brothers, relatives? We cannot know for sure. What is clear is that there was a French presence in Cape Town during Sara's time there, a presence very much enlivened by the exotic and theater.[43] This French connection between performance and the exotic was re-created in Paris, the epicenter of Europe, when Sara Baartman as the Hottentot Venus arrived in that city in September 1816.

If these were the contexts, financial and cultural, the mover and shaker behind the idea of a show called "The Hottentot Venus" was one Alexander Dunlop, a wily Scotsman with long experience in the seaports of the world, and now doctor at the Slave Lodge in Cape Town. The graying fifty-one-year-old surgeon came to the Cape in 1806 with the Pump and Tortoise, the Thirty-eighth Regiment of the Foot. He had served in the regiment since 1796 and in a few years would complete his military career. Dunlop earned little more than £7 per month, today's equivalent of less than $8,000 per year. Military surgeons required relatively little training, and their treatments often proved deadly. Dunlop's position was far from revered or coveted. Compulsory retirement came at age fifty-five; Dunlop would go on half pay beginning Christmas Day 1812, his eight thousand dollars shrinking to just to four. The Cape marked the end of Dunlop's career. He faced financial penury and very nearly outright poverty.[44]

In Cape Town Dunlop prowled around for other ways to increase his earnings. This was not unusual; for hundreds of years sailors and military men sought ways of supplementing their typically paltry pay with additional duties or through illicit activities like smuggling. Military and maritime economies had a considerable gray area between the legal and the illegal. What was unusual was that Dunlop had skills few others possessed. Within a short time after his arrival in South Africa, Dunlop was appointed as the medical superintendent of the Slave Lodge, tending to the medical treatment of its captives and receiving "a small allowance" in return. At least by the beginning of April 1808 Dunlop had begun treating "sick Hottentots and others" as well.

Dunlop's work at the Slave Lodge, just a few blocks from the African Theater, put him into contact with vulnerable women, including Khoekhoe women suffering from venereal diseases. In that capacity Dunlop would have been able to inspect women's bodies and study their genitalia, an eerie parallel to Cuvier's later persistence in trying to look at Sara Baartman's body. We think it was in the context of his medical work both with women and at the Naval Hospital near Papendorp that Dunlop encountered Sara Baartman around 1809. Dunlop no doubt watched the sailors' titillation and wondered at the possibilities of showing Sara Baartman not to hundreds of sickly people but to thousands of people with money in their pockets. Financial frustrations and schemes seem to have danced in his mind's eye: he was witnessing a potential commercial success, one that he could mold to the tastes of London. He could make a fortune and avoid ending his years an indigent retired military surgeon.

Dunlop began meeting with Cesars and looked to raise enough capital to bring Baartman to England.[45] It does not appear that anyone consulted Sara about these plans. A lieutenant and another surgeon who lived in a house near the hospital agreed with Dunlop to the plan. In 1808, the three men began putting together an agreement, tossing around fanciful figures. In early August, they offered Cesars 8,000 guilders, today's equivalent of more than $68,000 and eight times Dunlop's yearly pay. Hendrik assured Vos that he would clear his debts by early October 1808. But the plan collapsed no sooner than he returned to Papendorp. Orders arrived sending Dunlop's accomplices to Ceylon.

Dunlop persisted in his plans, now forging an agreement with a quartermaster of the Eighty-ninth Regiment and a soldier in the Ninety-third. Dunlop approached Cesars a second time, offering Cesars 6,000 *rixdollars*, beginning with an up-front payment of 2,000 and the last installment contingent on the "profits arising from the exhibition of the said woman." This was a princely sum, 6,000 *rixdollars* being nearly $100,000 today. Even the up-front payment represented nearly four times Dunlop's yearly salary. Hendrik had reason to start feeling he might be able to make money, repay his debts, send Sara off to England, and bask in the proceeds, perhaps even moving into the Cape Town proper. However, in October 1809 Hendrik's debts came due, and he had no money to fill his pockets. Vos once again granted him an extension.

The plans to finance the trip to London deteriorated. By November 1809, the two other military men faded from the effort, and the burden of the enterprise now lay solely with Alexander Dunlop. The medical man faced a barrage of problems. With the 1807 abolition of the slave trade the British had begun the process of closing the Slave Lodge, effectively ending one of Dunlop's positions. Dunlop was nearly constantly trying to increase his income, largely by memorializing the government for better compensation. In June 1809, for example, he requested more money.

With the departure of the two business partners, Dunlop's financial problems became acute. In early 1810, almost certainly as a scheme to raise capital, Dunlop submitted an invoice for more than 300 *rixdollars* for the treatment of sick Khoekhoe. He claimed that the treatment of one man with a bad foot had necessitated confinement for nearly a year. Each patient had been discharged just a month or two before the surgeon had submitted the bill. Dunlop knew the expenses were "high" and anticipated that the charge would not be received blindly. In fact the bill incensed his superiors, one of whom wrote that "Dunlop's conduct on this occasion has been particularly incorrect," instructing a subordinate that "you will not pay sixpence of the bill" and threatening to "name another medical officer" if Dunlop persisted in padding his compensation and in demanding outrageous expenses for splints, bandages, and dressings.

Dunlop faced additional problems. Hendrik Cesars, who saw his part of the deal as simply requiring the transfer of his rights in Sara to another man, seems to have had no intention of going abroad. Sara, however, had never been consulted on the details of the trip to England. According to Anna Staal, when Sara heard that Hendrik would be staying in Cape Town, she refused to go and insisted that Hendrik accompany her to England.

The threads of business and personal relations had created messy and near-intractable knots. Baartman refused to go without Cesars, and Dunlop could not conjure up the capital to entice Cesars to let go of his servant. But he recognized Cesars's financial woes and began to exploit them to his own advantage. We imagine he thought that if he could just get Hendrik on that boat, all would be well. Sara would be on board, with her master, and Alexander would be able to manipulate these colonials who, unlike himself, had never sailed from Cape Town.

Dunlop apparently drew up a contract with Hendrik about the conditions under which Sara Baartman would be taken to England. Vos asked

Cesars to see the contract. Cesars walked to Plein Street, contract in hand. Cesars would not have been able to make out the meaning of the words scratched on the parchment; he could neither read nor write. The piece of paper specified no sum to be paid Cesars, or to Sara. It was as much a contract to exhibit Sara as it was an agreement by which Cesars would become Dunlop's employee.

It was a fool's contract, but one that Cesars seemed unable to escape. Dunlop threatened him and said he would make certain Hendrik would end up in jail if he refused to go to London. Hendrik had little choice. He faced the wrath of one of the wealthiest and most powerful men in the colony. Sara Baartman refused to go to London without Hendrik. And Alexander Dunlop both threatened him with ruin and lured him with the chance of making money in England. Hendrik Cesars agreed to the plan.

On 7 March 1810, Dunlop wrote to the government asking either that Hendrik's pass to leave the colony for England be altered or that a new one be issued. The document mentions that Hendrik would be traveling with "a friend." Dunlop said that he and Cesars had planned on leaving earlier but had been prevented from doing so by the "sickness" of the "friend." This "sickness" likely was likely referring to the last-minute hesitations and resistance of Sara, who refused to leave the colony without Hendrik; it might also have related to new stalling by Hendrik. Hendrik tried to get another man to go in his stead. The man refused.

Hendrik and Sara were now destined for England. So, too, was a young slave boy Matthias, taken from the Slave Lodge by Dunlop. In 1809, Dunlop had petitioned the governor asking for permission to have Matthias transferred to his care on the grounds that Dunlop had brought him up "almost as a child." He was ordered to pay 150 *rixdollars* for the privilege.[46] In March 1810, Dunlop asked permission to bring to England the slave Matthias, now defined as Dunlop's apprentice. On 20 March 1810, Dunlop received his passport to travel "together with his Servant" the young Matthias. On the same day, Hendrik received his passport, which also authorized him to take with him the "Free Black Saar," almost certainly a misspelling of "Sara." On 29 March 1810, Hendrik and Ann deposited the will that they had drawn up five years earlier. Just over a week later, the couple bid their good-byes.

Important shifts and silences lay in these documents produced in the hurried last days of March and early April. A slave became a servant, thus allowing Matthias and the other youth from the Slave Lodge to enter an England that prohibited slavery on its soil. The draconian 1809 Caledon Code had expressly prohibited the movement of Khoekhoe outside the Cape Colony without official sanction. Dunlop had not secured this official permission. Designating Sara as "Free Black" deftly avoided the letter of the law, if not its spirit. The evasion became the basis of an investigation of the governor, Lord Caledon, in 1811 which yielded Staal's testimony, and so much information about the Cesarses and Baartman. As for Hendrik Cesars, departing the Cape erased his status as a Free Black.[47]

By 1810, Sara Baartman had lived in the Cape for more than a decade. She had had a relationship with a poor Dutch soldier. She had lost three babies in that decade. She had detailed knowledge of people's interest in her body and of the growing European fascination with all things exotic and "primitive." Sara had learned much about the customs of British men. Certainly, she was a victim of race, class, and above all her gender. But whatever the conditions of her life, by 1810 Sara Baartman had become a worldly woman in her thirties, not an innocent child recently brought from Africa's interior. Did the noble savage of Rousseau indeed ever exist in the way it came to resonate in Europe? Sara was a colonial woman. She walked, and worked, and lived in the commercial mélange that was Cape Town. She wore skirts and tops and dresses, humble yes, but European clothing nonetheless. She was multilingual, knowing her own language, Dutch, and probably a smattering of English, and had heard the many other languages in the cacophonous Cape.

Sara in 1810 owned nothing but the experiences of the pain and hardship of servitude. Her children were dead. Even her loved one had left. Dunlop promised her "Beads, clothes and support," in addition to money. Perhaps a more humane world lay across the horizon. The British, after all, had ended the slave trade and had tried to dull the brutalities of colonial life in the Cape Colony.

"Who will give me any thing here?" Sara apparently told Anna. Why not go? Sara Baartman and the others set sail on 7 April 1810 aboard the HMS *Diadem*,[48] a military transport ship that had assisted in the British capture of the Cape in 1806. Sara's life as the Hottentot Venus had begun. That life, and the representations of it that followed, would elide her varied experiences, her very being as a colonial subject, at the Cape of Storms.

LONDON CALLING

D unlop booked a passage for his party on the HMS *Diadem*, one
of many warships rolling at anchor in Table Bay. The ships were
headed for Chatham, the great naval base and yard on the
Thames River downstream from London. More than a half dozen other
military ships completed the convoy, including the HMS *Inconstant* that
sailed Napoleon into exile in 1814. The flotilla would escort East India
Company transport ships heavy with cottons and Asian silver.[1]

Weeks of labor had gone into readying the convoy for the six-thousand-
mile voyage. Cape Town did not have docking sufficient to support many
of the big ships. Instead workmen, many of them Free Blacks, loaded into
small boats thousands of pounds of vegetables, bread and biscuits, vinegar,
water, and lime juice to ward off the scurvy, as well as brined meat and
live animals. From the wooden jetty they rowed out to the ships. Sailors
then lowered the goods deep into the ship's hold.

The ship sat high in the water with two decks, a bowsprit pointing over
the water some 30 feet, and three masts well over 100 feet in the air. The
160-foot topsail schooner briefly served as Admiral Nelson's flagship and
in a single month captured no fewer than four Spanish vessels. It had given
good service in Britain's war with Napoleon.

The *Diadem* was one of the ships involved in the British takeover of
the Cape in 1806, under the command of Captain Popham. After taking
the Cape, Popham crossed the Atlantic Ocean to take part in the capture
of Montevideo and the disastrous invasion of Buenos Aires that left more
than four thousand British men dead on the streets and Popham court-
martialed back in England. The *Diadem* remained in the South Atlantic,
capturing and destroying French and Dutch vessels trying to sneak past
Cape Town. But three decades of military work had taken their toll as the

ship entered its final years traversing the North and South Atlantic. Cape workers converted the *Diadem* into a troop carrier, the sixty-four guns reduced to a mere twenty-eight. The cannons on the lower gun deck had been removed, the ports closed, and the small spaces turned into low-ceilinged cabins for troops and workers.

The ship could quarter as many as five hundred sailors, who braced themselves for the cramped berths and harsh discipline of shipboard life, the tedium of long journeys and apprehensions of disasters that might befall them. Many arrived on the boat with terrific hangovers. What loose money they had left went to drink and sex enjoyed under the blue skies of the Cape, as if memories of earthly pleasures might sustain them on the voyage home to the gray, churning seas of England.

Sara would have seen many vessels like the *Diadem*. From Papendorp she looked down at the ships arriving in the bay, sails dirtied and frayed by long voyages and the huge anchors breaking through the water. She probably had never stepped on a boat, much less a ship the size of the *Diadem*. To get to the *Diadem*, Sara returned to Cape Town's center. Walking down the hill, Sara Baartman would have passed the hospital where she had first met Dunlop before approaching the pentagonal Castle. In front of her lay the Grand Parade. Turning her back on Table Mountain, she saw the topgallant masts peeking over Cape Town's roofs. A mere five blocks away stood Elzer's house, Sara's first Cape home. To her left lay the burial ground cradling her children.

Sara, Hendrik, Alexander, Matthias, and we think one more boy from the Slave Lodge, boarded a small launch at the very end of March 1810. The oarsmen brought them to the *Diadem*, busy with the sailors on board making the final preparations for the voyage. The launch knocking into the great ship as it rolled back and forth, Sara grabbed the ladder and climbed some twenty feet to reach the main deck. Sailors brought Sara to her quarters, a space not much larger than seven feet wide and long, more a cell than a berth.

Sara was the only woman on the *Diadem*. Military law forbade women on board warships except by permission from superior officers or the lords commissioners of the Admiralty. Captains confined women to their cabins in the name of safety and discipline. Captain's wives and elite women were allowed to spend time on deck, not poor women like Sara. On the *Diadem*, Captain Phillimore would have sequestered Sara except for a few hours each day when she could stand on the aft deck with the three masts and dozens of sails before her. Mostly she sat in her dark cabin, listening to the noises of the ship and the relentless assault of wind and water.[2]

Under a fresh southeast breeze, the *Diadem* made a port tack out of the harbor. Table Mountain rose from the bay, hovering over the seascape like a dream. A few miles out amid swirling currents and shark-infested waters, the ship rounded Ladie's Rock at the southern tip of Robben Island. On those beaches and quarries, generations of political prisoners from the seventeenth through the twentieth century stared at beautiful Cape Town just out of reach.

Past Robben Island and into the cold waters of the South Atlantic Ocean, the ship changed its course. The *Diadem* now headed in a northwesterly direction for its first port of call, the island of Saint Helena, sixteen hundred miles and two weeks away. Strong South Atlantic waves and currents beat at the wooden hull, and the ship creaked and leaked under the fresh breezes. The deck hands trimmed the sails with a strong wind off the port stern. Table Mountain and its damask clouds retreated and then disappeared beneath the horizon.

The crew itself was every bit as diverse as the population of Cape Town. Sailors hailed from the United States, Africa, England, Ireland, Sweden, and Germany. Some of the sailors likely knew of Sara from her time at the Naval Hospital. Sara was not the only African, nor the only bonded person. At least four freed slaves worked on the ship. The British had outlawed the slave trade a few years earlier but slavery itself continued. One of the ships in the convoy, the HMS *Raisonable*, had thirteen slaves aboard.

Within a few days Sara likely fell seasick. All but the most experienced sailors suffered from seasickness in the early part of a voyage. Seasickness might continue for upwards of a week for those confined below deck and new to the constant swinging of the ship on the big seas of the South Atlantic. Just out of sight of Table Mountain a malaise would settle in, followed by cold sweats and then the nausea and vomiting. Dehydration, sleeplessness, and fatigue led to dry retching and vertigo, the small cabin spinning round and round as the waves rocked the ship.

Saint Helena appeared on the horizon in the middle of April 1810. While at dock, the crews spent two weeks making necessary repairs, taking on water and additional supplies. Captain Phillimore probably allowed Baartman to leave the ship in the care of Cesars and Dunlop. Sara ventured onto terra firma again, tasted better food, and regained her health somewhat after the fits of vomiting in her cramped, malodorous quarters below deck.

The convoy set sail again at the beginning of May, but not before Captain Phillimore transferred four former slaves to the *Raisonable*. The ships headed northwest toward Ascension Island in the middle of the South Atlantic, seven degrees off of the equator. Fresh breezes and good weather pushed the ships onward. They reached the little island in just less than a week. Ascension was far smaller than even Saint Helena, a dry, largely barren mass of basalt and volcanic cinder cones tipped with green and rimmed by brilliant white sand beaches.[3]

The next leg of the voyage was also its longest. Eight hundred miles of ocean separated Ascension Island from Port Playa on the island of Jago in the Cape Verdes. During the monthlong journey, light breezes becalmed the convoy. At other times, squalls and heavy rains lashed the decks. The *Diadem* faired poorly, at times falling out of sight of the other ships. For more than a week beginning on 19 May, the *Raisonable* towed the *Diadem* as workers made repairs.

From the Cape Verdes, the convoy set a northwesterly course, heading deeper into the Atlantic until the winds changed direction and the ships turned in a great arc in the direction of Lizard Point, England. Again the *Diadem* broke down, and again the *Raisonable* towed the aged ship.

Southern England appeared in early June. The voyage crept along for another month as the convoy made its way eastward. The ships moored finally at the beginning of July, some three months after setting off from Cape Town.[4] Sara and the two men had left in the Cape fall, when the days were beginning to cool. They crossed the equator, and fall became spring. The long days of the English summer had already settled in when the *Diadem* arrived on the coast in July 1810.

The convoy left the English Channel and eased its way slowly west along the river Medway through Kent. At Chatham, some thirty miles from London and the home of Charles Dickens's happiest childhood memories, Sara, Hendrik, Alexander, and the slave boys gathered their possessions and disembarked at the Royal Dockyard. Compared with those in Cape Town, the dockyards were massive, capable of servicing a hundred or more ships and employing nearly two thousand men. One wharf extended a full mile. Sara and the others negotiated their way around the three- and four-story brick buildings that lined the waterways, many with ropes and hooks loading and off-loading cargo.[5]

Following months of enforced solitude at sea, Sara now entered the hustle and bustle of Chatham dockyard that quieted only once she entered the town itself. Small inns and cobbled streets welcomed the visitors, the buildings leaning toward each other as if in happy conversation. The dockyard, with its streams of sailors bidding their good-byes or disembarking with their purses of coin, brought coaches and wagons to the town. Our travelers caught a coach for London, heading along the Old Kent Road that hugged the river Thames, going west past Gravesend, Greenwich, home of the Royal Observatory, and on to the great city.

Old Kent Road was the main thoroughfare connecting London with the Continent. The road was safe for the travelers, as it had not been in the eighteenth century when highwaymen regularly preyed on sailors returning home. Dunlop, Cesars, Baartman, and the boys entered London from the south though one of the poorer, rougher parts of the city, passing brick kilns, clothing manufacturers, breweries, and some of the early factories of the Industrial Revolution. These were among the meanest of streets. The road became ever more squalid and overcrowded, with people as well as animals living in the houses.

Even the worst areas of Cape Town could not match the dirt and sordidness of Old Kent Road, or the sheer size of London and the crush of its people. Hundreds of inns lined the streets of London, especially along the major roads, the work of coachmen and grooms adding to the activity of the travelers themselves. An eighteenth-century writer said of the area that it was "a most disgraceful entrance to such an opulent city. A foreigner, in passing this beggarly and ruinous suburb, conceives such an idea of misery and meanness, as all the wealth and magnificence of London and Westminster are afterwards unable to destroy."[6]

Finally the coach turned north onto Surrey Street, where conditions improved. The coach then crossed Blackfriars or Waterloo Bridge. To the right Sara saw London Bridge, to the left the Houses of Parliament. What fortunes would the city bring? Sara and the others would soon find out as they made their way from the mean streets of the East End, toward the West End of London and the streets of Piccadilly.

When Sara Baartman arrived in London in July 1810, the city was the capital of Europe, indeed of the world. Some three decades after losing its American colonies, Britain had strengthened its navy, had ended its involvement in the slave trade, and was beginning to see herself as morally superior to other countries for having done so. Britain was set to become the dominant player in world trade and politics for the next hundred years.

In 1800, an African wrote to his father of this great city, describing a dynamic London of display and wealth, and new opportunities. "London England," he said,

> is a very fine place but I have seen water hard & also I have seen Snow. . . .
> It is a very large town. . . . I have seen Bear Dance & Monkey dance upon
> his back & Coach Carry four weals and two horses carrying it. I have seen
> fish fly, & I have seen Apple Paire & Cherry and Waggon and Cart. . . . I
> wright and read I have seen peacock & I have seen the King and fine Garden
> . . . and we have seen Coaches & the Coachmen sit before & the footmen
> stand behind the Coach . . . I have seen the people from Seirra leoni [*sic*] I
> have seen kite [*sic*] fly.

Ten years later, those marvels, coaches, and shows were even more abundant.[7]

London reveled in its new centrality to international markets and fashion, fun, and political gossip. Sara arrived a year before Parliament made George Augustus, "Prinnie" the Prince of Wales, regent because of the madness of his father, King George III (1760-1820). The prince would also later rule as King George IV from 1820 to 1830. The king's illness and the political intrigues of the time provided near-constant grist for newspapers, cartoonists, and talk among the upper classes.

The city had undergone major renovation in the eighteenth century, much of it in the neoclassical style, with colonnades and reliefs and bold Greek pediments. From just over ninety-one thousand in 1700, the city had grown into a metropolis of a million people a century later, making London twice the size of Paris. No longer an old city surrounded by countryside and villages and more a sprawling suburbia spreading every which way, London quickly extended to the north and west past Piccadilly, where the city would welcome the Hottentot Venus. By 1810, Londoners were living even farther from the old city walls, the wealthy in the new West

End around Saint James's Park, the poor predominantly in the East End, and south across the Thames.[8]

On arriving, Sara, Alexander, Hendrik, and the two slave boys likely stayed first at the White Bear Inn. Long a major public house in Piccadilly for travelers to the West End, the White Bear Inn was situated a few doors down from 225 Piccadilly, the room that became Sara's place of exhibition in London. Dunlop soon secured cheaper and more permanent lodgings in Duke Street, Saint James's, in the heart of London's West End; the street connects Piccadilly to Jermyn Street and ends at King Street. Duke Street now is home to art galleries and specialty shops, still a street catering to the wealthy. Christie's, the international auction house, occupies much of the lower block of Duke Street between Ryder and King.[9]

Dunlop had lived in London as a young man and knew the importance of location. He had brought Sara into London's most exciting and elite neighborhood, with Piccadilly Street its crown jewel. Piccadilly had changed from a path in a rural area outside the city proper into a major route connecting the West End, the relatively new center of London, to the seedier Covent Garden. In the late eighteenth century, wealthy Londoners began moving into the area west of Westminster, building large mansions around central squares such as Hanover Square and Holland Square. The architect Henry Holland refashioned the Pall Mall facade with stone and Corinthian columns. In 1793, John Nash, the architect of Regent Street and London's famous terraces, started his architectural firm under the patronage of the Prince of Wales. Sara arrived just as the gentrification of the area to the east of Saint James's Square was beginning.[10]

The broad expanse of Piccadilly Street split Saint James's parish into two. To the north, bawdy neighborhoods of entertainment and prostitution beckoned the adventuresome and the addicted. To the south lay one of the wealthiest and most elegant sections of London, Saint James's, and Green Park, a luxurious neighborhood of great houses for the royal family, aristocrats, poets, and politicians. The new London unfolded as one walked the length of Piccadilly. The east of the city lay dark and ugly, with old buildings stained of soot and streets where people hurried along with no reason to pause except to buy roasted chestnuts or to watch a brawl among the city's dangerous classes. Light filled the new West End, buildings not yet marked by coal, and stores meant for lingering. In 1811, Jane Austen walked along Piccadilly.[11] Austen had Colonel Brandon from *Sense*

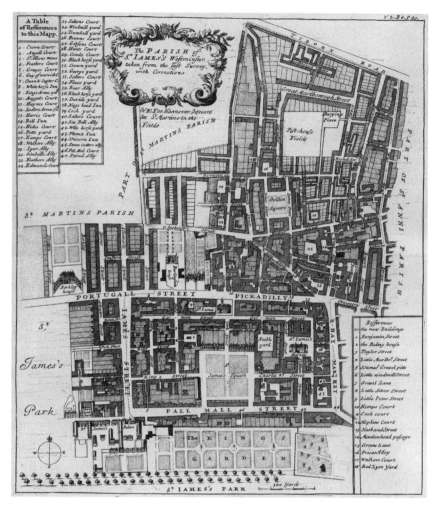

FIGURE 3.1. "The Parish of St. James's Westminster." (c) The British Library Board. All Rights Reserved. Maps. Crace.12.3.

and Sensibility own a house just around the block. Mary Shelley and Percy Bysshe Shelley, artists, diplomats, scientists, statesmen all lived in the area. Food left daily for the royal family from Fortnum and Mason, the venerable emporium still found at the corner of Jermyn and Piccadilly streets.

Sara, Alexander, Hendrik, Matthias, and the other slave boy from the Slave Lodge now lived in one of the busiest and liveliest places in all of

Europe, the center of the publishing and entertainment industries, the home of authors and poets and many of the royal family housed in Saint James's Palace. Piccadilly was a reputable street housing the mansions of the wealthy. Albany Street ran on the other side of Piccadilly from Duke Street and was home to an exclusive apartment building for wealthy bachelors. Byron, Prime Minister Gladstone, and more recently Graham Greene all lived there. Booksellers filled their windows with cartoons lampooning the foibles of the wealthy. Hatchards, the famous bookstore started in 1797 at Number 173 Piccadilly, moving to 190 in 1801.[12] It is still located on Piccadilly. Male artisans who made luxury goods lived above their shops, as did the innkeepers, some of whom were women. One John Smith owned an "eating house" in Jermyn Street, which he kept with his wife and niece. A widow owned Deal's Hotel a few years later.[13]

In between the great squares, artisans and shopkeepers as well as the poor lived in modest to neglected conditions, a bit of poverty hidden away in the wealthy suburb. The London working class made up about three-quarters of the total population of the city, and certain residential patterns were emerging: the West End overwhelmingly wealthy, the East End predominantly poor, the working classes scattered in every neighborhood. Limited transportation and the high demands of the wealthy for servants contributed to the persistence of "large pockets of poverty in the midst of areas of affluence."

In 1811, a visitor to London described with horror the poverty of Irish workers living near wealthy Portman Square just north of Oxford Street: " 'They fill every cellar and every garret . . . a family to each room, very poor, very uncleanly.' "[14] Sara and the men and children probably lived in a similar situation at Duke Street, which was two short blocks south of Piccadilly. Dunlop probably organized the lodgings, having connections through his naval career. Seamen and soldiers returning from duty overseas rented rooms in this neighborhood.[15] While the purpose of the household was to make money from her display, Sara was also Dunlop and Cesars's servant. Baartman would have risen early to make breakfast, sweep the rooms, wash clothes, chores she was accustomed to performing, responsibilities she shared with many black Londoners in this period.

The nineteenth-century black British community, based primarily in the port cities such as Bristol and in London, came from the far reaches of the British Empire, including parts of the Indian subcontinent, the slaveholding colonies of the West Indies, and Sierra Leone. People of African descent in Britain had primarily arrived as slaves, or as people fleeing their enslavement in the British Caribbean slave societies. The Somersett case of 1772 stated that a slave owner could not remove a person he owned without that individual's consent. This led many slaves as well as other antislavery activists to believe that this decision made slaves free once they came to British shores.[16]

The underlying tenor of racial prejudice molded the lives of all black Britons. While in the eighteenth century some men such as Cesar Picton, a coal merchant in Kingston on Thames, became wealthy, this was the exception rather than the rule. As early as 1731, for example, the Corporation of London forbade the apprenticing of black men. This meant that men found employment primarily as servants and sailors. Plans to resettle Jews in Palestine and Afro-Britons and freed slaves in West Africa were all part of a wider debate within British intellectual circles at the turn of the century about British citizenship. In 1786 the founders of the Committee to Relieve the African Poor in London, using a loose definition of skin color as a descriptor of "black," located far more poor Afro-Britons than they had anticipated. The unease over black citizenship helped facilitate plans fostered by the leading antislavery activist Olaudah Equiano to establish a self-governing colony in West Africa.[17]

In 1810, the black population of London was between five and ten thousand strong, and overwhelmingly male. The major campaigns against the British slave trade had achieved popular success under the leadership of William Wilberforce as early as 1788 with the first national petition drive to end the slave trade. By 1807, the antislavery lobby successfully orchestrated a law banning British participation in buying people in Africa and selling them for profit in the New World. With the ending of the trade, fewer Africans found their way to England until the ending of slavery proper in the mid-1830s.

In Sara Baartman's time, no churches or neighborhoods in London served an exclusively black community: most black Britons married people from the poor white working class. The few black women living in the city found employment as washerwomen and nurses. Sara may have encountered some of London's black working men and women in the streets of Piccadilly. Some men, such as Robert Wedderburn, participated in a black intellectual community through publications railing against racial and class injustice. Baartman's gender, working life, and domestic bondage would have allowed her little chance to participate in such activities, however. Beginning in September, Sara would add to these labors her work as the Hottentot Venus.[18]

Alexander knew, as did Hendrik and Sara, that marketing Sara Baartman as the Hottentot Venus could make money. The issue was how. Upper-class residents socialized in clubs, gaming houses, and coffeehouses, and at the theater. Men's clubs took up much of the landscape in Saint James's, their stately architectural graces belying some of the less reputable pleasures indulged behind the closed doors. Beau Brummell partied madly with aristocrats and lived on the credit of his tailors until he escaped for Paris to avoid debtor's prison. At 81 Piccadilly, home to the famous club Watiers, the Prince of Wales cavorted, drank, and ate too much. Upon Prinnie's death, he allegedly had slept with seven thousand women, taking a lock of hair from each one of them.[19] Aristocratic men with time on their hands wandered down the well-paved streets and sidewalks of Piccadilly looking for pleasure of all sorts: books, theater, food and drink, and women. The tendrils of an erotic economy spread out between the stately homes, where along some of the narrow streets men could find some of the most exuberant pleasures of London—if one had the means and the status.

London rents were among the highest in the world. Barely a month after their arrival, Alexander Dunlop contacted William Bullock of the Liverpool Museum at 22 Piccadilly, London's hugely popular museum of natural history. William Bullock had started the museum a year earlier to profit from the English public's taste for artifacts and things scientific. Bullock's immediate success came by exhibiting material from Captain Cook's exploration of the Pacific; by June 1810, some eighty thousand visitors had seen the exhibition. A decade later Bullock enjoyed similar success when he exhibited Gericault's huge and hugely controversial painting *The Raft of the Medusa*, with its dark tones that encouraged discussion of disasters and cannibalism.[20]

Dunlop walked the few blocks from Duke Street to the museum, first to sell a leopard skin to Bullock, who balked at the price. Dunlop returned to Duke Street, the animal skin rolled up under his arm, a good picture of the inside of the Liverpool Museum in his mind. If he could manage to get as many people to see Sara as the possessions of Captain Cook, Dunlop would be a rich man indeed. A week or so later Dunlop again

FIGURE 3.2. "Bullock's Museum, 22, Piccadilly." From *The Repository of Arts, Literature, Commerce, Manufactures, Fashions, and Politics.* London, 1809–29. (c) British Library Board. All Rights Reserved. C.119.f.1.

walked to Bullock's, with the animal skin and a proposition. According to Bullock, Dunlop said that he had "brought" a Hottentot woman from the Cape and that he was "under engagement to return her to the Cape of Good Hope in two years." She was, he continued, of an "extraordinary shape and make . . .an object of great curiosity and would make the fortune of anyone exhibiting her."[21]

Bullock bought the skin, at a lower price than Dunlop had originally offered. However, he rejected Dunlop's proposal to show Sara. He later said he feared "such an exhibition would not meet the countenance of the public." Bullock, it seems, fancied himself less a showman than an exhibitor of the exotic. Bullock looked more to the elite south side of Piccadilly Street than to the red-light district behind him, preferring to attract the upper class and the new bourgeois, who could marvel at his collection of scientific and exotic wonders.[22]

Dunlop needed to design a profitable arrangement as soon as possible. He had assured both Hendrik and Sara that they could make easy money in the great city. Instead, the group faced serious financial problems, if not impending collapse. Sara had no money and Hendrik very little. Alexander's retirement from the military grew near. He could scarcely live on half pay and could not support four people on such a meager income. London was an exorbitantly expensive city, and Dunlop would soon be responsible for two leases, the apartment on Duke Street, and a ground-floor room at 225 Piccadilly. Dunlop then seems to have decided to do something rather different, to combine the scientific and the extraordinary.[23]

Various representations of the Hottentot circulated in London in the early 1800s. Dunlop could have presented Sara Baartman as a "tame Hottentot" or a Christianized savage, given the fact that Baartman had lived most of her life within colonial culture. Just six years earlier, for example, a London Missionary Society missionary had displayed three "converted Hottentots" to London congregations. At a meeting in Scots Church in Swallow Street on November 1803, Johannes Kicherer presented the three people, now known as John and Martha van Rooy, and Martha Arendse, as "converted Hottentots."[24]

Kicherer clearly understood, as Dunlop did later, that Hottentot was a valuable cultural currency in London. Despite the fact that the two women were of partial slave descent and born into colonial society, Kicherer presented the three people as examples of what wonders Christianity could perform on the savage Hottentots of the world beyond the colonial frontier. In other parts of his narrative, Kicherer described Khoekhoe living outside of colonial society as "wild Hottentots" or Bushmen. For Kicherer "tame Hottentots" worked for wages, lived in houses, and adopted Christianity. He presented the "converted Hottentots" precisely as examples of the taming powers of Christianity. The show involved the three Africans also eloquently testifying to their religious awakening. The visit received coverage in the London newspapers, and according to Kicherer, the group left London very pleased with the reception they had received.[25]

In 1810, then, Dunlop could have shown Sara Baartman as another example of a "tame Hottentot." He could have put Baartman onstage as a Hottentot woman who could speak at least two languages, who could tell a fascinating story of journeying in one lifetime, from savagery to civilization, of a life traveled from Baartman's Fonteyn to the new British port of Cape Town. Dunlop no doubt reckoned that such a show, however, would not yield the kind of financial rewards he hoped to garner from a more lurid and distinctive production. Dunlop created an exhibition that combined science and the freak show, and alluded to the public interest in the figure of the prostitute.[26]

London provided many opportunities and examples for exhibiting the strange and the curious. Live shows and images were a key feature of popular entertainment for a mostly illiterate English public well into the nineteenth century. London was the primary venue for such exhibitions. As Richard Altick remarks in his *Shows of London,* "No English trait was more widespread throughout the entire social structure than the relish of exhibitions, and one might add, none was more effective in lowering, however briefly, the conventional barriers that kept class and class at a distance." For centuries, promoters throughout England had displayed striking animals such as lions, tigers, and bears, as well as people who seemed extraordinary and whimsical.[27] This interest predated the rise of evolutionary theory, with various showmen claiming such success in the course of the eighteenth century with displays as diverse as a "Man Teger" from the East Indies, a baboon from West Africa, and a monkey from "the Desarts of Arabia."

In August 1810, Dunlop, Baartman, and Cesars probably attended London's Bartholomew Fair, the most famous of all the pleasure fairs in England at this time. The fair took place for two weeks each August in Smithfield. Promoters brought people, animals, and collectibles to display to an eager public, who also came for the music, food, drink, and popular theater.[28] Bartholomew Fair was a place of bawdiness, rowdiness, enjoyment of pleasures of all the senses. The displays celebrated and marveled at the unusual even as they established the norm through contrast. The old ship surgeon no doubt had attended a few sideshows in his time. Nevertheless, Bartholomew Fair probably provided Dunlop with considerable practical knowledge. One of England's most famous theater owners, John Richardson, had a booth at the fair. He exhibited a child originally from the Caribbean island of Saint Vincent, "The Beautiful Spotted Negro Boy." The showman also displayed "dwarves" and "giants"; he also kept elephants and exotic animals. Richardson adorned his stage with green felt, crimson curtains, and no fewer than fifteen hundred lamps. Richardson's most expensive ticket was two shillings—for a seat in a theater box.[29]

Dunlop appears to have reached for a new model, one that would combine the bacchanalian elements of Bartholomew Fair with pretensions to scientific curiosity. Dunlop claimed, "Since the English took possession of

FIGURE 3.3. "Bartholomew Fair." Pugin and Rowlandson, illustrators. From *The Microcosm of London or London in Miniature.* Vol 1. London: Methuen, 1904.

the Cape, I have been constantly solicited to bring her [Sara Baartman] to this country, as a subject well worthy the attention of the Virtuoso, and the curious in general." Now Sara was in that country. Dunlop probably calculated that the residents of Saint James's would find a display that mixed sexuality and exoticism with a nod to science exciting and enticing and would spread talk and gossip across London. The challenge was to turn her into that "subject worthy of attention."[30]

The show invoked the public interest in the Hottentots of the newly acquired Cape, with Sara Baartman's body presented both as representative of all Hottentot women and as an example of an extraordinary individual body. Sara Baartman was an African woman in a city with a small black population and few black women. With the appropriate dress and presentation, her bottom could be rendered grotesque. The Hottentot Venus would stand at the line between the sexual, the wondrous, and the ethnographic.

The display of "Sartjee the Hottentot Venus" combined elements of the pleasure fair shows, which marveled at the unusual, but it also pointed to a future in which whole cultures became presented outside of history.

Into the nineteenth century, the term "freak" had a different resonance than the horrors it suggests to contemporary readers. "Freak" then implied interesting, affective, fanciful, or unusual; "freakery" was close to miraculous. People with disabilities, or those presented as having unusual anatomies or histories suggested as much the marvels of creation as the horrors of the abnormal.[31]

Like the freak show, the Hottentot Venus would need a showman. Cesars started in this role.[32] The show would require publicity and posters. Sara Baartman would have to appear in clothes that emphasized her bottom in order to render her strange and sexual, but not too risqué. But unlike the people who were displayed, or displayed themselves in the pleasure fairs of England, including Bartholomew Fair, the Hottentot Venus did not have a narrative of her life. Many exhibitors, such as Daniel Lambert, who in 1803 exhibited himself in Piccadilly as the fattest man alive, accompanied their show with detailed life stories. The show of the Hottentot Venus, however, was precisely to reach beyond the unique body Baartman presented, to a link with a whole culture of people living in the Cape. For Sara to have spoken of her history would have been to cast her more in the realm of the "converted Hottentot" who could be admitted into English society, and thus perhaps rendered less unusual. Dunlop, it seems, was determined to underscore the singularity of the Hottentot Venus ironically by placing her outside of history and into culture.

The Hottentot Venus created juxtapositions of difference around gender, race, the body, and culture in a way that created something new—the ethnopornographic freak show—and prefigured the later rise of the ethnographic show as spectacle. While freak shows continued to be a London favorite, the new century became ever more fascinated with innovative displays. An enfreakment of cultures, the process whereby whole societies outside of Europe came to be regarded as singularly peculiar, became a key feature of the most popular exhibitions. The first fifty years of the nineteenth century taxed promoters' talents. With the rise of the Enlightenment, displays came to be regarded as educational, based in science, but the public still wanted to be entertained.[33] The industrializing cultures of nineteenth-century Europe created larger cities, huge migrant populations, anonymous in ways unthinkable in the microcosm of village life. Exhibits such as Sara Baartman's and those of Tono Maria, the "Venus of South America," of "Bushmen," and Zulus, brought later to England, managed this public anonymity in new ways. In the structured setting viewers did not have to be responsible for their gaze, for their encounter with the unfamiliar. The whole point of a structured show was to permit staring in a way that caused little discomfort on the part of the viewer, and which downplayed, through the artifice of the display, empathy with the person staring back from the stage.[34]

In the middle of September, Alexander Dunlop was ready to blitz London with a shrewd advertising campaign. The highest returns lay with the wealthy, but volume went to the less well-to-do masses. Dunlop arranged the making of broadsheets, relatively easy to do in this era, in which publishers who had grown rich off the sagas of the Napoleonic era lined Piccadilly. By 1802 there were two hundred engravers in London, and prints of various sorts were ever more available to the public. Professional engravers often published their own prints or worked closely with particular print sellers. Saint James's Street, right near Duke Street, housed many print sellers. Satirical prints in particular appeared in bound collections and in magazines such as *Town and Country*. Individual prints were also popular and often put up on walls both in public and in private homes. These tended to have smaller print runs, of some hundred copies, print sellers often keeping the original engraving for decades so that they could make new prints if the market so demanded.[35]

Somehow, Alexander Dunlop secured the services of one of England's leading engravers to do the poster, perhaps through the connections already established with the wealthy. In September, Frederick Christian Lewis produced the first of two aquatints of Sara Baartman. He might also have done the original artwork. Lewis (1779-1856) had trained at the Royal Academy near Piccadilly Circle. He gained fame in the early 1800s with his work in *Original Designs of the Most Celebrated Masters in the Royal Collection* (1812) and had a good career doing aquatints of American landscapes. Lewis was not only famous: he was also well connected and worked on commission for members of the royal family.[36]

The aquatint of the Hottentot Venus outside 225 Piccadilly, less than a block away from Bullock's famous museum, with its emphasis on ethnic markings, conveyed the supposedly educational and aesthetic ethos of the display, removed from, but also connected to, the more vulgar traditions of the sideshow. The first broadsheet published on 18 September 1810, later circulated throughout Europe, has become one of the most well known depictions of the Hottentot Venus. This first engraving, fourteen by nine inches in size, depicts a seminude "Sartjee, the Hottentot Venus." Sara Baartman stands alone and sideways to the viewer. Baartman is mostly naked. Her buttocks occupy the center of the image. Her left breast is visible. A kaross or animal skin drapes down the shoulder opposite the viewer, serving as a foil for the naked body rather than covering it. A large headband circles the woman's forehead. Strokes somewhat bolder than one would usually have found among the early Gonaqua of the Eastern lands paint her face. She holds a staff, smokes a pipe, and wears shoes— the latter clearly not part of original Khoekhoe dress.

Lewis produced a second aquatint in March 1811, depicting Sara closer to how she was then being exhibited. Sara faces the viewer, no longer nude in the picture, but in a tight body wrap similar to the one she had worn in the first months of the exhibit. She wears beads, cloth to cover her pubis, a kaross hanging from her back. Sara's face is again painted in thick black lines to resemble the eland to which she had danced as a young girl. In both aquatints Sara's tortoiseshell necklace is clearly visible.

The aquatints represented an imagined Hottentot Woman. But for the tortoiseshell necklace and painted face, Sara's costume was more an amalgam than how the Gonaqua dressed before the colonial period. But the depictions also were not so far off. Who had the knowledge about Khoekhoe society? Dunlop and Cesars surely did not. The surgeon never ventured outside Cape Town. Nor could the men easily consult descriptions of Gonaqua. Hendrik could not read. Sara, on the other hand, had lived in the fading years of Gonaqua independence. According to Anna Staal, Baartman also had the experience of presenting the Hottentot Woman to eager sailors.

We think that Baartman sought to render her depictions with verisimilitude, even if the overall design of the poster was out of her control. And she went one step further. Both aquatints record S. Baartman as the publisher, not Alexander Dunlop or Hendrik Cesars. In a move most unusual for the time, the subject of a print managed to hold the copyright. Sara was the official publisher of the famous depictions. Sara had the rights to her own representation. In a context far from her choosing, she helped to fashion an icon for public consumption.[37] It is highly unlikely that Sara Baartman saw any of the royalties from the sale of her image. And the meaning of her being listed as publisher is hard to determine. The first

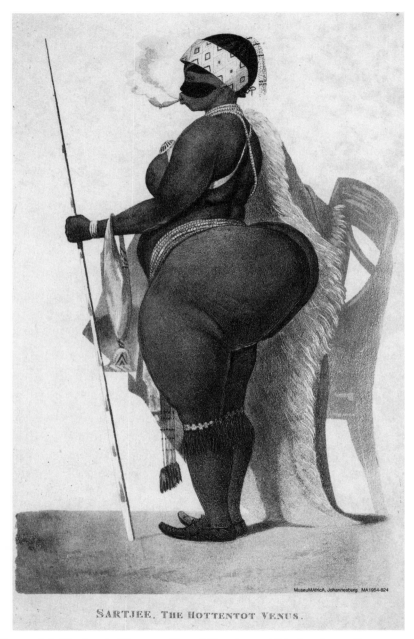

SARTJEE, THE HOTTENTOT VENUS.

MuseumMAfricA, Johannesburg MA1954-824

FIGURE 3.4. "Sartjee, the Hottentot Venus." "London, published as the act directs Sept 18, 1810 by S. Bartmaan." Aquatint. Courtesy of Museum Africa. MA 54824.

SARTJEE, THE HOTTENTOT VENUS.

EXHIBITING AT N° 225, PICCADILLY.

FIGURE 3.5. "Sartjee, the Hottentot Venus, Exhibiting at No. 225, Piccadilly." "Lewis Delin. Et. Sculpt. London, Published as the act directs March 14th, 1811, by S. Bartmaan, 225 Piccadilly." From Daniel Lysons, "Collectanea," (c) British Library Board. All Rights Reserved. C.103.k.11, no. 104.

poster, made early in her stay in England, might well have more genuinely represented her participation in the wider marketing of the production. By March 1811, however, she was contractually under Dunlop's authority, which makes one suspicious of her being named as publisher. Dunlop had reasons, in the wake of the court case about Baartman's liberty, to list her as publisher of the second print too. This might allay fears among members of the public that she was indeed particularly exploited. As in so many aspects of this history, we cannot easily resolve such questions.

Armed with an image that could be put up as a poster and sold also for profit, Dunlop set about informing the London elite and public that the Hottentot Venus had arrived. On 20 September, the first advertisement appeared in the London papers. It stated that the Venus "has been seen already by the principal literati in this Metropolis who were all greatly astonished, as well as highly gratified with the sight of so wonderful a specimen of the human race." Justifying the exhibit, Dunlop wrote "that the value of the exhibit has been fully proved, by the approbation of some of the first Rank and chief Literati in the kingdom, who saw her previous to her being publicly exhibited."

Sara traveled around London appearing in the houses of the wealthy and aristocratic, who nourished themselves on gossip, scandal, and exhibition. Dunlop also offered private showings at 225. Luring the elites, Dunlop figured, would tempt the bourgeoisie to visit 225, including "the ladies." "Parties of Twelve and upwards," said one advertisement, "may be accommodated with a Private Exhibition of the HOTTENTOT, at No. 225. Piccadilly, between Seven and Eight o'clock in the Evening, by giving notice to the Door-keeper the Day previous. A Woman will attend (if required)."[38]

Dunlop had divined the public interest well. His show combined both sides of Piccadilly Street, the posh and the bawdy, highbrow science and lowbrow freakery, Bullock's Museum and Bartholomew Fair. Sara would be clothed in tribal garb and in a way that would display her buttocks, the tight brown dress suggesting nudity. The aquatint of the Hottentot Venus outside 225 Piccadilly, less than a block away from Bullock's famous museum, conveyed the supposedly educational and aesthetic ethos of the display, removed from, but also connected to, the more vulgar traditions of the freak show while echoing the figure of the prostitute familiar to the rakes of Saint James's.

Around noon on 24 September, we can imagine that Cesars and Sara in her threadbare cottons left Duke Street, crossed Jermyn Street, and walked the few short blocks to 225 Piccadilly. A flurry of life swept across the West End streets, men and women shopping, merchandise moving in wagons, coaches passing the White Bear Inn, and ladies out walking accompanied by their maids. Sara entered 225, dressed her body as the Hottentot Venus, and walked onto a small stage.

How should one appear so that Londoners believed that this was a unique person on display? Did one turn one's head slightly to emphasize the bottom? Should one now and then utter some Khoisan or Dutch words? Singing and dancing seemed to make audiences believe that one was a woman from a very distant continent. But could one accomplish this without becoming the Hottentot? The doors opened, welcoming the public to the Hottentot Venus, a primitive Khoekhoe woman in metropolitan London, one of the wonders of the world. London poured in.

How strange to see the women's bosoms heaving desperately out of the high Empire line dresses. The discomfort: What were they thinking? How odd to promote the breast and then constrain arms in tight sleeves and enslave hair in ropes and jewels. Surely they were cold; it was so cold in London. At least the dress let go beneath the belt, floating down their legs in diaphanous folds. The men strutted in top hats. Their long frock coats bulged out in folds behind them and then down to their knees, their own silhouettes sharing much of the outlines of the Hottentot Venus. They laughed, but did they realize how much their own bottoms stuck out as they sought to look more closely at hers?[39]

Sara Baartman stood many long afternoons and into the evenings. People paid their two shillings, the same amount as the special boxes at Richardson's Theatre at Bartholomew Fair. They walked in gasping at the naughtiness of it all, women with eyes averted, men and women trying not to look too eager. Dresses swished on the floor, walking sticks clopping as couples crossed the room into the realm of the Hottentot Venus. Audiences stared at a woman in a very tight brown dress. They stared at her yellow-brown skin and the way it seemed to merge with the cloth. Elite women gawked, finally allowed to gaze at a female form and yet not lose their respectability. The men gawked, too: the dress emphasized the Venus's bottom, titillating the viewer with the semblance of nudity. What an opportunity to see, to feel, to intrude. "Turn around," Cesars demanded.

Sara mostly followed the order; if not, he brought her behind the screen and threatened to hit her. Pay extra, and touch her bottom. "Feel her posterior parts." Sara sighed in sadness even as the Hottentot Venus became "an object of great curiosity from the extraordinary appearance of her person and the unusual shape that belonged to her."[40]

An afternoon and evening was a very long time to endure when people looked at one not as a fellow human being but as an extraordinary object of nature existing at the edge of the exotic and the grotesque, a freak, a monster, an animal. Here was the icon of the adverts, this woman from the far-off Cape who seemed at once so sexual with her large breasts and bottom, and yet so very different from the feminine standards of London with their muted colors and long, slender lines.

The English public read the Hottentot Venus as a novel example of culture and nature, just as Dunlop had intended. Sara had become the "most correct and perfect Specimen of that race of people" that had begun entering Europe's popular imagination. The exhibit was so popular because it met so many and various criteria of public amusement and interest. And she was a black woman in a city with a small black population and very few black women, and parts of her body could be rendered grotesque. The Hottentot Venus was, in short, a perfect exhibit for the times.

The Hottentot Venus became the first figure from Africa to "win publicity" in the nineteenth century. From 1810, Sara stood for more than just herself, just as scientists, scholars, and the post-apartheid nation would again demand of her in different ways after her death. Her body became the foundation for the later far more stylized entrepreneurial forms that constituted the nineteenth-century freak show and for the development of racial science.

Trying to leave the Venus behind, Sara walked back to Duke Street. But work was never done, and ties still bound. By 1810, Sara and Cesars had known each other for some ten years. From the close quarters in the house in Papendorp, they were used to each other's rhythms, rhythms shaped by intimacy and domination. This household added Dunlop and the two African children. And fall with its wet and damp was coming. This was no Cape with its stretches of sea and mountain, and its winds that cleared the air.

Duke Street housed an uncomfortable group in tiny quarters in the warrens of London. Exploitation and intimacy held the household in their grip, a grip probably more representative of households at the time than we might like to consider. We can well imagine that the relationship between Cesars and Sara moved, if it had not been so previously, to one of sexual intimacy. Both Cesars and Sara were of roughly the same age, strangers to London, both colonial naïfs in a huge city. Speaking Dutch together, Cesars and Sara would have found they had something in common in London in a way they had not in Cape Town.

But things were not equal in Duke Street. After supper, Cesars and Dunlop wandered Piccadilly. Sara likely stayed inside: walking about subjected a woman to abuse and invitation both explicit and subtle. Respectable women did not walk out at night. If Sara had gone out, men likely would have seen her not as the Hottentot Venus but as a common prostitute—the dangers of Cape Town revived. Sara may also have heard stories of women murdered and bodies disappearing in the great metropolis, fodder for the anatomists' knives.

Exhausted from a long day's work, Sara went to bed to gather strength for another day. She shivered with cold and longed for warmer clothes. That winter was particularly cold and even colder for someone who had grown up in the warmer climes of southern Africa. On Sundays Sara rested. Sometimes she went for rides in the lovely Green Park and Saint James's Park. She consorted with, or at least mimicked, the wealthy as she rode in a carriage attended by the boys.[41]

By the end of September, the rhythms of the day and the week were being established. Dunlop had income; Sara Baartman was busy. Alexander promised lots of money, and the crowds were coming. And if Hendrik beat her, was that so different from his chastisements in Papendorp? Here, there was money in the beating, money not seen but promised. Life had never been perfect for Sara. It was far from perfect here, but it was perhaps a bit better than eking out a living at the edge of colonial society in Papendorp, three babies dead, one love vanished, only drudgery to fill the days. Perhaps too, though, Sara Baartman was becoming ever more aware of the differences between display in Cape Town and London. London consumed the objects of its gaze. The Hottentot Venus was not artifice, no, she was becoming real, in a way that Sara could not control.

4

BEFORE THE LAW

eptember 1810 began beautifully, with blue skies and warm temperatures and the pleasures of late summer. At the end of the month,
a rare tornado struck southern England, a harbinger of a difficult
season to come. By late October the fall chill had turned to storms and
snow stained gray by coal dust. London sank into its proverbial winter
darkness. The cool Indian muslin women had worn during summer disappeared beneath heavier woolens and linens. Men donned their overcoats.
October and November also saw changes in the lives of the people connected with the Hottentot Venus.

Dunlop took over as Baartman's official employer, and Cesars left Piccadilly, and the show, for the East End. Baartman met a famous duke and
other nobility and became the center of a legal investigation that enthralled London's chattering classes and established an important precedent in English common law. Britain had ended its participation in the
transatlantic slave trade only two years before Sara came to England. In
October and November 1810, controversy joined Sara Baartman's life to
this fundamental social and political transformation of the nineteenth-
century British Empire.

The hullabaloo began with a visit. On Thursday, 11 October 1810,
Zachary Macaulay traveled from his home in bucolic Richmond Park to
what he considered London's iniquitous center. People now tend to remember Macaulay as the father of the more famous Thomas Babington
Macaulay, but he was then a leading abolitionist, secretary of the African
Institution, and member of the Sierra Leone Company. Macaulay first
learned of Sara Baartman in 1810, through newspaper articles and other
"public statements." The aquatint and newspaper advertisements had
done their work. Macaulay wanted to learn how Sara Baartman had come

to England and whether she willingly made a "public spectacle" of herself or "whether she was compelled to exhibit herself."[1] The trip to Piccadilly took more than an hour. Macaulay arrived and paid his two shillings. The question for Macaulay was simple: Was Sara a slave in free England?

At 225 Piccadilly, Macaulay directed his questions to Hendrik Cesars, not Sara Baartman. He wanted to rescue an African woman, not engage her in dialogue. But he asked many questions of Hendrik. Where was Sara's birthplace? How did she end up in Cape Town? What did the Cape government know about Sara, the trip to England, the plans to exhibit her in London? Had the governor given his permission to bring Sara, this Hottentot, across the Atlantic? At the back of each question lay a suspicion if not already a conviction that Baartman's display was in fact an instance of slavery on British soil.

According to Macaulay, Cesars said that Sara Baartman was a "female of the Hottentot tribe" he had "obtained" from the Dutch Boers of the interior who traveled to Cape Town. The governor, Cesars claimed, had given him permission to bring Sara to London. Macaulay had his doubts. The Cape governor Lord Caledon had recently enacted the Caledon Code of 1809, a law that among other things prevented colonists from removing Khoekhoe from the Cape. Macaulay pressed the point. Where, he asked Cesars, was the written proof? Cesars refused to answer this, or any other, question.[2]

Cesars's behavior hardened Macaulay's conviction that Sara was a slave. Sara seemed "unhappy and dejected." The way Cesars treated Baartman particularly troubled Macaulay. Cesars commanded her to turn around on the stage, inviting visitors to touch Sara's buttocks. It seemed as if here was a woman on the slave block, mere chattel prodded by the interested. Zachary concluded that Sara had been "deprived of her liberty." He immediately began a campaign to have the attorney general investigate Sara's status. Letters began appearing in the London newspapers. Public discussion and debate ensued.

In late November, the highest common-law court in the Land, the King's Bench, agreed to consider a single question. Did Sara come to England and exhibit herself under duress or of her own free will? The investigation and hearings that followed created legal precedents that resonate to this day in international law. The legal investigation forever links Sara Baartman with the debate over liberty and freedom, compassion, and the right to intervene to stop the pain of others.

Macaulay was one of the Four Saints, so nicknamed for their combination of Evangelical fervor and political activism in the cause of reform. The Saints included Macaulay's dear friend and brother-in-law Thomas Babington, Thomas Buxton, and William Wilberforce, who had led the movement to end the slave trade. Through the African Institution, Macaulay now sought to bring "civilization" to Africa. Zachary Macaulay's work as a leading antislavery activist does not appear to have softened a man so unapproachable and self-righteous that he constantly invited hatred and vindictiveness. Macaulay had his own troubles, many of recent origin, others that lay deeper in his past.

Born in 1768, the third son of one Reverend Macaulay of Edinburgh, the young Zachary struggled to find a career. Like many second- and third-born sons from the middling classes, Zachary looked to the slaveholding islands to supply a richer future. Ties to the Caribbean and South Carolina ran deep in Edinburgh. At just sixteen, the future abolitionist became an overseer on a slave plantation on Jamaica.

Macaulay did not like becoming, in his words, the "vexatious, capricious, tyrannical, and pitiless . . . overseer." Nevertheless, he reconciled himself to the brutalities of plantation life for which Jamaica overseers were justly infamous. "You would hardly know," Macaulay wrote to a friend, that the man "with whom you have spent so many hours in more peaceful and more pleasant scenes, now works in a field of canes, amidst perhaps a hundred of sable race, cursing and bawling . . . the noise of the whip resounding on their shoulders . . . the cries of the poor wretches whose lives the overseer's whip often cut short."[3]

Macaulay seems to have been unwilling to take a stand of his own against slavery. He was therefore lucky that fate intervened and rescued him from association forever with being on the wrong side of history. After some four years of living in Jamaica, Macaulay received a letter from his uncle urging him to return to England, and so he did, arriving just as he turned twenty-one, in 1783.

Macaulay awakened to the evils of slavery soon after arriving home. Marriage helped. Thomas Babington, a member of the powerful antislavery group the Clapham Sect, had married Macaulay's sister. Thomas took his new brother-in-law under his wing. A powerful relationship developed between the two men as Macaulay entered the most activist circle of the British antislavery movement.[4]

HEROES OF THE SLAVE TRADE ABOLITION.

FIGURE 4.1. "Heroes of the Slave Trade Abolition." By unknown artist, wood engraving, middle to late nineteenth century. Given by W. M. Campbell Smyth, 1936. (c) National Portrait Gallery, London. NPG D9338.

Macaulay's new politics drew him to Africa and to the Caribbean memories of violence he had perpetrated on the backs of Jamaican slaves. Sierra Leone, the colony established by abolitionists, became the focus of Macaulay's interests. Activists against the slave trade, including Olaudah Equiano, established Sierra Leone on the west coast of Africa.[5] Their first attempt foundered, and in 1791, abolitionists, including Macaulay, started the Sierra Leone Company. Former runaway slaves from Jamaica, known as maroons, as well as people of African descent in Britain were among the first settlers in the new colony. Macaulay became governor of Sierra Leone for just over a year in 1794-95. He was then only in his early twenties. He again served as governor from March 1796 to April 1799. But faith in the future of Sierra Leone soon dimmed. The company struggled with mismanagement. Immigrants died of fever. Tensions with indigenous people proved intractable. Even the slave trade expanded. In 1808, the Sierra Leone Company transferred the colony to the Crown.

Activists' interests in Africa did not decrease. In the aftermath of the ending of the British slave trade in 1807, a small group of activists began turning their attention to the African continent, arguing that it needed reform and civilization in order to fully benefit from the ending of the slave trade. The African Institution became the key activist group in antislavery between 1807 and the 1820s. Macaulay was secretary until 1812. The ambiguity of abolitionists' views of Africans is evident in the first report of the society, which stated that the institution aimed to "introduce the blessing of civilised society among a people sunk in ignorance and barbarism."[6]

Abolitionist circles in Britain before the 1820s and the start of the major popular campaigns to ameliorate and then end slavery in the British Empire were very small and dominated by the London elite. The Duke of Gloucester, a prince, was the president of the African Institution, and "its committee consisted of the most respected and well-known public figures of the age—lords, bishops, political leaders, MPs, social and moral reformers." The same people often sat on a variety of organizations, effectively shaping public discourse on topics relating to slavery, Sierra Leone, and the people of African descent in Britain. Eight out of fourteen directors of the Sierra Leone Company between 1807 and 1808 were also members of the African Institution committee and "consisted of the most respected and well-known public figures of the age."[7] Thomas Perronet Thompson, the first governor of the crown colony of Sierra Leone, caustically if accurately remarked in 1809:

> The Sierra Leone interest is the leaven which sets all in motion. At the African Institution they impudently declare that they have no concern either with commerce or with missions; they step into their coaches and *presto*—they are the Sierra Leone Company—*hey pass* and they are the Society for Missions to Africa and to the East; another transformation makes them the Society for the Suppression of Vice; a fourth carries them to the India House, and a fifth lands them in the House of Commons.[8]

Mammon was indeed never very far away from virtue. Virtuous work took money. In April 1810, some three months before Sara arrived in London, Babington and Macaulay, already partners in the Clapham Sect and the African Institution, entered a partnership "as Merchants and Insurance Brokers" in order to benefit from Sierra Leone's environmental riches.[9]

It was toward the end of that year that Macaulay raised a public outcry about Sara Baartman's situation. Why did he do so, and why then? Is the answer as self-evident as it might appear—an abolitionist simply doing his activist work on behalf of a black woman, the very symbol of enslavement? We think not. Slavery and his complicity in it haunted Macaulay. We think that at least one reason why Macaulay seized on the situation of Sara Baartman with such alacrity in October 1810 was because his position as a Saint was in jeopardy. So, too, was the reputation of the African Institution as a whole given its entanglements with Sierra Leone.

The cloak of legislative victory over the trade in 1807 failed to protect Macaulay from his more recent past. Thomas Perronet Thompson, who the Saints had nominated to be the new governor of Sierra Leone, turned now into a foe. Even before going to the colony in 1808, Thompson had been troubled by his conversations with Macaulay. Thompson had reservations about the existing practice of apprenticing individuals in Sierra Leone. His stay in the colony did nothing to dampen his concern. He soon started investigating the role of previous governors and members of the Sierra Leone Company, including Macaulay, in sustaining this practice. The Saints were unhappy, to say the least. They had formidable enemies, to whom they did not want to give ammunition. The Duke of Clarence, the future King William IV, for example, delivered long, vitriolic speeches in Parliament defending the slave trade and the West Indian planter interests.[10]

Wilberforce soon wrote to Thompson: "Instead of having to congratulate you on the auspicious commencement of your government," he began, "I am bound to declare . . . that you make me tremble . . . by the temper and spirit you appear to have assumed." Wilberforce's alarm at Thompson's activism caused him to recall the governor. Wilberforce hoped Thompson would hold his tongue upon his return to England. Thompson did not.

Thompson returned to England in May 1810, full of venom for Macaulay and other members of the Sierra Leone Company whom he saw as supporting slavery in the colony, and determined to get a hearing from the government. Thompson charged that contracts of apprentices in Sierra Leone were never actually ended and that apprentices were thus in a de facto state of slavery. In letters dating from July 1810 through January 1811, he implicated Macaulay and the directors of the Sierra Leone Company in supporting slavery in the colony. At roughly the same time, the chief justice of Sierra Leone also brought charges of libel against Macaulay. The charges were so "widely disseminated that it became necessary for Macaulay to vindicate his character."[11] The Saints had managed to end Britain's participation in the Atlantic slave trade only to suffer accusations of practicing slavery under the cloak of a linguistic sleight of hand. Wilberforce and especially Macaulay, lay in the crosshairs of attack.

It was in this context that Sara Baartman's display offered Macaulay a wonderful opportunity to demonstrate the vitality of the African Institution's concern to end slavery and to defend his honor as a man of principle. Creating a cause out of Sara Baartman continued the work of the African Institution and muted the political controversies that swirled about the Saints. Macaulay's interest in the status and plight of Sara in 1810 certainly was also part of an enduring commitment on his part to ameliorating the conditions of slaves. But his interest was limited only to Baartman's status. Macaulay's interest in Sara Baartman's situation resonated well both for Macaulay and for the antislavery lobby, with a long abolitionist history of representing slavery through a suffering female figure. Appealing to the public on behalf of a Khoekhoe woman also fit well with the claim that the British takeover of the Cape had rescued the Khoekhoe from Boer domination.[12]

It is striking that neither the court nor Macaulay took up the position of the two black boys resident in the household at Duke Street—Sara even referred to them in her testimony. We have seen that at least one of the boys, Matthias, came from Cape Town. These children might well have been in a state of slavery in London, yet Macaulay did not find their case compelling. Investigating the status of the boys living with Sara Baartman would perhaps have been to open up also for investigation, at least by Macaulay's conscience, his own complicity in a similar practice. In 1799, Macaulay himself had brought to England African boys from Sierra Leone and had become embroiled in controversy.[13]

Macaulay's crusade was thus also a defense of that narrative of the beneficent humanist that he had so sorely constructed in the aftermath of his experiences as an overseer in Jamaica. The identities of both Macaulay and Sara Baartman were at stake in the investigation that soon followed.

On 12 October 1810, a day after Macaulay's visit, a letter appeared in the *Morning Chronicle*. The author, "An Englishman," was in great likelihood Macaulay. He explained that Sara, this poor "wretched creature . . . has been brought here as a subject for the curiosity of this country. . . . This poor female is made to walk, to dance, to shew herself, not for her own advantage but for the profit of her master, who, when she appeared tired, holds up a stick to her, like the wild beast keepers, to intimidate her into obedience." Macaulay knew obedience and violence well. He argued that while people did show themselves for profit in London, they did so of their "own free will." Baartman, on the other hand, "this poor slave," was "obliged to shew herself, to dance to be the object of the lowest ribaldry."[14]

Macaulay's visit seems to have alarmed Dunlop since on 13 October 1810 the *Morning Chronicle* now published a letter purportedly from Cesars, defending his display of Baartman. It is unlikely that Cesars was the author; the will he drew up in March 1810 shows that he could not write. Free Blacks at the Cape had virtually no access to education. Hendrik could not write his name in Dutch, let alone compose a letter in English. Perhaps he dictated the letter to Dunlop, but the rhetoric's appeal to conventions in English public life suggests that Dunlop was both scribe and author.[15]

"Having observed in your paper on this day, a letter signed 'An Englishman' containing a malicious attack on my conduct in exhibiting a Hottentot Woman, accusing me of cruelty and ill treatment exercised towards her, I feel compelled, as a stranger, to refute this aspersion, for the vindication of my own character, and the satisfaction of the public." Dunlop was no stranger. Pretending he was Hendrik offered Dunlop a claim to colonial authenticity and knowledge about the Khoekhoe. It also perhaps created the ruse of a visitor innocent of the moral complexities of England. Both positions offered sanctuary from the moralizing of "An Englishman."

The "Englishman," Dunlop continued, "betrays the greatest ignorance in regard to the Hottentot, who is as free as the English. This woman was my servant at the Cape, and not my slave, much less can she be so in England where all breathe the air of freedom; she is brought here with her own free will and consent, to be exhibited for the joint benefit of both our families."[16]

On the technicalities of Sara's status at the Cape, the letter was correct, although whether Sara Baartman ever saw wages from Cesars in Cape Town is highly doubtful, and we have already seen she was gifted, as chattel, from Elzer to Pieter Cesars. In Britain, money was at least theoretically available to Baartman through the sale of broadsheets and from proceeds from the show. Dunlop/Cesars could report that a slave she emphatically was not. Dunlop had turned the table on Macaulay, using a clever bit of logic. Since Sara was in England and England was the home of freedom, it naturally followed that Sara was free. So "that there may be no misapprehension on the part of the public," Dunlop concluded, "any person who can make himself understood to her is at perfect liberty to examine her, and know for herself whether she has not been always treated, not only with humanity, but with the greatest kindness and tenderness."[17]

Dunlop perhaps believed that a strong offense served him best. He was sorely mistaken. Macaulay returned with renewed vigor to 225 Piccadilly on 15 October, now with two other members of the African Institution. One was Thomas Babington. The other man, Peter van Wageninge, spoke Dutch. Interview Sara they would, since they now had someone who could indeed "make himself understood to her."

The three men stayed for more than an hour. They watched Cesars make Sara Baartman leave the little recess where she went to hide. They observed her unhappiness. Her "Exhibitor" treated her very badly, "as he would to any of the brute creation." Sara sighed deeply several times in the course of that hour and seemed distressed. Van Wageninge asked Sara questions in Dutch. Did she have any relations? Was she happy? Did she want to go back to the Cape?

Sara refused to answer.[18]

The men left, convinced that they had just witnessed slavery in free England. Further campaigning followed. More letters appeared toward month's end, from "A Man and a Christian," "White Man," "Humanitas," likely all by members of the African Institution, perhaps all from the pen of Zachary Macaulay. The letters introduced no new themes, reproducing only clichés of the female victim—a perspective taken up by much of the scholarly research on Baartman. This woman was wounded by slavery, a "wretched object advertised and publicly shewn for money—the 'Hottentot Venus,' " "an unfortunate being," a "poor creature," a "helpless" black woman.[19]

Dunlop began responding to the newspaper attacks with his own letter on 22 October. He connected the exhibition with London's popular exhibits. Referencing the tall Irishman, Patrick O'Brien, who had entertained London with his size in the early 1800s, Dunlop asked has "she not as good a right to exhibit herself as an Irish Giant, or a Dwarf?"[20]

Dunlop did change the exhibition, apparently in order to forestall additional criticism. He got rid of the tight body stocking that suggested a nude Hottentot Venus. He also rid the show of Hendrik Cesars. The interaction between Cesars and Baartman onstage seems to have been a distraction for audience members otherwise eager to look at the Hottentot Venus. On 29 October, "A White Man" charged that two letters from the foreigner who claimed to be "her keeper" were so equivocating that they did not satisfy the queries of the public.[21]

At least some viewers seem to have mistranslated Cesars. The way they understood identity did not render his Cape status visible in London. Cesars, as we now know, lived in the Cape context as a Free Black. In London, some spectators rather saw in the tableau of Cesars and Sara Baartman a vignette of Boer-slave relations, which the British takeover of the Cape in 1806 was supposed to have helped end. Sir John Barrow, traveling in the Cape at the turn of the century, popularized the notion of the Boers as European savages, rendered uncivilized through their many years of living in Africa.[22] Now, letter writers cast Cesars in the role of the awful Dutch farmer who had slid into barbarity. Some members of the London public understood Cesars as a foreigner and, it seems, a Boer, not a man of acknowledged slave descent himself wounded by inequality and prejudice.

For a brief while in England, one might imagine that Cesars enjoyed his new status freed from the shackles of Cape classification. However, London rendered Cesars's foreignness problematic. The public cast Hendrik as a colonial brute, not as fully civilized as the English. His performance of race in England was thus double-edged. It gave him status that he could only dream of in the Cape, the status of whiteness, but it was a whiteness supposedly sullied by colonial power. This rendition complicated his public relationship with the display of Sara Baartman—to the extent that he withdrew from his public role. The letter of 22 October, purportedly from him, announced that "as my mode of proceeding at the place of public exhibition seems to have given offence to the Public, I have given the sole direction of it to an Englishman, who now attends."[23]

Perhaps Alexander misunderstood, however, the cause of public unease. He seems to have interpreted the difficulties of display as concerning only Cesars's "foreign" status. He does not seem to have registered that it was Cesars's threatening tone toward Baartman that caused discomfort among some viewers. With a history as a surgeon working in the Slave Lodge, Dunlop perhaps took for granted a certain brutality that did not sit well on a London stage, in an England beginning to pride itself on a certain romantic humanism and identification with suffering.

Their defense lawyer later better understood some of the dynamics. He argued in the investigation by the King's Bench that most of the affidavits against Baartman's display referred to "an occasion when the keeper had been observed to hold up his hand to the woman in a menacing posture; the fact being, that . . . the person alluded to, had from that very circumstance, been removed from his situation."[24] The threatening interaction, as much as the identity of the showman, caused disquiet. Both factors came into play no doubt. The perception that Cesars was a colonial foreigner confirmed his viciousness toward the Hottentot Venus. He had to go.

Shortly thereafter, on 29 October 1810, Dunlop drew up a contract with Baartman employing her as a domestic servant. This change in showmanship did not mollify critics, who wanted to know who "the real Agent" was. "All farther concealment can only awaken the indignation of the public."[25]

There was nothing like controversy to attract the curious. Even unfavorable press could be very good publicity indeed. The Hottentot Venus became the talk of London. The controversy and Dunlop's advertising campaign succeeded in creating a steady stream of visitors, some titillated by the Hottentot Venus, others both stimulated by and concerned with her plight. "They ill-use that poor creature!" the actor John Kimble wrote, "how very shocking!" Sara apparently appreciated his empathy.[26] In November, one Henry Grimston wrote to his brother, "Some of the papers have written much about the impropriety of shewing a poor unfortunate stranger, as they think her, against her will because, in this blessed country, however a person may have been a slave in an other [sic] clime 'if their lungs receive our air that moment they are free.' Yet nobody prevents it!" Despite his disgust, Grimston sent his sisters "an outline of the Hottentot Venus."[27]

Dunlop claimed that London's "Literati" had seen Sara. Many of England's greatest writers lived in the immediate vicinity of Piccadilly. If they did not personally see the exhibit, they certainly would have read about the controversy and likely discussed it. Mary Shelley, soon to begin writing *Frankenstein*, lived near 225. The great poet Lord Byron moved to Saint James's in 1811. Coleridge visited London on and off while Sara stood on exhibit. Keats lived on the other side of town in the Swan and Hoop. While visiting her brother Henry, who lived on Sloane Street, Jane Austen traveled along Piccadilly in 1811, passing 225 on her way to the British Gallery.

London imbibed the spectacle of the Hottentot Venus. Londoners moved from poking Sara Baartman's bottom onstage to lampooning it in popular print. Cartoons and songs also appeared. One famous cartoon lampooned the rump Parliament. Another cartoon, breathtaking in its rudeness and insult, lampooned what pundits called "The Broad Bottom Ministry." A commentator remarked that the "printshops are full of her measuring broad bottoms with Lord Grenville." Cartoons linked the bottom of the Hottentot Venus with the corpulence of the prince regent. On 13 November, a cartoon directly referred to Cesar/Dunlops' statement comparing Sara Baartman to people who showed themselves for money. "The Three Graces" depicted the Hottentot Venus in the middle of a trio, a little person on her right, a thin albino woman on her left.[28]

Just before England's highest court discussed whether Sara Baartman lived free or as a slave, whether this woman was capable of free will, the Hottentot Venus had a most important showing, before the Duke of Queensberry, one of London's most infamous rakes. Then in his eighties,

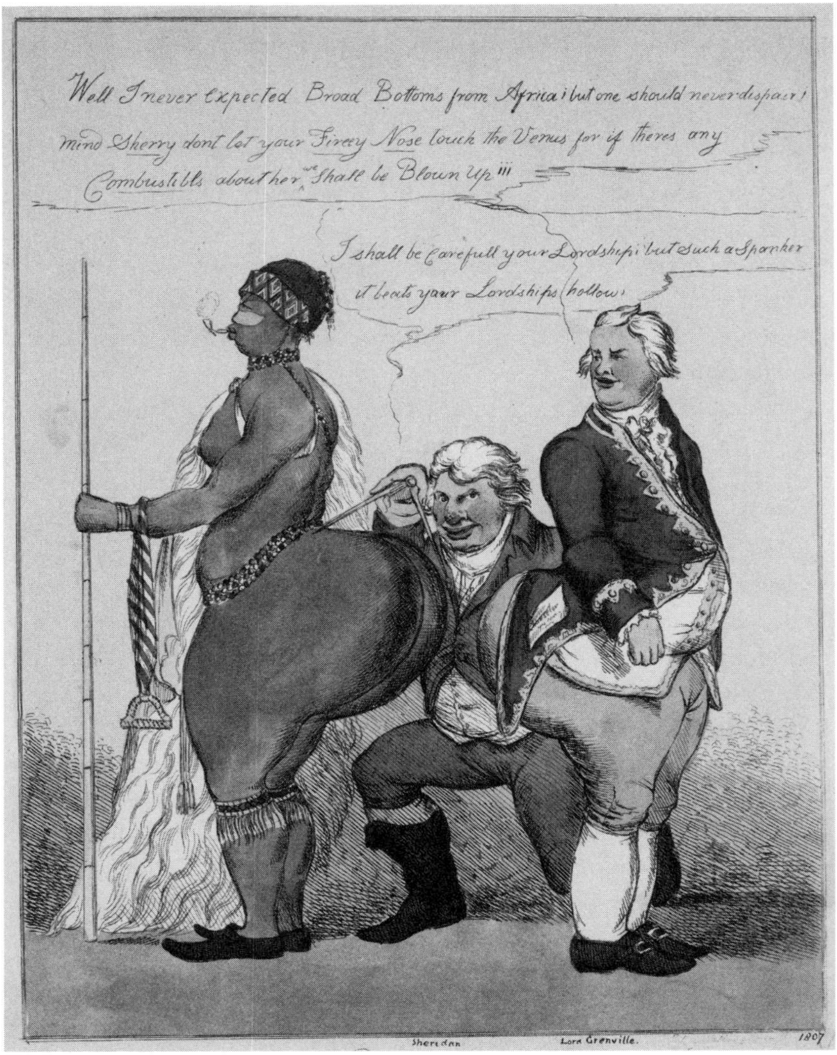

FIGURE 4.2. "A Pair of Broad Bottoms, 1810." Cartoon by William Heath. (c) The Trustees of the British Museum. 00136490001.

and near death, in late November he sent a chair for Sara Baartman to bring her to his mansion in Piccadilly. She boarded a chair held by four men and with thick cloth shielding her from the early winter's breezes coming off the Thames. The Hottentot Venus was carried down the street like a lady, a far cry from the miles of walking Sara Baartman had done in Cape Town. Sara Baartman stood before the duke and his guests. They demanded that she dance. She complied, performing "an African fandango in a style of true savage simplicity," which the duke much enjoyed. The duke and his guests examined the woman who had caused such a brouhaha. The duke subjected Sara to a "microscopic" inspection, a visual dissection, particularly of her bottom.[29]

What degradation and fame, juxtaposed. Sara had been carried like nobility to the duke's mansion, only to be treated like a slave on a block. In this context, perhaps the ascension of the Hottentot Venus, a phantasmic being, offered protection, the fantasy figure hiding Sara Baartman. A cartoon soon appeared in which the Hottentot Venus rejected the offer of marriage from no less than the Duke of Clarence, the future king. Bags of money hang from her hips, the duke claws at her, desperately, but to no avail. Perhaps the Hottentot Venus has here the last laugh, but what of Sara Baartman?[30] If Sara had thought before that she could to some extent control the results of showing her body to an audience, she surely could do so no longer as her body became the stuff of jokes and humiliation.

Macaulay remained convinced that he had discovered slavery in London. If high and popular culture embraced the Hottentot Venus, perhaps the law would rescue Sara Baartman. The scandal Macaulay sought to generate came to a head that month, in November 1810, when he persuaded the court of the King's Bench to intervene. After considerable pressure by the Saints, the attorney general submitted a writ of habeas corpus, an application to the court requesting that the judges collect evidence concerning Saartje Baartman, the Hottentot Venus.[31]

The King's Bench pointed out to the attorney general that an interested party could bring a case of public indecency. Sara had first appeared in a very tight-fitting brown dress that echoed nudity. People literally had poked at her bottom. The attorney general did not take the court's advice and instead followed the leaders of the African Institution. The Saints cared less about decency than liberty. The investigation proceeded on the grounds of slavery and freedom, an investigation into pain and the obliga-

FIGURE 4.3. "King's Bench." Pugin and Rowlandson, illustrators. From *The Microcosm of London or London in Miniature*. Vol. 1. London: Methuen, 1904.

tion of others to intervene to alleviate suffering. Britain as triumphant defender of virtue and liberty would come to the rescue.[32]

"It is much to the credit of this Country," the attorney general argued, "and particularly to the credit of that Society who instruct me to make this application that a person in the condition in which this unfortunate woman is placed is not without friends here." "These Gentlemen," he continued, "will receive her under their protection and will restore her to that Country from which she has been brought and they will also take care in the interim that she be properly disposed of."[33] The court would release Sara into safety.

This hardly was a legal argument. But the attorney general had powerful evidence of Sara's enslaved status. Appearing before the justices, the long rays of autumnal light passing through the immense windows of the high-ceilinged hall, the African Institution presented the depositions of William Bullock of the Egyptian Museum, Zachary Macaulay, his brother-in-law

Thomas Babington, and Pieter Van Wageninge, who had the benefit of knowing Dutch.

Bullock's deposition recounted how Alexander Dunlop had approached him in August, first trying to sell the leopard skin, and then returning to offer Sara Baartman for display in his museum, as if she could be bought and sold like any other piece of property. In the second, more damning, deposition Macaulay, Babington, and Van Wageninge described their visits to 225 Piccadilly. They portrayed a woman manifestly unhappy, treated inhumanly, exhibited under duress and compulsion, and living in a state of bondage. According to Macaulay, Sara "was produced exactly as any beast would be—that some sort of control was practiced over her as would be practiced by a man leading a Bear by a chain . . . that he has no doubt whatever that this Woman is in a state of absolute control to her keeper and has no will of her own."[34]

With this evidence, the attorney general applied to the King's Bench "for Rule to shew cause why a writ of habeus corpus should not be issued." The King's Bench agreed. The investigation proceeded. The key witness would be Sara Baartman, the central actor in the legal drama. The court ordered an interview with Baartman. They ordered it be done "out of the presence of her keeper," by whom they appear to have meant Cesars. The attorney general wanted the interview to be conducted in her natal tongue, but the court determined that Dutch would have to suffice.[35]

Dunlop knew he needed a lawyer once Sara's life came under the legal gaze of the attorney general and the King's Bench. He also knew that the brouhaha concerned less decency than the more abstract issue of slavery and freedom. He needed an agreement; a contract would be a trump card. As always, Dunlop was prepared. He had the contract he had drawn up shortly after the beginning of the controversy in October. The contract marked Dunlop's mastery and Cesar's marginalization. Hendrik Cesars left Duke Street and moved to rough Minories in London's East End.

No longer Hendrik's servant, Sara now moved decisively into the realm of naked profit, a realm less touched by the complex bonds of history and intimacy that marked her life with the Cesars family in Papendorp. The contract, retroactively dated to just before Sara departed Cape Town in April 1810, stipulated a term of service of five years in length. In its duty to the laborer, it is a model of contractual language; it traffics in a kind of fantasy of the good nineteenth-century employer, a romance subverted, however, by context. The original agreement, dated 29 October 1810, was in English. Sara Baartman thus was highly unlikely to have understood it well at this time. We have no evidence that she could read, and her English was probably not very good, certainly not in March, before her leave of the Cape. We also have no evidence as to whether Dunlop read it to Baartman or translated it initially to her. The agreement superseded the one alleged to have been entered into (we find no record of this contract) while Sara, Dunlop, and Cesars lived in Cape Town, by which Sara was to receive a portion of the money from exhibiting her body in England.

The new contract spoke to the different forms of labor expected of Sara Baartman. She was expected to do domestic chores, and to exhibit herself in both England and Ireland—Dunlop was clearly already planning a trip to that country, one that eventuated in April 1812. He was supposed to pay Baartman twelve guineas, equal to just over twelve pounds, and all expenses of the trip to Ireland. Dunlop also promised to pay for her return to the Cape should she wish to go before the five years were up. But Baartman probably knew little of the contents of this contract of service; it was only when court officers came to interview Sara that one of them made a Dutch translation of the contract and then shared it with her. Sara carried this document all the way to Paris, where after her death it came into the possession of the Musée de l'Homme (Museum of Man). The contract was perhaps a sad talisman of that moment when the law knocked at her door in London town.[36]

On 27 November, several men knocked at Duke Street, Saint James's Square. The coroner of the court and a notary accompanied two merchants fluent in Dutch. The court had stipulated that her "keeper" not be there. Cesars was not: he had been living in Minories, near the Tower of London, for more than a month. The men also confirmed that they interviewed Sara Baartman out of the presence of Dunlop. This is unclear, however, as Gaselee, Dunlop's advocate, said that Dunlop had attended the interview.[37] The solicitors of both parties were present. We can imagine that Sara Baartman felt the weight of Dunlop's power looming in the figure of his attorney, George Moojen, perhaps even in Dunlop's very presence.

The men spoke to Sara for three hours. They asked her to recount her life story. How did she end up in the Cape? (Had Sara been enslaved by frontier Boers?) And what of her trip to England? (Had Sara been sold? Did she leave Cape Town under duress?) Did she remain in the city willingly? (Was there a slave in free England?) Did she have any complaints about her situation and treatment? (Was Sara unhappy, in distress, physically or mentally abused?)

After all the publicity, the controversy, the renderings of Sara as a victim of slavery, she finally speaks. Sara Baartman's voice finally enters the archival record, but perhaps not in ways the antislavery activists wished. This is one of only two records we have where Sara had an opportunity, however compromised, to leave a statement about the story of her life.[38] The statement is a paraphrase of the interview, and a translation from Dutch into English. Even here, we see Sara Baartman at a remove, through the lens of Europe. The context in which she produced this account of her life, as well as the huge absences in the archival record, confound our ability to know her.

So let us listen, aware of the yawning gaps of history that separate us from Sara's account of her life, and of the context in which she spoke. She gave it before four European men, one being now her formal employer, Alexander Dunlop, and before two African boys who had journeyed with her from Cape Town across that big sea to the capital of the world.

Sara spoke in Dutch, her second language. As recounted by the interpreters, "The Brother of her late master, Peter Caesar, brought her to the Cape." The late master here was Hendrik. Sara registered in this interview the feature that the court seems to have most wanted to secure: that she had no ties anymore to Hendrik, the man who others had seen abuse her and who probably had enslaved her. He was now "her late master" living in the East End. Sara said she had gone to Cape Town "of her own consent" and had been Hendrik and Anna Staal's "nursery maid." Sara Baartman did not speak of the years when she lived in Elzer's household and was then passed on to Pieter Cesars, given as inheritance. The language of contract and freedom was clearly the register demanded of this interview. The questions posed assumed a world of contract, even in its denial; Dunlop no doubt had also coached her to speak of freedom. Sara did so.[39]

As to England, Sara said she had traveled there "by her own consent." The agreement was that she "was promised half of the money for exhibiting her person. . . . for a period of six years." As to the issue of whether or not the Cape government allowed Dunlop and Cesars to bring Sara to England, Sara stated that she "went personally to the Government in company with Hendrick Caesar to ask permission to go to England." And how would Sara return? "Mr. Dunlop promised to send her back after that period at his own expence [*sic*] and to send the money belonging to her with her."

Sara stated that she had "everything she wants; has no complaints to make against her master or those who exhibit her; is perfectly happy in her present situation; has no desire whatever of returning to her own country not even for the purpose of seeing her two Brothers and four sisters; wishes to stay here because she likes the Country and has money given her by her master of a Sunday when she rides about in a Coach for a couple of hours." Sara was "not desirous of changing her present situation—no personal violence or threats have been used by any individual against her; she has two Black Boys to wait upon her: One of the boys assists her in the morning when she is nearly completely attired for the purpose of fastening the Ribbon round her waist." Sara's only complaint was that she was often rather cold.[40]

Ah, what a lovely picture Sara Baartman painted. The court officers, perhaps reveling in the picture of merrie London, listened with apparent equanimity. Finally the notary asked the simplest of questions. Did she want to go back to the Cape of Good Hope or stay in England?

"Stay Here."[41]

Sara evaded answers that would bring her into conflict with Dunlop: she was unwilling to talk about whether she could choose to end her exhibition. Solly and Moojen said that she understood "very little of the agreement made with her by Mr. Dunlop on the twenty ninth of October 1810—and which Agreement she produced to us." She told them that she could neither read nor write.[42] Nonetheless, the legal representatives involved in the investigation for the King's Bench took what appears now as a statement made in a context of power and probably coercion, and by a person who did not fully grasp the nature of the contract she was now entered into, as a transparent expression of Sara's will. The court did not reflect on the fact that Sara had grown up in conditions of slavery, a state that sought indeed to deny enslaved individuals the capacity to exercise free will. Nor did they consider how Sara might have felt having white men interview her in her home. Would she have felt safe to truly say what she felt?

Colonized people survived colonial cultures through dissemblance of their motives and hopes from settlers and slaveholders. Would Sara indeed have considered, in 1810, just some six months after leaving the Cape, that it would be politically feasible for her to speak truth to power? If she had wanted to stop being displayed, what were her options? Perhaps Sara saw humanitarian self-righteousness hijacking her chance to make money in London. Perhaps she feared the reprisals of Dunlop should she say she was unhappy. Perchance unhappiness in London was not as bad as in Cape Town, or was it worse? About these important issues of perception, as in so many other instances, we can only surmise. The context deeply constrained Sara Baartman's chance to talk to history. Her words slip away; they mimic what might have been. They caution history, and those who believe in the power of the historical fact, that individuals rarely can speak truth to power.[43]

The King's Bench discharged the rule the next day, 28 November 1810. The investigation ended.[44] Macaulay and the other Saints of the African Institution washed their hands of the entire matter. In saying she was content to exhibit herself for money in London, Sara Baartman refused what was to become one of the most potent sites of self-representation for the British public in the early nineteenth century, that of liberators of black women from the abuses of slavery. Instead of hailing Sara as the martyr who Britain could save, the public rendered her now only an oddity. Sara returned to Duke Street, to Dunlop, to her life as the Hottentot Venus.

The decision regarding the Hottentot Venus had lasting implications in law. The case helped establish law with regard to habeas corpus—a writ that authorizes a court investigation into whether a person is being unlawfully detained. The decision on the Hottentot Venus influenced social welfare law in England. The United States invokes the case to this day, in cases dealing with the foreign nationals' relationship to the state.[45]

Far from conferring liberty, or rescuing Sara Baartman, the abolitionists' campaign propelled the Hottentot Venus into notoriety. The English public clamored to see her through April 1811. Cartoons, a Christmas pantomime, and ditties lampooned the gentry, politicians, and the Hottentot

Venus. In 1810, a ballad appeared retelling the story of the case. "The storie of the Hottentot ladie and her lawful knight who essayed to release her out of captivitie and what my lordes [*sic*] the judges did therein."[46] By 1812, however, the Hottentot Venus had declined to a sideshow of the provinces. It was perhaps there, ironically, that Sara Baartman found community and companionship in England. If so, it lasted only for a short while.

5

LOST, AND FOUND

From the end of 1810 through April 1811, Sara continued her work at 225 Piccadilly, walking the few blocks each day from the Duke Street apartment. Newspaper letters, detailed reports of the legal proceedings, and the royal family's interest in the Hottentot Venus secured an eager market. With the start of the new year, crowds continued to view the exhibit. In March, Lewis fashioned the new poster of Baartman, now facing the viewer and covered in beads, her breasts no longer visible, with the two black marks across her cheek. As with the image of September 1810, Sara Baartman remained the publisher, retaining copyright over the dissemination of her image. The Hottentot Venus remained highly popular. One ballad called "The Hottentot Venus" took a cue from the now famous letter of October 1810 in which the author (probably Dunlop, but purportedly Cesars) compared the Venus to a giant or a dwarf. Compared with other sights, the ballad declared, the Hottentot Venus was as "unrivalled" as "the Queen." The chorus repeated, "We'll go no more to other shows while Venus treads the stage, We'll go no more to other shows while Hottentot's the rage." William Bullock, Covent Garden, the Opera, and others, all seemed "but shilly-shally, to Venus."[1]

Dunlop, however, must have found himself in a dilemma. Exhibiting Sara nearly naked had almost elicited charges of immorality; he thus advertised that he had changed the display. As his attorney had promised before the King's Bench, Dunlop altered the display to conform to the tastes of "proper" London. The show was now quite "suitable for ladies."[2] If elite women could see the show, anyone could. The "false idea of indelicacy," stated the last London advertisement in April 1811, was "now entirely, and very properly, got over, from her having been visited as a truly interesting object of natural curiosity by some of the first Ladies of distinction in the Kingdom."[3]

The display no longer suggested an explicit spectacle of flesh and touch. Advertisements from December through early spring 1811 continued to represent Sara as that rare individual from an equally rare "Tribe," but a veil of decorum now descended over the exhibit. Under the new regime, the spectacle of ethnography was perhaps to dominate pornography. However, it was the Hottentot Venus's body that provided the authenticity of primitiveness and exoticism. The more like Londoners Sara seemed, the less interested they were in viewing the Hottentot Venus.

One viewer expressed disappointment at the show's respectability. A dress with beads did not suffice to conjure the exotic Khoekhoe woman from the newly colonized Cape. In early 1811, Lord Porchester of Hampshire visited London, making sure to see the exhibit. "Since the trial" of the Hottentot Venus, Lord Porchester wrote to his wife, "she is so well clothed as to be little worth seeing, she is short and square but very oddly made behind." Nonetheless, he did say that the Hottentot Venus's "shape is enough displayed," Porchester continued, "to prove her make to be very little like as human shape and more like a Camel's hump in the stern, she has a thick stripe of black paint across each cheek which does not improve her countenance."[4]

Lord Porchester's account lacks the empathetic imagination of Macaulay's description of the show. He depicts a peculiar object of study, understood better through reference to the animal kingdom than the realm of humankind. Cuvier's later scientific writings on Sara Baartman shared this interest in species and location. The new show, it seems, rendered the Venus as an example of attenuated humanity—a perspective that science and popular culture more fully elaborated in France.

By the time the spring of 1811 finally made its London appearance, interest in the Hottentot Venus had waned. More interesting developments were unfolding. King George had gone stark raving mad. Prinnie became regent in February. London gossip soon turned to the assassination of Prime Minister Percival as he entered the House of Commons. England remained held in the grasp of Wellington's battles with Napoleon in the War of the Spanish Ulcer.[5] For Sara and Alexander it was time to move on.

The show closed for a time in London in April 1811. We know little of Baartman's subsequent travels, but for a time she seems to have followed the movements of wealthier audiences. In summer, the wealthy deserted London for their residences in the ancient city of Bath, famous for its

Roman architecture and sulfuric baths. (Only later did people realize that reclining in the waters in fact led to death, the lead seeping slowly into the skin along with the restorative water.) We know Sara went to Bath; a Jack Higginbotham published a ballad talking of the interest in the Hottentot Venus by the ladies of that town.[6] As autumn approached, the aristocrats returned to London or to the promise of good hunting on their country estates. Sara and Alexander did not return then, however. London promised controversy, but no longer easy money. Sara Baartman disappeared from the public eye. By December 1811, she and Dunlop were in Manchester, the heart of England's industrial revolution.[7]

If one needed to disappear for a while, Manchester was the place. The city had sold itself to cotton. Barges moved up and down the Irwell River from Liverpool, bringing raw cotton and taking finished cloth. Migrants from the countryside streamed into the city looking for work, sweat joining coal and cotton in England's industrial revolution. Filthy and dangerous, Manchester made London's East End seem safe and salubrious. Pestilence and disease besieged the poor, children, and adults dying of tuberculosis, overwork, and starvation. Sewerage ran through the streets and into the river. In many areas, the buildings, still mostly of wood and thatch, grew so close that they leaned over roads and into each other. Children played in streets that rarely saw sunlight. The city was in a constant state of rebuilding as weekly fires destroyed the old buildings, which were replaced by the clean lines of red brick.

Manchester lived for profit and seethed with discontent. The Luddites had been very active there in 1811, meeting outside the city, where they discussed their low wages and planned industrial sabotage. Riots in April 1812 led to considerable destruction. In June, eight rioters were hanged for mill burning and for breaking into houses to obtain food. One of those executed was a woman who had stolen some potatoes.[8]

What a journey, from the tip of Africa to the place of strangeness in a northern industrial city. However, Africa was present also in Manchester. For example, the *Liverpool Mercury* in March 1814 featured John Campbell, the very man who left us a sketch of the Papendorp cottage. Reporting on Campbell's trek into the southern African interior, the *Mercury* advocated that the men of the London Missionary Society, "by carrying forward the line of their settlements in to the interior," were "making constant advances upon the barbarism of this vast continent."[9] The Africa that came to England through the newspapers was one that confirmed Sara's roots in a "barbarous" continent, and it was with that Africa that Sara had to negotiate in England and France.[10]

In Manchester, Sara and Alexander likely found accommodation in Strangeways, a working-class area across a tight bend in the Irwell River. Behind the neighborhood lay open land, in front buildings crowded together at the water's edge. The small community of black Mancusians lived at Strangeways. Black men in Manchester were mostly former seamen who had landed in the city off one of the barges from Liverpool. They worked on the city's docks. The largely Irish working class would not allow people they saw as black to work alongside them in the dye works and cotton mills.

To get into the city from Strangeways, Dunlop and Baartman would have walked over the bridge past Chetham College, with its ancient library where Daniel Defoe, Karl Marx, and Friedrich Engels studied and wrote some of their greatest works. The great cathedral of the Collegiate Church stood on the left. Renovations enlarged the building over time so that it had become a huge edifice of stone and glass windows with multiple wings. Beautiful wooden arches and cornices disclosed its Gothic origins and contentious past; in the mid–seventeenth century during the English civil war, Oliver Cromwell and his men galloped on horses round the pews cutting off the heads of the wooden saints.

The cathedral served the wealthy but tended to the poor, largely because of the enduring leadership of an eccentric priest, a man whose ministry touched Sara's life too. At the end of 1790, the Reverend Joshua Brookes (1754-1821) became chaplain of the Collegiate Church and assistant master of the grammar school. A famously unpopular teacher (the students once rioted and threw him from the building), Brookes committed himself to single-handedly baptizing and marrying the entire working class. The ceremonies very often took place en masse, with crowds of people waiting beneath the great Gothic ceiling. Usually Brookes did not meet the individuals beforehand. By 1811, Brookes neared sixty years old but still worked tirelessly to bring the poor into God's fold, even if it meant boxing their ears and cursing them in his broad accent. He was known to yell and excoriate parents at the baptismal font and insist on giving the crying infant a name of the reverend's own choosing. Over the course of his long

FIGURE 5.1. Interior of Manchester Cathedral. Photographer Clifton Crais, 2005.

career, Joshua Brookes baptized and married, it was said, more people than any other man in England.[11] Sara Baartman was one of them.

On 1 December 1811, Sara Baartman entered Manchester Cathedral. She stood at the very front of the baptismal line—the individuals baptized after her were babies born the same year. Brookes dipped his finger in the holy water of the font and christened Sara with the sign of the cross. Sara or Saartje Baartman became "Sarah Bartmann." She made the papers again, this time as a Christian convert.[12]

"Sarah Bartmann" is a strange conflation of British and German spelling; it probably resulted from a phonetic interpretation by the scribe. Around the time of Sara's reburial in 2002, the South African government said that any other rendition of her name was insulting and should be avoided. Sara, Saartjie, Saartje—all were assigned to the dustbin of the offensive. This name, hastily scrawled in a baptismal register, was now proclaimed the official name.

Unlike most of the other people, Sara had met Brookes before he christened her. Brookes was not a man who normally consulted his superiors.

In Sara's case, however, he wrote to the bishop of Chester requesting permission to welcome Sara into the church. Perhaps he did this because Sara was foreign, perhaps because she had been the subject of a public investigation, and her baptism might therefore elicit attention. Brookes waited for His Grace's approval before baptizing this "Female Hottentot from the Colony of the Cape of Good Hope, born on the Borders of Cafraria."[13]

Why was Sara Baartman christened? We can only surmise. By December 1811, Sara had been in England for over a year. She was an African woman in a time when few other women of African descent lived in England. Perhaps through baptism, she sought divine protection from quotidian evils. Perhaps she sought to join a wider community. Baptism would have joined her both to England and to the experiences of other individuals of African descent who crossed the Atlantic. From the time of Equiano, people of African descent from the slaveholding colonies had moved to England imagining it as a break with slavery, shown partly by being able to embrace Christianity. Sarah signified Sara Baartman's geographic and conceptual migration from that far-off periphery of the Eastern Cape. Christening also offered Sara connection to the promises of missionaries at the Cape who sought to protect Khoekhoe from settler violence.[14]

Sara might have been baptized in order to also connect her back to her family of the frontier. One can read her baptism as a way in which Manchester Cathedral was appropriated into a Khoekhoe history. The Khoekhoe of the Eastern Cape were among the first Africans to accept Christianity. In the early nineteenth century Sara's brothers moved to Bethelsdorp, one of the first Christian missions in the Eastern Cape. One brother later also became a famous rebel fighter against the British. By being baptized, and in taking on an English version of her name, Sara Baartman perhaps sought to connect her story back to her natal home to signify her ties to her family, also with the knowledge that baptism could coexist with a critique of British policies.

The baptismal certificate conferred no legal privilege except for permitting marriage, and marry she did, although no record of the marriage certificate exists and we do not know the spouse.[15] Alexander Dunlop signed the copy of the baptism. Was he the husband?[16] Perhaps Sara was pregnant. This would explain the silence in the archives about her exhibition. Sara had left Bath in the summer of 1811. The next time she was on exhibit

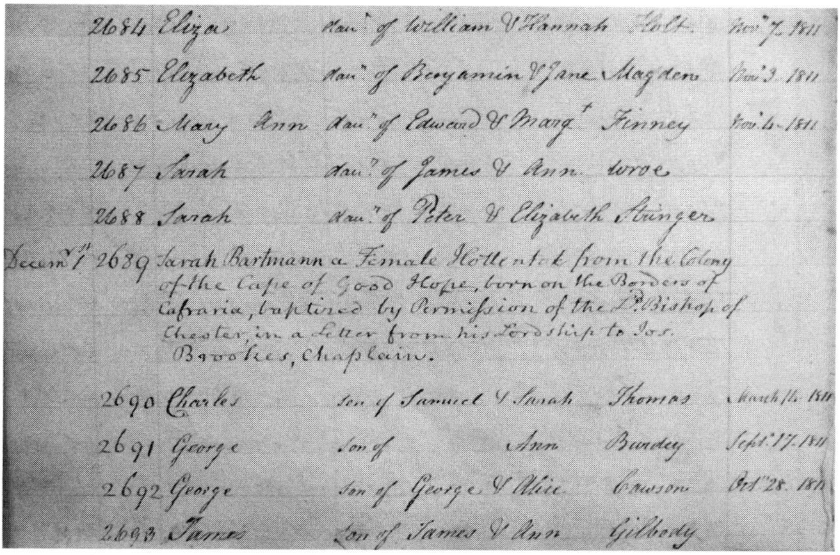
2684 Eliza dau.r of William & Hannah Holt Nov.r 7. 1811
2685 Elizabeth dau.r of Benjamin & Jane Magden Nov. 3. 1811
2686 Mary Ann dau.r of Edward & Marg.t Finney Nov. 6. 1811
2687 Sarah dau.r of James & Ann Lowe
2688 Sarah dau.r of Peter & Elizabeth Stringer
Decem.r 1st 2689 Sarah Bartmann a Female Hottentot from the Colony of the Cape of Good Hope, born on the Borders of Caffraria, baptized by Permission of the Ld. Bishop of Chester, in a Letter from his Lordship to Jos. Brookes, Chaplain.
2690 Charles son of Samuel & Sarah Thomas March 16. 1811
2691 George son of Ann Burdey Sept. 17. 1811
2692 George son of George & Alice Cawson Oct. 28. 1811
2693 James son of James & Ann Gilbody

FIGURE 5.2. Baptismal certificate. Photographer, Clifton Crais, 2005.

would be ten or twelve months later, in early April 1812 in Limerick, Ireland. The Manchester papers neither reported her arrival in their city nor advertised her presence among them. The dates and silences, the fact that Sara came to Manchester but was not shown as the Hottentot Venus, suggest that Sara had fallen pregnant while still in the south of England.

If Sara Baartman was pregnant, the child apparently perished, joining its siblings in early death. The father of Sara's child as well as her betrothal remains a mystery. This period in her life clearly meant much to her, however. Seven days after her baptism, Sara and Alexander returned to obtain a copy of the document. She carried that copy, along with her contract of service to Dunlop, with her until her death in Paris four years later.[17]

The contract Dunlop had drawn up with Sara Baartman in October 1810 already foresaw a visit to Ireland. In April 1812, Sara finally arrived in that country. She and Dunlop probably boarded a ship at Liverpool, one of the many ships that ferried Irish workers to and from the entry point for England's industrial towns. The Limerick fair, held around Saint Patrick's Day, was one of Ireland's largest, with people selling produce and animals and searching for work. In the British Isles and throughout Europe, spring and summer were a time of fairs and merriment welcoming winter's end and the arrival of days when the sun seemed to go on forever. A circuit of pleasure fairs had emerged since at least the Middle Ages, when people combined amusement with the sale of animals and produce. The most famous remained London's Bartholomew Fair in August, but scores of other fairs mixed fun with commerce and even employment.

Sara's visit to Limerick probably would have been more successful had she attended the fair, but she arrived shortly after it closed. The birth of a baby, or its death or illness, possibly delayed her arrival at the fair. Whatever the cause, the visit was not a success. The Hottentot Venus exhibited in Limerick for five days, five sad days. Unlike her earlier triumph with the public in London a year or so earlier, the Hottentot Venus now "was seen by very few."[18]

That disappointment must have put an end to Dunlop's dreams of becoming rich exhibiting the Hottentot Venus. By the summer of 1812, Dunlop, now a relatively old man in his fifties, was living in Portsmouth, home of the Royal Navy, a town where many a sailor spent his final years. It was in that port that he died in July 1812. Hendrik Cesars had disappeared the year before. With Alexander's death, Sara lost her last strong connection to the world and people she had known at the Cape. What future awaited her, alone in England, well known only for her display as an icon, "a symbol of African exoticism"?[19]

What else was there to do but continue to perform the part she had become so adept at re-creating? In August 1812, Sara probably returned to London to Bartholomew Fair. We do not know if she went alone, or with Henry Taylor, the man who later took her to France. We can find no hint of him in the records before Paris. Records for Sara Baartman in England become increasingly difficult to trace, too. A new rendition of an older song inserted a reference to her at the fair. "Here, here the only booth in the fair," sang a ballad, "the greatest curiosity in all the known world— the Wonderful and Surprising Hottentot Wenus [sic] is here, who measures three yards and three quarters round."[20]

Two months later, the Hottentot Venus appeared at Bury Saint Edmunds, near Ipswich, Suffolk, at the famous and boisterous fair that had long attracted young Cambridge men for revelry. The fair, first held in 1149, unfolded over an October fortnight. It included stalls selling various merchandise and the staging of three balls at the time of the fair, two for the public and one especially for the "nobility and gentry."[21]

"The Most Wonderful Phenomenon of Nature, The Hottentot Venus," the broadsheet for the Venus show announced. The "Female Sex" had "so liberally patronized her exhibition," as had various princesses and even the prince regent. Shorn of the earlier lewd pitches to attract audiences, the poster advertised the Venus as a "perfect Specimen of that most extraordinary Tribe of the Human Race, who have for such a length of Time inhabited the more Southern Parts of Africa, whose real Origin has never yet been ascertained, nor their Character, which has been so differently described by every Traveller who has visited those remote Regions of the World."[22] "Considering the natural morose Disposition of those People (who are scarcely ever observed to laugh)," the broadsheet continued, the Hottentot Venus was "remarkably mild and affable in her Manners."

Times had changed for the Hottentot Venus in England. Few muslin dresses were in the audience this time, though maybe a few top hats. Villagers and passersby peered into the canvas tent. People could buy copies of Lewis's aquatints. Now, audiences only had to pay one shilling to see the Hottentot Venus, the same price they paid to buy the broadside ballads distributed at the pleasure fairs and half the price of the London show. Half price, half used, the Hottentot Venus had become a sideshow traveling the circuits of minor pleasures in the wet English provinces.

Ironically, as the Hottentot Venus became less popular, and as Sara Baartman haunts rather than inhabits the historical record, Sara might well have found a greater sense of community in England as she traveled the circuit of pleasure fairs. Such fairs were rowdy events. Fairs were filled with many performers and sights, rough places of gossip and revelry as much for the performers as the audiences, far from the isolated setting of the London show. Accounts from the late eighteenth century through the following century described local fairs as places of coffeehouses, of music, of wondrous shows, "Buildings for the Exhibition of Drolls, Puppet Shews, . . . Wild Beasts, Monsters, Giants, Rope Dancers, etc."[23]

Rather than being prodded out of a cage on a bare stage as in Piccadilly, in the provinces Sara would have been surrounded by other individuals similarly exhibiting themselves, the smell of horses and cows lingering among the pies. In the setting up of the stall, the finding of drink and food, sleeping nights under the stars, or even lashed with rain in Bury, Colchester, and all the other places she moved through, Sara Baartman

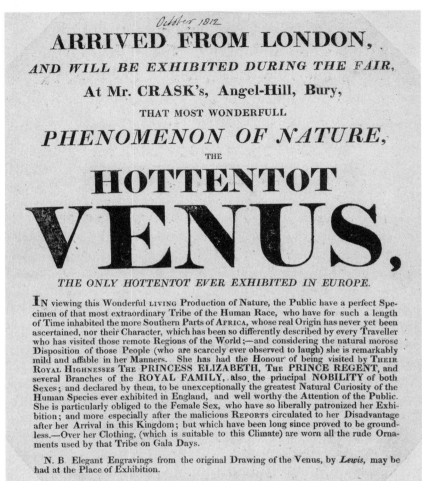

October 1812

ARRIVED FROM LONDON,

AND WILL BE EXHIBITED DURING THE FAIR,

At Mr. CRASK's, Angel-Hill, Bury,

THAT MOST WONDERFULL

PHENOMENON OF NATURE,

THE

HOTTENTOT
VENUS,

THE ONLY HOTTENTOT EVER EXHIBITED IN EUROPE.

IN viewing this Wonderful LIVING Production of Nature, the Public have a perfect Specimen of that most extraordinary Tribe of the Human Race, who have for such a length
of Time inhabited the more Southern Parts of AFRICA, whose real Origin has never yet been
ascertained, nor their Character, which has been so differently described by every Traveller
who has visited those remote Regions of the World;—and considering the natural morose
Disposition of those People (who are scarcely ever observed to laugh) she is remarkably
mild and affable in her Manners. She has had the Honour of being visited by THEIR
ROYAL HIGHNESSES THE PRINCESS ELIZABETH, THE PRINCE REGENT, and
several Branches of the ROYAL FAMILY, also the principal NOBILITY of both
Sexes; and declared by them, to be unexceptionally the greatest Natural Curiosity of the
Human Species ever exhibited in England, and well worthy the Attention of the Public.
She is particularly obliged to the Female Sex, who have so liberally patronized her Exhibition; and more especially after the malicious REPORTS circulated to her Disadvantage
after her Arrival in this Kingdom; but which have been long since proved to be ground-
less.—Over her Clothing, (which is suitable to this Climate) are worn all the rude Ornaments used by that Tribe on Gala Days.

N. B. Elegant Engravings from the original Drawing of the Venus, by *Lewis*, may be
had at the Place of Exhibition.

⁎†⁎ Admittance ONE SHILLING *each.*

FIGURE 5.3. "Arrived from London . . . the Hottentot Venus." Angel Hill, Bury
St. Edmunds." Suffolk Record Office, 1783/91.

would have lived among a community of performers all struggling to make
enough to ward off hunger. Lost to history, she might have found friends.[24]

Nearly two years after appearing in Bury, Sara left England for good.
She was used to traveling, riding in carriages, sleeping in rough inns, trying
to make enough money to keep going. She had seen much of southern
England, had lived in the north in Manchester, sailed across the Irish

Channel, returned to London, visited rural England. Now, in August 1814, Sara left London, passing Greenwich, Chatham, and her earliest memories of England on the way to Paris. Perhaps Sara remembered Alexander Dunlop, now two years dead in a Portsmouth cemetery. Or Hendrik—or Matthias and the other boy from the Slave Lodge.

Now we think she was with Henry Taylor, a man who dodges most of the archival record except for the transaction in Paris. Past Chatham, the coach entered the summer hills of the Kentish countryside, green with wheat and barley and pasture for the county's famous sheep and cattle. The route took Baartman and Taylor through Canterbury with its great cathedral and numerous small villages dotted between the great religious city and the port of Dover.

Somewhere along the line, the travelers spent the night and then another before boarding a small packet or merchant vessel headed for the Pas de Calais in the early morning hours. With good westerlies the channel crossing might take four or five hours. In bad weather, they might have to spend an uncomfortable, wet night at sea. The tides dictated whether the boats would be able to enter the Calais basin with its jetties or lay at anchor. In the latter case Sara would have descended a rope ladder into a small rowing boat, the men barking orders in French and trying to rush the travelers along. Once on the mudflat, rough men and women would have carried Sara and her possessions to shore.

Sara and Henry were among the first wave of travelers heading to France following Napoleon's defeat and the Treaty of Paris, which was signed just a few months earlier. By 1815 more than fifteen thousand British subjects were in Paris, the great majority of them tourists fulfilling their "travelling propensity." Others traveled for political reasons. Macaulay also headed to Paris in May 1814, just a few months before Sara Baartman, hoping to persuade the French to abolish the slave trade.

Calais's economy mostly depended on ferrying travelers. The French might love their theater, but the "grand tour" of Europe was a decidedly British passion. Mary Shelley and Percy Bysshe Shelley traveled to the Continent. As the *Edinburgh Review* commented on their book *History of a Six Weeks' Tour* (1817), "Our countrymen are pouring in swarms over every part of the Continent, carrying with them their sons fresh from College, and their daughters full of romance, and eager for composition—in countries which, two or three years ago, were wholly locked up from our inspection." The grand tour was reserved mostly for the aristocracy and the nouveau riche, though some commentators deplored the fact that "dashing *milords* of the last age are now succeeded by a host of *roturiers*," mere commoners, "who expatriate themselves for the sake of economy."[25] It was probably that motive exactly which Henry Taylor sought to pursue in Paris.

The trip from Calais to Paris was not cheap, nor the route without its own challenges. The two first had to contend with the formidable French bureaucracy. Customhouse employees searched through luggage, the cost ten sous per bag. Those traveling with passports went to the Grande Place—two francs per passport, the equivalent of a shilling. Exchanging money, or having coin made from your own gold and silver, was subject to additional taxes. The government divided the trip to Paris into twenty-four posts, the shortest just over five miles, the longest just over ten. Travelers had to pay at each post to proceed farther, thirty sous per horse to the government and fifteen sous to the postillion. A thousand sous later in Paris, one had forked out nearly an English pound just in taxes.[26]

Sara and Henry may have been able to travel with a driver who brought the mail between Calais and Paris and who, as a right, had "the privilege of taking two travellers with him." This was the cheapest way to travel, but even this was expensive. The price was five louis each, or nearly ten English pounds, roughly what one hundred visitors to 225 Piccadilly paid to view the Hottentot Venus in 1810.

The coaches made but four or five miles to the hour, stopping at each post to pay taxes and to exchange horses. Getting to Paris took anywhere from three to five days to make the 180-mile trip. The roads were generally poor, and wealthy English travelers very often took few valuables with them in fear of highwaymen. In the fields mostly women labored, their triangle hats protecting them from the sun, their men only just beginning to return from Napoleon's wars.

Many towns and some villages bore the scars of the Revolution, homes burned to the ground or abandoned and in disrepair, aristocratic estates broken up and sold bit by bit. After Boulogne, the coach headed to Abbeville on the Somme River and then eastward to Amiens. (Twelve years earlier the British and French had signed a peace treaty that ended the first round of war with Napoleon.) Here Sara and Henry likely spent the night, the great Gothic cathedral plainly in view, before entering the coach for the southward leg to Paris.

South of Amiens, the villages and towns appeared more frequently, particularly south of Clermont. Paris began to appear once they reached Saint-Denis, passing through a series of gates and along straight tree-lined roads. Barracks appeared on the right. The Ben Inn and the French Flag Inn welcomed strangers. The famous Abbey of Saint-Denis lay near the road. Just a few miles farther Sara and Henry reached the gates of the great capital, Paris, City of Light.[27]

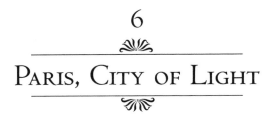

6

Paris, City of Light

ara Baartman arrived in early September 1814 to a Paris that could
know her only as the Hottentot Venus. After some four years in
England, the Hottentot Venus was now an object for public consumption, a European fetish wrapped in a garb of ethnography, sex, and
science. Sara Baartman lived for eighteen months in the city's vibrant cultural and intellectual heart, when Paris was still the center of European
culture and letters. Unlike London in 1810, in which various roles were
available for the presentation of a "Hottentot," this was not as much the
case in Paris of 1814: Sara Baartman arrived in France already the Hottentot Venus, and the fame of that figure only increased. Vaudeville dramatists
crafted a new opera *La Venus Hottentote*. Articles and cartoons again appeared in the popular press. The fiction of the Hottentot Venus became
so powerful that it ended up capturing the very person who enacted it.[1]

One of the many tragedies of Sara Baartman's life is that the more she
grew accustomed to Europe, to being European, the more Europe rejected,
for her, the possibility of change and becoming. Shortly after her arrival
in France, Sara could speak Dutch, English, and a little French. Writers
remarked on her facility with language, but they could not see beyond
the Hottentot Venus.[2] Unlike, for example, the English celebration of the
transformation of Pocahontas into Rebecca in the seventeenth century,
Europeans now insisted on Sara Baartman being primitive and savage. Sara
had to learn to acculturate herself to a self that Paris imagined her to be.
Both scientific and popular understanding placed her within an imaginary
Khoekhoe culture that allowed for no learning, no movement, no history.[3]

Any hopes Sara might have had that a different life would be possible
in France were surely dashed by the time she set foot on French soil,
with its papers heralding the arrival of the Hottentot Venus. Indeed Sara

"understood" what early nineteenth-century Europe wanted from her. She was to provide solidity to their imaginings of the Khoekhoe as a step below humankind, to be a "pristine native woman" whose body seemed to reveal the supposed horrors of the primitive state or who perhaps could enchant them with images of a primordial Eden of the noble savage.[4]

No controversy swirled about Sara in the City of Light. Her slave status had once been an issue in London. In Paris, in the heart of the country that produced the greatest revolution in the idea of the individual and of men's inalienable rights of freedom and liberty, there was no debate about who this woman from Africa "was." The "rights of man" did not extend to black women, and certainly not to a Hottentot, no matter how important they might be to the European imagination of itself.[5]

Despite the Revolution, the Terror, and Napoleonic excess, Paris remained the place where the most radical and profound ideas were considered and debated, both in the halls of learning and in the salons and cafés. The city drank the exotic, fed on intrigue, and starved on crisis. In September 1814, when Sara arrived in Paris, Napoleon had only just relinquished his title as emperor. Crowned in 1804 after rising during the 1790s to be one of three consuls who replaced the Jacobin terror, Napoleon had threatened English supremacy with his plans to conquer Europe. Admiral Nelson had thwarted the emperor in the Battle of Trafalgar in 1805, but into the next decade Napoleon continued to look east to Russia and to neighboring states such as Spain. The Congress of Vienna in 1814 finally ended Napoleon's expansion, sending him off to the island of Elba.

Sara's first six months in Paris therefore witnessed the Bourbon restoration of Louis Philippe. The royal family again ruled France after a long hiatus and the chopping off of various royal heads during the Revolution. However, in March 1815, during the last year of Sara's life, Napoleon again set foot on French soil, in Cannes, and launched his final attempt to reclaim his control of France. News of his advancing armies and reports of English retaliation dominated the newspapers, which, at the bottom, carried advertisements for various forms of popular culture and displays including that of the Hottentot Venus. In October 1815, Europe finally vanquished Napoleon. He spent his final six years exiled on Saint Helena impassionedly reading the European newspapers. Perhaps he read of the death of Sara Baartman in December 1815.

Napoleon gave Parisians a sense of distinction and order after the ravages of the late revolutionary years of the guillotine. He created a new civil law, a civil service, and revamped education. He began rebuilding Paris as an imperial city, later consolidated by Haussman's large boulevards and magnificent symmetry. Paris seemed like a vast building site. When the king of Württemberg, ruler of the city in which Georges Cuvier was born, was asked, on a visit in 1810, what he thought of Paris, he replied tersely, "Fine, for a town that the architects have taken by assault!"[6]

However, life under Napoleon had been exhausting. From 1806 through 1811, France was constantly at war. Public celebration of victories required state prodding of a Parisian populace no longer so enthusiastic about their grandiose ruler and ready for some relief. Russia defeated the emperor in 1812. Napoleon's long retreat through Holland, the Italian states, and Switzerland stopped in Paris in March 1814, just six months before Sara's arrival. Nearly one hundred thousand Prussians, Russian Cossacks, and other allied troops defeated Napoleon's soldiers on the hills of Montmartre during an unusually cold spring. Thirty thousand men lay dead there and at the other battle sites around the city. Farmers took solace in the fact that the hard frost protected the winter seeds as men, horses, and cannons trampled the land and soldiers fought and died. Spring brought bounteous crops emerging amid the dead.[7]

Sara entered an occupied Paris, the first time foreign troops had taken the city for some four hundred years. The Duke of Wellington led his troops back across the channel. Tens of thousands of soldiers, especially Prussians and Russians, loitered in the city, waiting for orders to return to home. Regiments bivouacked in the great parks of the Tuileries, Luxembourg, the Bois de Boulogne, and the Jardin des Plantes. Grenadiers walked about with their long brown and white rifles and tall hats of black topped with red plumage. Even a division of Egyptian Mamluks roamed the town, scimitars at hand, curved stirrups at the sides of their Arab stallions. Parisians feared the Cossacks with their mounts and capes and the rumors of massacres and plunder in the French countryside. Boisterous, heavy drinkers, the Cossacks slammed their fists on restaurant tables yelling "Bistro," "quickly," bequeathing the world a new kind of dining.

The miasma of troops living among half-built public works begun by the emperor, but abandoned by war and defeat, left the city in a state of considerable unrest, curbed only by a roll of drums announcing the nine

FIGURE 6.1. "Jardin du Palais Royal." David W. Bartlett. From *Paris: with Pen and Pencil; Its People and Literature Its Life and Business.* New York: Hurst and Co., Publishers, c. 1880.

o'clock curfew. The city was less than half the size of London, but utterly confusing. While imperial architects had turned Paris into a vast building site, destroying houses and entire communities to create grand streets celebrating Napoleon's military victories, disorder ruled in most neighborhoods. Beyond streets like the Quai d'Orsay and the great boulevards, the city in fact had very few major roads and very poor sanitation, with open sewerage running down the middle of streets.

As wily as Alexander Dunlop before him, Henry Taylor, who remains so elusive to us in the historical record, ignored the poorer and more remote quarters of the city and made his way to the extravagant Palais-Royal, the heart of European decadence. The palace began its long history innocently as a collection of different buildings and gardens brought together and rebuilt by the famous Cardinal Richelieu, consul to King Louis XIV, as the Palais-Cardinal. After Richelieu's death in 1642, the king took over the palace and fittingly renamed it Palais-Royal. In the next hundred years, architects redesigned the gardens and constructed facades along rue Saint-Honoré on the southern edge.[8]

The palace remained largely untouched until the eighteenth century. Throughout the Enlightenment, the Palais-Royal was the center of political intrigue and power where revolutionaries discussed politics and plotted against the ancien régime. The philosophes Voltaire and Diderot frequented the *palais*, as did many more thinkers who considered such lofty ideas as the meaning of freedom and liberty, and the nature of man and the history of civilization. In 1776, the year made famous by the fall of the Bastille and the start of the French Revolution, the architect Victor Louis, on commission from the Duke of Chartres, began building the shopping arcades and restaurants that formed one of the first commercial shopping centers of revolutionary Paris. Nine years later, the south sides of the square witnessed the building of some one hundred shops, most with lower rents and catering to a more diverse population. Between 1800 and 1807, the *palais* served as the headquarters of Napoleon's tribunal.

If France ushered in the modern era, then the glorious "Bazar" of the Palais-Royal was its birthplace. The great cultural theorist Walter Benjamin saw in the galleries of the Palais-Royal the very markers of the modern era, their arches and stages providing a cinematic view of the vices and wonders of urban cultures, the crossing of pleasures and consumerism and architectural beauty, indeed the very heart of the modern consumer culture. A dizzying, intoxicating spectacle where time and space seemed compressed and the world became available all at once, in the *palais* "all that is solid melts into air."[9]

In the *palais*, where reality and performance blurred into a kaleidoscope of sensation, one could delight in all pleasures, licit and illicit. The famed galleries hosted prostitutes, jewelry stores, printers, and restaurants. Brizzi's at 36 rue Neuves-des-Petits-Champs offered more than one hundred dishes. Nearby, the "most splendid" Veri's was one of the most expensive restaurants in all of Europe. A good meal at Brizzi's cost twenty francs, at Veri's two or three times as much. The Café Chartres and the Café Mécanique lured luxury customers, while the less affluent or the more risqué went to the Café of Savages, or the Café of Fools, one of the best in Paris. Until the restoration of the royal family in 1814, the Palais-Royal attracted dramatists and actors who often let the apartments of the palace's Theatre Française to their left-wing friends. At the Café de la Paix actors performed scenes from plays or concocted impromptu theater by free association a century before surrealism.[10]

On the ground floor were the shops, restaurants, and gambling houses. Here, men and women drank coffee, read the paper, gossiped. In the evening, they danced and amused themselves. The owners of the Café of a Thousand Columns lined the walls with mirrors, creating an optical illusion of infinite columns and a dizzying array of light and artifice. Rich and poor flocked to the Wax Museum and beheld representations that, in their three dimensions, seemed real.

An English visitor in 1802 complained that the *palais* was a "nursery of every loathsome vice, that abomination of all virtue and profanation of all religions";[11] he nevertheless lingered for a good while. At the Palais-Royal,

> one could find All the necessaries of life, without exception, and all the inventions of refined luxury; every sensual, and almost every mental gratification; the means of becoming in a few hours a Croesus or a beggar; an Exchange and a Theatre; gaming houses and money-changers; reading-rooms and brothels; blind virtuosi and sharp-sighted loungers; sumptuous tables for the gold of the wealthy; moderate ones for the less opulent: the productions of all the quarters of the globe, are here concentrated, for the crowds that pass into and out of this place like the tides of the ocean.[12]

The palace had "no parallel in Europe," an English visitor remarked in 1815, for "it contains every thing to inform the understanding, and corrupt the heart."[13] At night men sought out other men for gambling and drink, men sought out women, and gay Paris found solace in the palace's dark corners. The "crowd that thronged the Palais-Royal . . . was doubly transgressive . . . by combining sexual licence with political radicalism." One contemporary described the *palais* as "the temple of sensual pleasure."[14]

Sara had moved to an extraordinary place where propriety was no issue and spectacle was everything. Henry Taylor and Sara lived in a building that housed apartments, one at least serving as a brothel. The basement apartment on the cour des Fontaines (now the place de Valois) was located near the canals that ran along the Palais-Royal.

As in London, Sara joined a city in which few black women resided, in a country with a very small black population. Only between thirteen hundred and two thousand people who were legally recognized as mulatto or black lived in France as a whole during the first two decades of the nineteenth century. Men were overwhelmingly in the majority, and as in England, most men of African descent in France were either servants or ex-soldiers. Very few historical records from the time addressed the black or mulatto population as a group. Sara Baartman might have met ex-soldiers

FIGURE 6.2. "English Visitors in the Palais Royal 1814." From Grego in Gronow's *Reminiscences*. Courtesy of Mary Evans Picture Library, www.maryevans.com. Image no. 10008056.

or servants in Paris; it is highly unlikely, however, and we will probably never know if she ever had the opportunity to make friends with people from the French slave colonies.[15]

Sara lived in the Palais-Royal and worked there too: upstairs in a room at 15 rue Neuves-des-Petits-Champs, the street bordering the northern side of the *palais*. Number 15 was a busy place. The building housed a Monsieur Olivier's variety show—he charged three francs as an entrance fee. Other showmen exhibited panoramas and mechanical inventions. People also paid three francs (the equivalent of three shillings, one shilling more than at 225 Piccadilly) to see the Hottentot Venus, enough to buy a tea breakfast for two at one of the coffeehouses or half the price of a good seat at the Comic Opera.[16]

For ten hours a day, from eleven in the morning to nine at night, Sara endured the gaze and the prodding of strangers as she stared out at this new public and the masses of people who turned the palace's gardens into a muddy mess. Sometimes she moved downstairs and to one of the cafés, including the posh Café de Chartres, still an expensive restaurant. There she mingled with guests who watched her sing, poked her, and marveled at her bottom.

Taylor seems to have arrived in Paris with a two-pronged strategy. He must have expected to make money exhibiting Sara at the *palais*. Taylor also planned to approach the leading scientists of the day. Biology was then the king of the sciences, and human history his queen. As we have seen, even in Cape Town in 1809 the Frenchman Villet had combined these interests for profit with his shop and menagerie. Both biology and comparative anatomy were firmly ensconced in Paris; indeed, the city was the world center for the study of natural history. With the Hottentot Venus, Taylor had what some thought might be the missing link separating humans from lesser animals.

Shortly after their arrival, Taylor wrote to the head of the Museum of Natural History. In a report dated 10 September, Taylor informed the museum that he had with him "the original" of the picture he now enclosed. The picture he referred to was presumably a copy of the engraving by Lewis that had circulated through England and had been sold at the fairs. Taylor alleged that the Hottentot Venus came from the region of the Gamtoos River and said she was going to be on public display. He invited the illustrious Georges Cuvier, the museum's head, the Renaissance man of French science, and the founder of the discipline of comparative anatomy, to see the display the following Tuesday afternoon, 13 September, at rue Neuves-des-Petits-Champs. Cuvier did not then take up Taylor's offer. As we shall see, a few months later Cuvier changed his mind, however, perhaps persuaded by the public curiosity about the Hottentot Venus.[17]

The first advertisements for the exhibition appeared on 18 September 1814. They copied the earlier broadsheets from London and the English countryside with claims about the Venus's distinction as an "extraordinary phenomenon." The advertisement in *Affiches, Annonces et Diverse*, for example, now claimed a more specific ethnicity for Sara: she was now "the only one that has ever appeared in Europe from the Hauzannana tribe. In this woman, as extraordinary as [she is] astonishing, the public has a perfect model of this tribe, which inhabits the southernmost regions of Africa. . . . She wears all the ornaments that serve the tribe to which she belongs as jewelry on holidays."[18]

Henry Taylor fashioned Sara's introduction to Paris precisely by paying attention to dress and manner and by playing on preexisting popular and academic "knowledge" of Hottentots. Taylor's knowledge of how to market Sara Baartman suggests that he had read his Le Vaillant, the romantic explorer and naturalist who had passed near Baartman's Fonteyn in the 1770s. Le Vaillant had written about the Houswanna society, supposedly a group of San, and had alleged that they suffered from steatopygia, a supposed medical condition of great amounts of fatty tissue on the bottom.[19] Taylor, therefore, did not describe Sara as Gonaqua, around whom a romanticist literature had formed, but as a Houswanna, a supposedly more primitive being.

The *Journal de Paris* urged people to see the Hottentot Venus who had "newly arrived from London." Four days after the advertisement, the newspaper reported in a full column on the second page that the Hottentot Venus had "a very engaging manner." However, the paper cautioned readers that since "ideas of beauty vary according to the climate, amateurs should not expect to discover in the Hottentot Venus the forms of the Venus de Medicis."[20] Print sellers also saw opportunities to make money. Prints depicting Sara Baartman began appearing throughout Paris. One displayed a version of the Lewis engraving alongside a picture of a popular actor of the day, Anne-Françoise-Hippolyte Boutet.

The print proposed humor by juxtaposing the woman no Parisian was supposed to desire next to the sixteen-year-old Mme Mars whom everyone loved. The *Journal General de France* stated that "if we were to be taxed . . . we would prefer the French Venus over the Hottentot one." This of course was also a juxtaposition of generation, although the newspaper did not remark on this. Sara was thirty-six or thirty-seven by 1814, Boutet only some sixteen years of age.[21]

Sara Baartman's movement through empire and different commercial contexts helped create her racialization within Europe. The advertisement affirmed steatopygia as a trait of ethnicity and race and science. In the course of her lifetime, Sara Baartman moved from being an individual, to being a person with steatopygia, to being steatopygous because of her ethnic makeup, to being the living missing link in the natural history of humankind.

Parisian newspapers enthusiastically understood Sara Baartman as an ethnographic wonder. *Affiches* recounted the standard story of her life, again with the emphasis on her time in Europe and displaying little interest in her childhood apart from naming her supposed ethnic background: "A young Dutchman took her and she stayed with him until her departure for Europe. She was displayed in the major cities of England for 3 years.

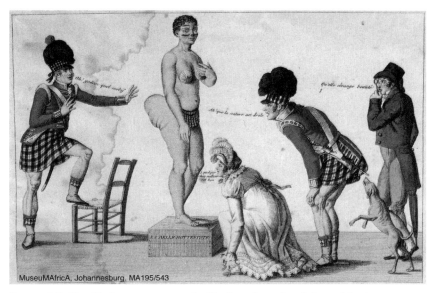

FIGURE 6.3. "Les Curieux en extase ou les Cordons de souliers." Aaron Martinet. Courtesy of Museum Africa, Johannesburg. MA 195/543.

She speaks Dutch, English, and her natal language, in which she sings several songs. Her manner is lively and pleasant with her audiences." The paper also commented on the fact that she painted her face and covered herself with glass beads and noted, "Her color is closer to that of the Peruvians than to Africans, whose hair and traits she has."[22]

Sara and the men who displayed her knew they were purveying fantasy. They engaged, in different ways and with different degrees of willingness, in performance art of an early nineteenth-century sort. The public, on the other hand, consumed the Hottentot Venus not as a brilliant if tragic marketing ploy but as a rendering of the "real" primitive. It was as if the more modernity unhinged the accepted truths of religion, authority, and historical change, the more people sought something absolutely certain and fixed. When Sara was on show to the public, her handlers were careful to sustain the fiction of her primitiveness, her fixedness in a kind of eternal ethnographic present and past that allowed for no personal or historical growth. Sara had to sing in her native language, wear the tortoiseshell necklace that signified her relation to the Khoekhoe, to wear a kaross and other artifacts that flagged her status as a true, ethnic exemplar.

These elements of her costume became the standard by which later ethnographers and cultural historians would understand and render to a wide and nonscientific audience the ethnic garb of the hunter-gatherers and pastoralists of southern Africa. Racinet's 1888 compendium of folk costumes from all over the world included portraits of supposed "Bushmen" women. For Racinet, Sara Baartman's presentation established authenticity. He said that wealthy women wore a double kaross such as that which one saw on "Sarah Bartmann" when she was in public in the salons of Paris in 1815.[23]

By the end of September, the Hottentot Venus had become a success. In November that icon moved onto a different stage: on the nineteenth a vaudeville opera entitled *La Venus Hottentote, ou Haine aux Francais (or the Hatred of French Women)* opened at the Vaudeville Theater right opposite the Palais-Royal, a theater nicknamed the Wit's Box.[24] The conceit of *La Venus Hottentot* centered on a young Frenchman who was supposed to be marrying his young cousin, a woman he did not find sufficiently exotic. The cousin disguises herself as the "Hottentot Venus," whereupon the young man falls in love. The sexuality of the Hottentot lured the man to reveal his true desires; primitiveness helped disclose truth. Secure in his enchantment, the cousin reveals her identity, the young man comes to his senses, and the couple marries. The leading Parisian papers advertised the play, which was on show "tous les jours" with prices ranging from one to four francs. Reviews of the play referred to the real Hottentot Venus appearing in Paris while they discussed the fantasies explored in the vaudeville.

Even when not onstage, the Hottentot Venus of rue Neuves-des-Petits-Champs hovered in Paris's cultural ether as fantasy and as truth. *La Quotidienne* reviewer remarked that the audience particularly appreciated the parts of the play that discussed the traits of civilized women, or "women who were not savage." The reviewer did chide Mlle Rivière, who played "the Hottentote," for misrepresenting a Khoekhoe by being "extremely pretty."[25] The reviewers all took for granted that the "real" Hottentot Venus was a "female monster" incapable of enticing a man so easily to love.

One reviewer decided to see "the original" Hottentot Venus before he attended the vaudeville. He hoped to encounter the Hottentot Venus. Instead, much to his disappointment, he found Sara Baartman. On the morning of the premiere, he visited "Mademoiselle Sartjee." He thought

her pretty. She wore simple clothes and no ornaments. What a disappointment for someone who had believed in the truth of the Hottentot Venus:
"alas, my hopes cruelly evaporated. Instead of the imposing and majestic
Venus of the Cape of Storms, I found only a svelte Venus."[26]

The visit to Baartman's apartment revealed the acting skills she pursued
so well onstage. This was not what Paris wanted, an act, a display of cun-
ning artifice, a facsimile, a mere verisimilitude. Paris sought not an actor
they could admire but rather a native truth, an indigenous essence, a performance of the real amid modernity's endless flux.

Sara could not escape the Hottentot Venus. Her penultimate decline
began with a transaction. Early in a legendarily frigid winter, Taylor abandoned Sara to a showman of animals named S. Reaux. This name is
haunting. Was this a relative of the Reaux who Sara probably encountered
in Cape Town? He was the ballet master sent off by the Cape governor for
too enthusiastically celebrating the French Revolution. That Reaux had
been associated with the African Theater and Villet's circle. The S. Reaux
whom Sara Baartman encountered in Paris owned a curiosity shop, similar
to Villet's shop in Cape Town. We have to entertain the idea that Sara
agreed to go to Paris because she thought that there might live a man she
had known in Cape Town, a remaining connection to the land of her birth.

"The Venus Hottentot has changed owners," the *Journal General de
France* reported on 23 January 1815, the year of Sara Baartman's death.
The paper also casually remarked that her owner was her husband. Showmen often claimed to be married to the people they exhibited in order to
forestall precisely the kinds of issues that troubled the display in London.
No whisper of such a marriage emerges in the historical record, and it is
highly unlikely that one occurred. But, if this was the Reaux from Cape
Town, or his brother, perhaps we have to give the story more credence
than the records lend it.[27]

Reaux kept a shop on the cour de Fontaines near where Sara lived and
contributed to the phantasmic world of the Palais-Royal, where truth and
fiction seemed so unclear. He had far better connections than Taylor did.
Reaux exhibited Baartman for the whole of 1815, and he widened his
audience for the Hottentot Venus. He arranged for Sara to star in a soirée
reserved exclusively for high Parisian society. He paraded her at cafés and
restaurants in and around the *palais*. At times he placed a collar round her
neck, showing her off to aristocrats and plebeians, anyone who would pay.

Here that public mark of slavery, the collar, elicited no complaints. Reaux sold the Lewis aquatints at his shop, as did another shopkeeper on rue du Coq.[28] Sara surely made no money off these transactions, displayed as little more than a living fossil.

Reaux also seems to have made Sara available for interviews, thus marketing her to a broader audience. In the first three months of 1815, two purported interviews with Sara Baartman appeared in Parisian newspapers. The articles represented extreme reactions to her display: one talked of her in awful, demeaning terms, the other used her plight to indict Paris. However, one was a satire, not necessarily based on an interview at all; the other appears as an imagined conversation, although the journalist seems to have met Sara.

On 15 January 1815, the satire appeared, written by one so-called émigré by the name of Monsieur Musard. "Mr. Lazy" wrote a long article using the Hottentot Venus as fodder for his critique of Parisian society. This Venus he rendered as having "a dull square figure and horrible scars on the cheeks, made with gun powder as a form of adornment." He managed, as so many commentators did, to insult her further by mentioning "her huge protuberances" even as he claimed not to speak of them. He supposedly asked Sara Baartman about her love life, but whether he imagined this or made it up, we cannot be sure. The journalist wanted to know if Sara had a "Hottentot lover." Sara replied that she had had three daughters by an African prince, but that her children were dead.[29]

If Sara professed such history, she had become even more adept at reading the interests of the French public in the idea of the noble savage and their loss of innocence before Western civilization. Perhaps Sara also registered her pain of losing her children. She spoke of three deaths, the count of her three babies, dead, at the Cape. However, one wonders of the African prince, the mention of royal blood. Sara was no queen, though the story fits well with French fantasies of exotic loves and Africans of noble blood. Perhaps Baartman told Musard what he wanted to hear, but more likely, given the deeply satiric tone of the piece, M. Musard simply invented his story on the basis of just a few fragments of information.

Musard, of course, was not alone. Various Europeans had created stories about Sara's life. Macaulay had done so in creating a narrative of enslavement and oppression. Dunlop had countered with his own story centering on free will. In Paris, where a few decades later the modern novel would

emerge, fiction became more real than reality itself, the writer using observations and other information to create a verisimilitude so believable it
reached to something essential about the world around us.

The Paris stories about Sara were small fictions parading as truth, just
as Sara's own performance as a Hottentot elided the many complexities
of her life. A little later in the month, a second journalist met Sara at a
fancy party where Reaux made her walk round the room, singing and
dancing at the request of patrons. Sara's sadness moved the journalist to
write of his meeting. He wrote that she was a poor Hottentot Venus who
sang and danced for money. "We are cruel in our pleasures," he wrote.
"We laugh at exactly that which should sadden us."[30] Having made his
moral point, the journalist re-created Sara's life, indeed speaks as Sara in
a fictive first-person narrative.

"My name is Sara, poor Sara. Sara who does not deserve her fate," he
has her say. "The sun had turned twenty times in the sky" before she first
saw the whites who took her from her natal shore. The author depicts a
father hunting, a mother organizing celebrations, and a lover torn from
Sara during a barbaric attack by colonists. The journalist then details how
he wanted to discover more from her, alerting the reader to his commitment to finding the truth. After the party he gives Sara a lift back to the
palais and her apartment. (Reaux is conveniently absent from the story;
there is no interlocutor between author and subject.) Sara speaks to the
journalist in a mixture of Dutch, English, and French. Sara offers an account of a happy childhood and a happy adolescence. She speaks of a party
to celebrate her forthcoming marriage to a man called Solkar. But the Boer
commando interrupts the narrative of bliss. Innocence is shattered, and
slavery ensues. The final part of the story reads as a narrative of the slave
trade. "We unfortunate victims, which death had not taken, were attached
with strong bonds and taken away by malicious men from our cherished
forests, carried through many insults on floating trees where we saw nothing but sea and clouds. . . . On each of our voyages, I thought I would
find [the] palm trees and sand" of her African home.[31]

Here was a human Sara, even if a Sara that did not exist except in the
romantic imagination of a journalist. If Sara did in fact talk to the journalist, she seems to have invoked not so much the details of her own life as
the adolescence and adulthood Europe wanted to read about. This is a
fictive story of a happy Africa, of sexual awakening and dancing, one that

conforms to Europeans' yearning to believe in another place altered in time where civilization had no bearing and no chains. It is civilization, or at least civilization's dark side, that intervenes in what reads as a classic story of European vice and the slave trade.[32]

Compassion might be fiction's close cousin, but the article did nothing to elicit public concern and humanitarian intervention or to forestall Sara's transformation into exotica. Paris had many churches but few saints. Parisians wanted to know Sara's body, not her history, her location in the order of the natural world, not her thoughts or her feelings. In her years in England and then in France, Sara had found a way to project "Hottentotness" onstage. The public who visited Sara Baartman marveled at her singing ability, at her curious shape, at her apparent exemplification of a Hottentot woman.

The public understood Sara Baartman in the context of a wider cultural enthusiasm for the exotic sustained by Napoleon's many campaigns. Alongside advertisements for the vaudeville, for example, Parisian newspapers also advertised plays such as *The Arabs of Liban* or the display of Zumbo in the anatomical and natural history cabinets at the Museum of Natural History, and carried reviews of books on "African" customs and dress.[33] The relationship of the show, the Hottentot Venus, to the history and culture of English freak shows with their shenanigans of veracity and illusion seems not to have translated in France. Sara Baartman's presentation of the Hottentot Venus was so convincing that audiences saw her performance not as artifice but as essence. Ironically, Sara's great acting talent, and her increasing skill at interpreting the desires of her audience for authenticity, solidified her audiences' prejudices about the opposite: her supposed inability, as a Hottentot, to interpret or to create culture.

There were many stories that Sara could have told, and that her body could have demonstrated. But tales of childhood, of work, of romantic love with a soldier, and terror, were not the stories Parisians wanted to hear from her. In the age when science and romanticism became bedfellows, the public was convinced that it was the buttocks and sexual organs of the Hottentot Venus that had stories to tell. These stories were about humankind's history, of the relationships between animals and plants, humans and apes, stories of the natural world.

When Reaux approached Cuvier in March 1815, the scientist now was far more interested in what the Hottentot Venus might have to offer his science of comparative anatomy. Georges Cuvier was *the* man of nine-teenth-century French science, and his influence spread far beyond the era in which he lived, and beyond the boundaries of France. Of modest, nonaristocratic background, Cuvier was a protégé of Napoleon. Cuvier famously navigated his way with aplomb through changing administrations from the time of the Revolution, through Napoleon and on to the Restoration. Cuvier was a profoundly important scientist, an amazing man. When he met Sara, Cuvier held a plethora of posts. He was professor of comparative anatomy at the Museum of Natural History, served on the council of the University of France (a political appointment of Napoleon), and was vice rector of the Faculté des sciences, Université de Paris.

Working with his colleague Étienne Geoffroy Saint-Hilaire, who in 1798 accompanied Napoleon to Egypt and returned with famous mum-mified cats and ibises, Cuvier made Paris the world center of comparative anatomy, biology, and zoology. He enjoyed fairly tumultuous and intimate relationships with the other leading scientists—Saint-Hilaire was Cuvier's patron, but later the two men emerged on opposite sides of a key debate; similarly, Cuvier mentored De Blainville, who then also later broke with Cuvier. Though younger than Cuvier, Saint-Hilaire became his mentor, but not forever. In 1830 at the Academie Royale des Sciences in Paris, they publically debated two interpretations of nature, a nineteenth-century version of the famous Valladolid debate between Bartolomé de las Casas and Sepulveda over the question of whether the Indians had souls. Like de las Casas, one might say that Cuvier won the battle but lost the war.

In the course of the century, his belief that organisms are integrated wholes that the environment cannot alter receded from the mainstream of science. However, Cuvier remains a central figure in modern science. By the time of his death, he was Baron Cuvier. Cuvier created the discipline of vertebrate paleontology—the study of vertebrates' fossils, the comparative method of organismal biology—and proved for the first time that the extinction of species was a fact. Without Cuvier, Darwin may well not have discovered evolution.[34] Cuvier's grand purpose for the *jardin* and the museums was to assemble in one spot an example of every mineral and especially every animal and plant on the planet, and then to catalogue and organize every specimen to create a complete knowledge of the order and history of the natural world. He classified everything; even heaps of soil and manure had labels describing their content. Cuvier's attention to detail was legendary: he even designed his various uniforms. He organized the Museum of Natural History around the three kingdoms of nature, minerals, plants, and animals. The *jardin* had a series of separate halls, each devoted to a different aspect of study.

Cuvier worked in a large building near the amphitheater of the Jardin des Plantes—he had his own domain. Cuvier lined the walls of the laboratories with boxes into which he put all the bones he received and labeled. In his laboratory, Cuvier strove to have a "complete skeleton of every animal," as well as their fossilized ancestors. On large tables, he prepared and arranged bones, placing them neatly in a box shelved in a wooden cabinet. In one room there was an Egyptian mummy, recently unwrapped, its desiccated skin and flesh open for examination, nearby several preserved bodies of male and female Guanches, people who had once lived on the Canary Islands. The scientist's cabinets held 11,486 "preparations, 6231 of them dried and 5255 preserved in alcohol. There were human skeletons and skulls of different ages and races, 1500 skeletons and 1041 skulls of vertebrates. . . . Preserved in alcohol were 172 preparations of muscles, 216 brains, 327 eyes, 220 hearts, 80 fetuses in their envelopes."[35] The final room of the Museum of Comparative Anatomy held the unborn and the "monsters."

What Cuvier did not have in what was the largest collection of specimens anywhere in the world was a Hottentot woman. From the middle of the seventeenth century all the major biologists and zoologists had engaged in discussion of the nature of the Hottentot. The Cape had become part of the European scientific imagination. The Cape was the landscape, the body on which zoology and botany focused their scientific endeavors. The famous Linnaeus dreamed up the notion of classification that inspired nineteenth-century racists in their attempts to classify people according to geography, skin color, skull features, and so on. His student Sparrman traveled to the Cape in the late eighteenth century. Now Cuvier's examinations of Sara Baartman contributed to this kind of historical layering, a geologic formation around the meaning of the Khoekhoe woman's body.

Enlightenment intellectuals Denis Diderot, Montesquieu, Voltaire, and Jean-Jacques Rousseau had been fascinated by the place of the Hottentot in history and culture. Hottentots seemed to European philosophers to exist at the very nexus of nature and culture. In Dutch, Hottentot meant "to stammer." Naturalists and European philosophers wondered, did the

Khoekhoe have language, considered to be the most basic gift that distinguished man from beast and thus civilization from the rest of the animal kingdom? In short, were they human? How could humans smear their bodies with fat? And in the age of classification, how does one measure the breadth of the human world? Was skin color the way to classify humans into discrete races, or some other physical marker such as the skull or, in the case of the Hottentot Woman, their genitalia? Man was to woman what civilization was to nature. Ergo, woman was closer to beasts. Could not her genitalia serve as the marker of humankind?

Scientists occasionally discussed the Hottentot's breasts, but increasingly they focused on the buttocks and the genitalia, the "organs of generation." They held that the more primitive the mammal, the more pronounced the genitalia and the bodily enticements to procreation. They saw hypersexuality and uncontrolled drives in the female Hottentot body. The scientific community already had decided that Khoekhoe had no culture and that they were a race separate from "Negroes." Europeans understood the Khoekhoe woman as embodying (in all its senses) the meaning of that absence of culture.[36] Scientists married primitiveness to sexuality, the instincts, and urges revealing the essence of the lower species. The question concerned their precise location in the gradations of human and animal variation. Might Hottentots belong to the family of monkeys and not humans? The female body held the secret.

Sara Baartman had the great misfortune to arrive in Paris just when these kinds of questions moved from travel literature into the center of scientific inquiry. She "arrived" from London already packaged as a female Hottentot, the very case study that scientists thought might be the supposed missing link between animals and humans. (It is probably no coincidence that Saint-Hilaire, who worked with Cuvier, founded the study of "monsters," or malformation, teratology.) Sara arrived well advertised, well presented. Sara's handlers had always been careful to sustain the fiction of her primitiveness and racial purity.

Cuvier had seen a Hottentot boy in 1807. Now he could examine an adult and, especially, a woman. He had at his disposal a vast library. Cuvier had read deeply into travel and scientific writings on the Hottentot. He assumed a function for Sara's bottom. He wanted to know about the composition of the fatty tissue and do further research on its alleged function. In addition, did she have the famous Hottentot apron, or tablier, the elon-

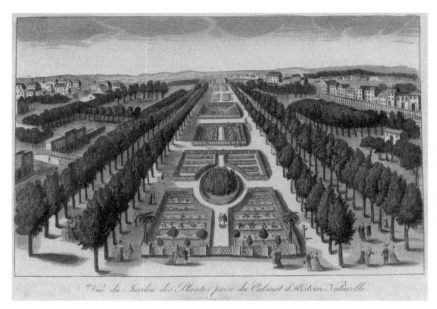

FIGURE 6.4. "Jardin des Plantes." Engraving by an unnamed artist sold by Chereau, c. 1805. Courtesy of Mary Evans Picture Library, www.maryevans.com. Image no. 10068312.

gated outer labia that would provide anatomical proof of the unrepressed sexuality and essential animal character of the Hottentot? Now Cuvier seized his opportunity to add to his collection and knowledge of the world beyond France and to study a Hottentot in his own laboratory. In this woman, the scientist knew what he wanted to find.

In March 1815, Baartman and Reaux went to the Jardin des Plantes situated on the far east side of Paris, near the Seine. They likely walked on one of Napoleon's great quays running along the Seine, past the Île de La Cité with its famous Hôtel Dieu and Notre-Dame. Crossing the river either at the boulevard du Palais or perhaps at the rue d'Arcole, they saw the Jardin des Plantes and its magnificent menagerie before them. The Museum of Natural History stood at the end of the *jardin*. To the right lay the Museum of Anatomy, Cuvier's laboratory.

Sara Baartman walked up the steps of this great hub of scientific activity, a monument to France's great age of science, a foreigner, and a woman subject to the curiosity of Europe. Sara entered no doubt dressed like other

French working-class women in long skirts, a shawl perhaps to ward of the wind. She passed through, walked among, thousands of bones in the world's most extensive collection of the natural world—skeletons and wax renditions of people long dead, mummified in burial or in the wax of the anatomist. Across this landscape of death and history, Sara walked to meet the greatest scientist of the day.

In ways that could scarcely have been imagined, Sara Baartman's meeting with Cuvier changed the course of history. For more than a century a rendition of her figure would become the template through which European culture understood the Hottentot, and how authors sought to describe "the primitive." Throughout Europe and America, Cuvier's writings would become foundational texts in comparative and evolutionary anatomy and biology, anthropology, as well as racial science and sexology. Cuvier's central question was simple. Was Sara of "the last race of the human species, or the negro race and the first of the apes" just above the orangutan? Cuvier thought that a key part of the answer lay in Sara's genitals.

Cuvier and his assistant Henri de Blainville stood by while four artists drew Sara Baartman for some three days.[37] The great halls of the museum were cold and damp. Showing little empathy for the woman they wanted to study, the scientists wanted Sara to disrobe completely. Sara, however, refused to allow Cuvier to examine her.

"She kept her apron concealed," Cuvier would write, "either between her thighs or still more deeply." Sara Baartman refused to give the greatest European scientist what he wanted. She managed to deny him this even as the artists painted her portrait from all angles and the scientists minutely measured her body. In that gesture of refusal, we read a profound statement of self.

Baartman made an impression on Cuvier: he apparently thought that she had a good memory and an outgoing personality. He described her as drinking brandy, playing on the harp, and dancing—although perhaps he engaged in hyperbole to diminish the humiliating circumstances of the examination. Sometime in those long hours in the Museum of Natural History, the young De Blainville asked Sara about her life, perhaps to put her sufficiently at ease to stand naked in front of the men. Reaux, it seems always aware of a marketing opportunity, asked De Blainville to write up his observations. Reaux perhaps wanted to sell stories of her life along with the prints.[38]

De Blainville also made use of his interview. He delivered his account as a lecture in 1815. He published the lecture as "Sur une femme de race hottentote" in the *Bulletin des Sciences* for the Société Philomatique de Paris in 1816. The article began with a rationale of his interest in Baartman, continued with a short account of her life, and then described her body in detail, always reflecting on the relation of Baartman's body to other humans and animals.

De Blainville started by trying to give "this woman as detailed a history as it was possible to make with the materials he had obtained from her." In answer to his questions, Sara said that she had been born to "Bushman" parents near Algoa Bay and had been abducted at the age of six. She lived "between the lands of the Dutch and the English, because she spoke the language perfectly." Later she married an African with whom she had one baby, "which she said resembled his father perfectly."[39]

We wonder if in the telling and the ommissions, Sara constructed a tale redolent of the past she was supposed to be representing. Talk of loves and her working life in Cape Town might have seemed disruptive of the narrative that scientists were so eager to construct. Or, perhaps Sara did speak of Cape Town, but De Blainville did not listen. He did listen, however, once the story veered toward Europe. Baartman identified Alexander Dunlop, although rendered as English not Scottish, as the driving force behind the project. De Blainville said that "she came to Europe with an English doctor, with the intention of earning money, and displaying herself in public, and then to return to her country." Baartman confirmed Anna Staal's claim that Sara went to earn money in London.

Ignoring questions of intent, of the very desires that made Sara human, De Blainville then immediately moved into a kind of classificatory language that emerged fully blown later in the century as scientific racism. He stated that he wanted to do a "detailed comparison of this woman with the lowest race of humans, the Negro race, and with the highest race of monkeys, the orangutan." Those words, together with Cuvier's later writing, helped seal for posterity the ambivalence Europe had long held about the place of the Khoekhoe in human history. The article also helped leash Sara Baartman's fate to the rise of scientific racism. De Blainville allied Sara Baartman, as representative of her "race," more closely with the orangutan than with "Negroes."[40]

If Sara arrived to meet Cuvier in any small measure as a woman, as Sara Baartman, despite her resistance she left the *jardin* ever more the Hottentot Venus. Baartman returned to her squalid quarters near the *palais*, suffering through a long winter. The Seine froze over and thawed slowly. The spring crops failed, the price of food skyrocketed. Some Parisians rioted over the price of bread. Paris conversation turned to the unusually cold weather, price gouging, the Bourbon king, and especially the possibility of Bonaparte returning to power.

Napoleon escaped from his island prison on Elba and entered Cannes in March 1815. He reached Paris on 20 March mounted on his great white horse. Back in the capital, Napoleon forced the occupying armies from the city, overthrew King Louis XVIII, and restored the empire. The emperor quickly raised more than a quarter million troops and issued a decree drafting 2.5 million more before setting off for Belgium.

In June, the French forces defeated the Prussians, only to collapse before Wellington at the Battle of Waterloo. At the end of the month Napoleon abdicated for a second time. Napoleon finally surrendered to British troops at Rochefort on 15 July 1815. Nearly one million French soldiers had died serving the emperor. Another million French civilians had died in the long wars. Allied forces had entered Paris for a second time on 7 July, though skirmishes continued outside the city for a few more days. The whole length of the Champs-Elysées "was covered with tents, horses, picketed by thousands, innumerable troops (mostly British) cavalry, infantry, and artillery." The Prussian army encamped in the Luxembourg Gardens and at Cuvier's beloved Jardin des Plantes. Paris had again become "a British and Prussian garrison."[41]

A somber quiet fell over the city, as if Paris had become "a vast mourning family," with three out of five people walking in the street dressed in black. Parisians bundled themselves up against the unusually cold weather. Allied military patrols surveilled the city. Troops placed cannons on many of the bridges. Even the Palais-Royal closed at eight in the evening for fear it might once again become a haven for revolutionary and seditious talk. The allies dispatched Napoleon for good: he arrived on Saint Helena in October and died there on 5 May 1821. In November 1815, France and the allies signed the Second Peace of Paris, marking the end of the Napoleonic Wars. Peace offered little succor to the citizens of weary Paris. War and crop failure created great dearth, and a veil of crisis hung over the city. Famine arrived in the countryside.

In the course of 1815, the French newspapers stopped covering the Hottentot Venus with as much interest as they had paid before. *La Quotidienne* briefly mentioned Sara in mid-September, but by then she already had faded from the public's attention. Sara's life had been decidedly miserable for some time now. War had robbed Sara and many others of possible income and in less than six months had thrown the city into economic depression.

The Hottentot Venus had become little more than a minor attraction in a city seemingly always on the move to the next controversy or titillation.[42] Reaux tried exhibiting Sara on Saint-Honoré and in the cafés of the *palais*. He also made her available to be seen, and perhaps hired at the brothel in Cours des Fontaines. There was little loose money in the fallen city. The prostitutes struggled to find customers and lowered their prices. He may well have have offered Sara's body for a few francs to buy food.

At the end of the year Sara Baartman died her first death. Sara Baartman, Sarah Bartmann, Saartje, Sartjee, the Hottentot Venus, all those personas in the one, dead, far from the wide countryside of her birth. For a century or more, only the Hottentot Venus would see a resurrection. Parisian newspapers wrote more obituaries about Sara Baartman than for any other African woman throughout the nineteenth century. A few rehearsed Europe's fascination with the Hottentot Venus. The *Manchester Mercury* mentioned Sara's baptism at the Collegiate Church and that she had been married "at the same time." Most articles were short.

Like so much else about Sara, when it comes to a detail that matters to the person, the evidence is lost, or conflicting, as if no one really cared to get it right at the time. Georges Cuvier said that she died on 29 December 1815. *Annales, Politiques, Morales et Literaires* said that she died the following day of a fever. An even later date was offered by the *Journal General de France*, which reported on 31 December, on its second page, that "the Venus Hottentote, who was exhibited to the public . . . died this morning at 7am after a short illness of 3 days." The major English papers also covered Sara's death. Of what did Sara die? Newspapers reported that she died of smallpox, which her doctors had mistakenly understood to be some form of respiratory ailment. The cause of death did not interest scientists.[43] With a poor diet and terribly cold, most likely Sara died of pneumonia.

Sara Baartman might have faded into the past, joining the many other indigenous people of the world whose lives and deaths were so shaped by the violence that inaugurated the modern era. Posterity likely would have forgotten Sara Baartman and the Hottentot Venus had it not been for Cuvier and the other scientists at the *jardin*. They secured permission from the police to obtain the corpse. Sara Baartman's body was wrapped in cloth, bundled into a cart, and brought to Cuvier's laboratory.

Cuvier was at the height of his fame. Still revered within biology as a leading scientist, Cuvier is no marginal figure. He remains a very important scholar who left a legacy of accomplishment. He did not empathize with a woman from Africa. Science and the unethical, science and the theatrical, discovery and passion, obscenities and curiosity coexisted— Mary Shelley's *Frankenstein* was born in this era. Europe as the observer of Africa created so many stories of disrespect and exploitation. For example, Pierre Delalande, a famous naturalist, traveled to southern Africa a few years later, collecting human skulls and skeletons to bring back to France. His nephew Jules Verreaux, who worked for a while in the South African Museum in Cape Town, corresponded with Cuvier. In 1830, some fifteen years after Sara's death, Jules stole a cadaver in South Africa and brought it to Paris. El Negro, as the corpse was now named, stood in the shop for years until taken to Spain, where it was displayed into the 1990s before being returned to Botswana—weird science, insulting science, nineteenth-century science, twentieth-century science and popular culture; racism invented and sustained through the body.[44]

In January 1816, over the course of a number of days, Cuvier minutely dissected the corpse of Sara Baartman. A journalist viewed the body lying at the museum. He remarked that her corpse showed no trace of the illness that killed her, a good indication Baartman did not die from smallpox. He predicted that Cuvier's dissection of the body would furnish an extremely interesting chapter in the history of the variety of the human species.[45] Before dissecting Sara Baartman, Cuvier had made a full cast of her body, fixing the new, eternal Hottentot Venus to a small, heavy platform. Artists painted the cast so that it seemed as a close to what they saw as possible. Aureole and nipple imparted on her breasts, a trompe l'oeil of hair added to her head, even a small animal skin protecting her genitals. Sara Baartman's eyes are closed, but she seems to be downcast. Her lips are parted as if she were about to speak. What tales would she tell, what triumphs, perhaps, what endless sorrows?

With his scalpel Cuvier sought to bring to a conclusion the long-standing scientific debate as to the real nature of the Hottentot and their position in the tree of biological life. Cuvier made incisions around the bottom of the skull and from the top of the chest to Sara's vulva. A saw separated the skull from the rest of the head. The scientists removed the brain. They examined, weighed, and then it placed in a medical jar for preservation and future study. Cuvier thought the brain important, so also the shape and size of the cranium. Cuvier's own brain had a similar fate, the zeal of science in this case knowing no boundaries of status, race, or gender.

Other cuts radiated out from the long body incision. Cuvier weighed all the major organs and inspected them for secrets that might reveal similarities and differences between the Hottentot, humans, and apes. Cuvier was not interested in all of Baartman's body. He directed his most intense concern to the buttocks and the sex organs, which Sara had refused to show him ten months earlier. Did the Hottentot Venus have the "Hottentot apron" made famous by travelers' tales? Now she could no longer resist their entreaties. Spreading her legs open, the men examined Sara's genitals, to their delight discovering her "apron."

Science as rape, institutionalized. Scientists excised Sara's genitals, placing them in a separate jar of preservative. The dissection complete, the academics removed limb from limb and placed the remains of Sara Baartman's body in large vats. Hours of boiling water dissolved connective tissues, separated flesh from bone. They then carefully reassembled the bones into Sara Baartman's skeleton. This skeleton joined the many others in Cuvier's great collection.

By 8 June 1816, Cuvier had finished writing up his "dissection of the Hottentot Venus." As the *Times* reported, "This new object of curiosity for the amateurs of natural history will be placed in the museum of this fine establishment." Cuvier's writing added to De Blainville's account of the earlier examination of Sara Baartman while she was alive; these writings re-created the Hottentot Venus for posterity. While Cuvier determined that the Hottentot "apron" resulted from culture, not nature, he concluded from his study of Sara's body that the Hottentot was a closer relative of the great apes than of humans.

Science now fixed forever, it seems, European travelers' stereotypes of Hottentot women. Darwin, writing so much later said that many Hottentot women were "steatopygous."[46] The Hottentot Venus had indeed become a racial type. In their compulsion to link the Hottentot Venus to larger scientific interpretations, Cuvier and the other scientists at the *jardin* ensured that Sara Baartman and the Hottentot Venus would never die. The Hottentot Venus became the foundation of racial science. Yet Cuvier argued that Sara Baartman was not a Hottentot but a Bushwoman. Ironically, the man who solidified the identity of the Hottentot Venus did not hold her to be a Hottentot. Even the icon now became a reference for something else.[47]

The stroke of a pen, the mark of print, the authority of science, silenced Sara Baartman's life story of traveling across South Africa, of loving, giving birth, of suffering. It did not, could not, account for her journeys across the Atlantic, and through much of England, the woman baptized in Manchester, the Sara working at the Palais-Royal, the story of the woman who braved a Europe of industry and revolution and died alone at the center of Parisian pleasure and politics. People would tell part of that story in a new era: that of the postcolonial world, when the formerly colonized confronted Europe and demanded restitution.

7

GHOSTS OF SARA BAARTMAN

She stood there for nearly two hundred years, lips sealed in plaster and paint, her naked body exposed to the multitudes. Thousands of people, scientists and tourists, children, families, writers and artists, stared at her while visiting the Jardin des Plantes, the world's premier museum of natural history and the site of some of the most extraordinary scientific advances in the natural sciences. At Case Number 33, visitors viewed her brain and the skeleton stitched by wire and held erect by a simple metal pole. A few beheld the excised organs that lay well preserved on a shelf in one of Cuvier's wooden cabinets.

In 1889 she greeted the millions of people who came to the Universal Exhibition of Paris celebrating the Revolution's centenary and, ostensibly, the birth of modernity. In 1937, she moved from the *jardin* to the Musée de l'Homme, opposite the Eiffel Tower, that was designed for the International Exhibition of Arts and Technology in Modern Life, a rebirth of modernity after the disastrous Great War of 1914–17. More than thirty-one million flocked to Paris, where they could see her, or Picasso's *Guernica*, or the German pavilion designed by Speer with its powerfully austere and massive columns crowned by an eagle and adorned with swastikas and a huge Nazi flag.

In 1994 she traveled a short distance across Paris to the Musée d'Orsay, the great museum of modernism, where she participated in the exhibition La Sculpture Ethnographique au XIXeme siècle, de la Venus Hottentot à la Tehura de Gauguin. And always "she" was the Hottentot Venus, never Sara Baartman, always a symbol and never a human being. In the Musée de l'Homme a simple plaque read by millions memorialized an illusion, a spectral being, someone who never existed except in the minds of others.

In the many years between her life and death in Europe and Sara Baart-man's triumphant return to South Africa in 2002, the Hottentot Venus became an important part of European and American culture. We will turn shortly to the location of the Hottentot Venus in ideas about race, women, and sexuality. Less is known about the legacy of the legal decision rendered in 1811, and the ways it has shaped Anglo-American jurisprudence. On behalf of the African Institution, Zachary Macaulay had brought a writ of habeas corpus before the King's Bench, arguing that the conditions under which Sara Baartman lived in London should come before the court and that she should be released from unlawful restraint. Depriving Sara Baartman of agency, the humanitarian Macauley spoke for Baartman and requested the court to protect her inalienable rights.

Although the action failed, "The Case of the Hottentot Venus" (along with the 1772 *Sommersett* decision outlawing slavery in England) helped establish two precedents. Macauley's intervention represented an early instance of a third-party application to intervene in order to mitigate the conditions of someone who could not otherwise speak. The humanitarian was neither related to nor even knew Sara Baartman beyond his visit to Piccadilly Street, but he believed she was ill-treated and implored the state to intervene. In the nineteenth century this empathetic imagination ending in a legal action was highly distinctive. Today it is an unquestioned part of our moral and legal culture where the concern of strangers has helped save the lives of abused children, battered women, and the aged and infirm. It is a part of our humanity, the terrain of human rights, a simple act of caring and of worrying about the fate of people we do not even know, of extending our imaginations beyond the immediacies of everyday life.[1]

A second precedent centers on the status of foreigners. Do non-nationals have the protection offered citizens under the rights of habeas corpus? The King's Bench ruled in the affirmative, in part because Sara Baartman as a colonized subject was a member of the British Empire. Recently, the status and legal protection (if any) of aliens has become an extraordinarily volatile legal and political controversy growing out of the United States' military intervention in Afghanistan and Iraq, the predicament of thousands of prisoners held at the Guantánamo Bay prison, and the morality of the current "war on terror." In a series of court cases before the U.S. District Court (District of Columbia), the U.S. Court of Appeals, and ultimately before the Supreme Court of the United States, attorneys and judges have invoked "The Case of the Hottentot Venus." In *Rasul v. Bush* (2004), arguing for the majority, Justice Stevens asserted the centrality of habeas corpus within common law, including its exercise concerning "the claims of aliens detained within the sovereign territory of the realm." Stevens cited as an authority "The Case of the Hottentot Venus" before the King's Bench.[2]

A string of other cases, petitions, and briefs resurrected Sara Baartman's history in London. In March 2006, the Supreme Court heard *Hamdan v. Rumsfeld* (2006). In June the court issued its decision, denying a writ of habeas corpus and remanding the case to the district court. In December 2006, Judge James Robertson in the U.S. district court held that, under the Military Commissions Act, which has withdrawn the statutory protection of habeas corpus, Hamdan "has no constitutional entitlement to" protection.[3] The legality, let alone the morality, of the Military Commissions Act remains the subject of ongoing congressional, legal, and scholarly controversy, in which various actors invoke "The Case of the Hottentot Venus" and speak yet again for the African woman living in London nearly two centuries ago.

The presence of Sara Baartman continues within the labyrinthine world of the law, in which her experiences have helped shaped some of the most basic protections offered within Anglo-American jurisprudence and now challenged by contemporary world events. It has been, however, the absence of Sara Baartman and the presence of the Hottentot Venus that have figured most powerfully and visibly. Throughout the nineteenth century and well into the twentieth century, the Hottentot Venus participated in the great debates on evolution, race, and female sexuality. Cuvier's dissection of Sara Baartman and the Hottentot Venus discussed in works such as *Observations on the Cadaver of . . . Hottentot Venus* (1817) and the four-volume *Natural History of Mammals* (1824–47), edited by Cuvier's brother Frederic and Étienne Saint-Hilaire, concluded that the Khoisan were closer to the great apes than to humans.

These were very widely read and exceptionally influential texts produced by some of Europe's greatest thinkers and from the world's premier laboratories in the natural sciences. Cuvier's writings, for example, were particularly influential to Charles Darwin as he began elaborating his theory of evolution. And his prior understanding of the Hottentot shaped Darwin's ideas on human diversity and sexuality.[4]

The Hottentot Venus's greatest notoriety came with the spectacular proliferation of scientific racism in the second half of the nineteenth century. All of the most prominent writers on the supposed inferiority of non-Caucasoid races knew of the Hottentot Venus and very often explicitly discussed the Hottentot in elaborating their ideas on race and on the dangers of racial mixing. These ideas helped bequeath racial intolerance and hatred in the American South, in South Africa, and in Germany in the infamous 1935 Nuremberg Laws prohibiting marriage and intercourse between Germans and "non-Aryans." The Germans had their own history of genocidal violence against southern Africans, and the Hottentot figured in the eugenic science of European fascism and the Final Solution that destroyed Europe and condemned millions to firing squads and concentration camps.[5] The Hottentot still figures in contemporary neo-Nazi propaganda.[6]

The Hottentot figures as well in the work of scores of writers and artists over a period of some two centuries, as a marker of difference and as an object of subjection and fascination. "Marry that mulatto woman," scoffs George in Thackeray's *Vanity Fair*. "I am not going to marry a Hottentot Venus." In *Les Misérables* Victor Hugo draws a portrait of a Paris that "accepts everything royally; it is not too particular about its Venus; its Callipyge is Hottentot; provided that it is made to laugh, it condones; ugliness cheers it, deformity provokes it to laughter, vice diverts it." The characters Dr. Mortimer and Sir Charles spend "many a charming evening . . . discussing the comparative anatomy of the Bushman and the Hottentot" in Arthur Conan Doyle's *Hound of the Baskervilles*. "Let us take woman," wonders Stephen in Joyce's *Portrait of the Artist*. "The Greek, the Turk, the Chinese, the Copt, the Hottentot . . . all admire a different type of female beauty. That seems to be a maze out of which we cannot escape."[7] Decades later, and much differently, writers as diverse as J. M. Coetzee and Thomas Pynchon returned the Hottentot to Africa as colonized people, exploited by South African farmers or quite literally destroyed by the Germans in the 1904–7 Herero genocide.[8]

Well into the twentieth century the Hottentot Venus continued to shape French and especially Parisian culture, particularly with regard to female sexuality. Writers on prostitution consistently tied it to the savage woman, the "terrible voluptuousness" of the "wild Venus," according to a 1903 play.[9] Ideas about the primitive, sexuality, and women folded into scientific and popular fascinations with hysteria, particularly from the 1860s and 1870s when Parisian women seemed "as foreign as a Hottentot" and dance began imitating the movements of female hysterics in the Salpetriere Hospital. In 1878, the play *La Vénus noire* enjoyed considerable success at the Théâtre du Chatelet. In Emile Zola's most famous novel, *Nana* (slang for "chick"), the heroine is a "blond Venus." Edouard Manet's *Nana* depicts the woman with an enlarged derriere and a gentleman customer gazing from the painting's edge, mentally undressing the prostitute and imagining the mysterious folds of her flesh. And Picasso, who frequented the Jardin des Plantes and the Museum of Man with its African sculptures and masks and who made African art his own, produced scores of work displaying the essence of female sexuality . . . women with large buttocks and swollen genitalia.[10]

When Josephine Baker conquered Paris in the 1920s, the great actress became the "Brown Venus." At the Théâtre des Champs-Elysées, Baker quite literally crawled onto stage as if an animal in heat, wearing few clothes and with her bottom erect and inviting. Later in the performance Baker appeared mostly nude and, with the dancer Joe Alex, performed a "savage dance." Paris went absolutely wild with Dionysian delight. Josephine Baker was continuing the tradition of the exotic, hypersexual black woman begun with the exhibiting of Sara Baartman a century earlier.[11] Indeed Baker, like Sara, was known particularly for her bottom, according to Georges Simenon, "the most famous bottom in the world. It must be the only bottom which has become the centre of a cult. And it is everywhere."[12]

Unsurprisingly, Sigmund Freud knew of the Hottentot Venus, who had a ghostly presence in his ideas on female sexuality as the "dark continent" of psychology. Freud had studied the work of the famous neurologist and founder, in 1859, of the French Anthropological Society, Paul Broca, particularly his writings on aphasia and hypnosis. Broca used Sara Baartman's skeleton in his work on comparative anatomy.[13] Freud moved to Paris in late 1885, drawn especially to the research of Charcot, when ideas about the Hottentot, the savage woman, female sexuality, and the body saturated Parisian scientific and popular culture.[14] Charcot's work at Salpetriere Hos-

pital on women, hysteria, and the body greatly influenced Freud, who
wrote an obituary of the master following Charcot's death in 1893. The
Austrian doctor's Parisian experiences powerfully shaped Freud's ideas on
human sexuality and genitalia, particularly that of women.[15]

Sara Baartman had been reduced not simply to men's image of her body
but to men's image of her genitals and the ways the organs of sexual pleasure stood for character, her very being. White women, even the most
civilized, were liable to fall victim to their animal instincts and passions,
to revert to their Hottentot selves. European prostitutes became degenerate
women, literally women who had become more Hottentot. Just look at
their genitals, even their rough faces. Politicians and bureaucrats devised
laws throughout Europe to control the biological deviance of prostitutes
and female sexuality. In Europe and in the United States doctors cut or
burned women's clitorises off with acid. Surgeons destroyed women's genitals to make them less pronounced, less like the Hottentot Venus to control
the sexual cravings and brute drives of these "unmanageable" women. In
some cases, doctors argued, castration was warranted; in the United States
the practice continued through the 1950s.[16]

In Anglo-American popular culture women remain hypersexual, partic-
ularily if they are black. For the British rock band Queen:

> Left alone with big fat Fanny
> She was such a naughty nanny
> Heap big woman you made a bad boy out of me. . . .
> Fat bottomed girls you make the
> rockin' world go round.[17]

More recently, in 2004, the misogynist rap artist Nelly came out with a
line of jeans ostensibly sculpted for black women's bottoms; protests invoked the Hottentot Venus. "Black women know the sister very well,"
went an article in *Essence*,

> Sometimes, when we are walking down Main Street feeling pretty and
> strong, we pass young Black men, and suddenly we see her in their eyes, in
> their leers. "Can I come with you, Mama?" And we know what they see.
> Big thighs, big butt. No need for foreplay, she's ready anytime, all the time.
> Spits out babies just to collect a check. Been doing it since she was a kid.

She screams when she comes; gets funky and sweaty. Her hair goes back. Don't matter. She ain't nothin' but a born whore. Black woman. Whore. Whoreblackwoman.[18]

The Hottentot Venus is a figure so pervasive as to become nameless, a ghostly presence in modern Western culture. The history of the Hottentot Venus is one of tragedy and paradox, of necessity and artifice, a history of our own times and our deepest held prejudices and predicaments.

For two centuries Sara Baartman had disappeared from history. Virtually no one cared about her history, her life in South Africa, her experiences in London, her display in Paris, or even the remains of her body preserved in so many medical jars. Nor was there any effort to bring Sara back home.[19] The famous Harvard paleontologist and comparative biologist Stephen Jay Gould reintroduced the Hottentot Venus to a wide public in his *Mismeasure of Man* (1981) not to explore Sara's life but to critique racialized science. Following protests that the exhibit debased Africans and women, in 1982 museum officials removed Cabinet Number 33 from public viewing.

In the 1990s, the figure of the Hottentot Venus would loom in America's "culture wars," as part of the rise of black and feminist scholarship and cultural studies, with its concern with the "Other." In 1990, the acclaimed African American poet Elizabeth Alexander published a collection titled *The Venus Hottentot*. A year earlier, a poem by the same title appeared in *Callaloo*, a leading journal of African and African American writing, in which Alexander speaks as the Hottentot Venus, attempting to reverse the negative stereotypes of black women. The poem begins with Cuvier, where the poet imagines the scientist measuring Sara's cranium and how Baartman's "genitalia will float inside a labelled pickling jar." "Monsieur Cuvier investigates," Alexander writes toward the end of the poem, "between my legs / poking, prodding / sure of his hypothesis."

But then Alexander turns the table, stigmatizing the scientist in order to destigmatize Sara Baartman and to return personhood and agency to the silenced woman. "If he were to let me rise up" from the dissecting table,

> I'd spirit his knives and cut out his black heart,
> seal it with science fluid inside

a Bell jar, place it on a low
shelf in a white man's museum
so the whole world could see
it was shriveled and hard,
geometric, deformed, unnatural.[20]

A cloudburst of journalistic, artistic, academic, and popular work on her life and legacy spread knowledge and sowed debate on and about Sara Baartman as the Hottentot Venus. A few years later a different Baartman surfaced. In 1996, Susan-Lori Parks (who later, in 2002, won a Pulitzer Prize) produced the play *Venus*, which opened at Joseph Papp's Public Theatre in New York City. Parks's play attempted to represent Baartman as, ultimately, "complicit" and to convey that the world of race was "more complicated than 'that white man down the street is giving me a hard time.'" The theater critic for the *New York Times* complimented Parks for seeing Baartman "as [not] just an uncomprehending victim." For Parks, the issue is "about a woman who makes choices."[21] Others disagreed and found Parks's representation intolerable: "Baartman was a victim and not an accomplice, and the portrayal of her as complicit recapitulates the travesty of objectification or 'Otherness' perpetrated by the nineteenth-century exhibition of Saartjie Baartman."[22] Perpetration and power-lessness, agency and its absence, would become defining ways by and through which people and communities across the globe, and in South Africa an entire nation, imagined Sara Baartman and brought to life a person dead if not buried.

It was as if Sara Baartman had begun talking from beyond death's horizon. Writers, artists, and academics adopted Sara Baartman, producing everything from sculptures to essays to exhibitions. In October 1998, *The Life and Times of Sara Baartman* became one of the very first films produced by a black person, about a black person, to appear in post-apartheid South Africa.[23]

South Africa had faced the specter of an all-out race war following a decade of intense and protracted violence. A negotiated settlement between the African National Congress (ANC) and the Afrikaner Nationalist Party (NP) led to elections in 1994 and the beginning of a constitutional democracy at Africa's southernmost tip. The following year saw the formation of the Truth and Reconciliation Committee (TRC) aimed at public healing, where, ostensibly at least, the evils of the past would no longer be secreted away.

How South Africans understood Sara's life and the history of the Hottentot Venus shaped discussions about democracy and identity, citizenship and ethnicity, about memory and how people might face, or efface, histories of violence and oppression. What was the "new" South Africa? Who was this woman trapped in a Paris museum? How would Sara Baartman be returned home? To whom did she belong?

It seemed as if one could touch worlds that lay broken and scattered across the horizon. For people of Khoisan descent, the promise of return and renewal had long been part of their sense of themselves and their history, no more so than in the years immediately after apartheid's collapse when earlier state and racialized ascriptions melted away. "Coloured" disappeared as a legal category. But who one was in history's detritus and in South Africa's political quagmires was less than clear.[24]

For some there was the palpable feeling the prophecies people had kept alive for well over a century might finally come true. And there was a sense, a terrible fragile vague sense, that somehow one might connect the present to a now distant time before the violence and dispossession of colonial conquest . . . when Sara's parents had been a free people in the Camdeboo. What stories had they spoken, what stories did Sara hear—the winds, the moon carrying the soul away, the stars the spirits of departed women and children? Which star was Sara?

People saw in Sara and her return to South Africa the revelations from the book of Ezekiel where the Spirit becomes a wind blowing across the land that breathes the Lord God into our hearts. Ezekiel sees the bones of a genocide, a land of horrible, violent death that annihilates memory and creates a holocaust so vast and lonely that the living are unable to care for the departed. But he also sees the promise of reconciliation and rebirth. In a valley "full of bones" the Lord God instructs Ezekiel to "prophesy unto the wind, prophesy, son of man, and say to the wind." These bones were "the whole house of Israel," and the wind "came into them and they lived." And the Lord God would bring the people of Israel "into their own land" and "make them one nation" again. The scattered bones of people once cursed reconnect, one bone bumping into another until each found its proper place. Muscles and skin reappear. Ligaments reunite what had been sundered apart. God's breath makes the dead come alive again.

Sara likely had heard of the words of Ezekiel during her years living in Cape Town. Those of her family who had survived the deafening silences of colonial violence believed in them. Now, almost exactly two centuries after she journeyed to the port city, people imagined in Sara Baartman the book of Ezekiel, in the violence perpetrated against her and in the redemptive possibilities of coming home. Baartman's return heralded the arrival of a new era, for many Khoisan quite literally when the scattered bones of the oppressed might come together again and the chasms of history finally traversed.

People claiming Khoekhoe descent, and especially the Griqua, took the lead in claiming Sara as their own and in demanding her return, and they often did so through the words of Ezekiel. The Griqua emerged in the eighteenth and nineteenth centuries among people who fled colonial power across the borders of the Cape Colony. Khoekhoe, slaves and others, initially had been known as "Bastards" or "Basters," an indictment of their mixed descent. Around 1813 they adopted the name "Griqua," and many recognized the strong leadership of men like Adam Kok and the Le Fleur family. Over the decades Boer and British chased them from one spot to another, from the Orange Free State to Griqualand East, later to Plettenberg Bay along the Indian Ocean and as far as Vanrhynnsdorp in the Western Cape. Each time the Griqua believed they had finally found a land of their own, the authorities pushed them away again.

For two centuries the Griqua have spoken of the stories and prophecies of Ezekiel and of their leader as "die kneg," as a servant of God. In 1889, A. S. Le Fleur received a calling from God to gather together the bones of the Griqua founder Kok as the first task of gathering the Griqua as a nation, "so that they can be my people and I their God . . . and that the word of Ezechiel be fulfilled." Women have long fashioned blankets recalling their history of dispossession and scattering, bits and pieces of cloth which they wear around themselves during the winter, fragments of the past stitched together reminding them of their history and that, one day, their land shall be returned and restored.[25]

Following his 1903 release from Robben Island on charges of sowing unrest, Le Fleur had a vision that God called him to a desolate place some three hundred kilometers to the north where the Griqua should gather, where the bones of the past would one day come alive again. A final trek led to the scrub of Namaqualand near Vanrhynnsdorp, where in the short spring the plants bloom to create an extraordinary quilt of brilliant yellow, oranges, azure blues, and magentas before disappearing back into the greens and browns of the veld. Here Le Fleur began to acquire part of the farm Kranshoek, where they established their sacred site of Ratelgat, named after an animal that leads one to water. At the farm he prophesied a new world, that this barren dry land would become a Garden of Eden for the Griqua headed by his organization, the Griqua National Conference (GNC). Since 1905, the Griqua have struggled to come together to reaffirm their history and conviction that the world will be made anew, that one day they will make blankets of whole cloth. In 1941, the Great Reformer died. The faithful buried Le Fleur at Ratelgat. Even this piece of land, as richly symbolic as it is barren, they lost to a white farmer who God later punished with a violent death.

Before the 1990s, no Griqua leader knew of Sara Baartman. A man named Mansell Upham brought her story, and the location of her remains in a Paris museum, to the attention of the Griqua leaders. An attorney by training, a former diplomat, and an extraordinarily skilled genealogist, Upham claims descent from Eva or Krotoa, the seventeenth-century Khoekhoe women who worked as a servant for Jan van Riebeeck and who, in 1664, married the Dutch surgeon Pieter van Meerhof. In Sara Baartman, Upham conceived a Krotoa for the nineteenth century, the plight of indigenous peoples, and a story of dehumanization and the tragedies befalling black women in colonial societies.

Upham had seen Sara Baartman standing alone in the Musée de l'Homme. His travels and diplomatic career exposed him as well to international movements and developments relating to indigenous peoples, for example, the United Nations Working Group on Indigenous Populations in 1982. Upham returned to South Africa shortly after the 1994 elections and continued his great interest in genealogy. He also became a legal adviser to the GNC at the very moment many people in South Africa were asserting indigenous identities and "Coloureds" especially were imagining pasts independent of racial prejudice and state classification.

In Cape Town, Upham "alerted" the Griqua National Conference to the "Sarah Baartman issue as a possible indigenous people's issue."[26] The timing of the campaign to bring Sara Baartman home was perfect. The politics of Khoisan identity and history, and with it Sara Baartman's past and present, had become an international issue. It also dovetailed with local and national politics. In South Africa's first democratic elections in 1994, the African National Congress failed to win the Western Cape. Instead the province remained under the control of the National Party, the very party responsible for apartheid, for persecuting "Coloureds" even as it provided them with preferential treatment within the labor market. The "Coloured" vote swung the balance against the ANC.

Politics within the "Coloured" community remained fraught and fragile. Many thousands had fought against apartheid; hundreds had lost their lives. But many also shared much of the culture of white Afrikaners, including a language and a common, if also divided, history in the Cape. The movement of Africans into the Western Cape from the 1970s, an area previously under the "coloured labor preference policy," created anxieties and conflicts over jobs and housing. At least many in the older generation wondered if the wave of black nationalism and government declarations of an "African Renaissance" included them. Claims to ancient blood and land, and shameful histories like that of Sara Baartman, offered one way of negotiating an uncertain present.

Politicians clearly knew that securing the province for the ANC was impossible without the "Coloured" vote, and in the ensuing years they became acutely sensitive to the demands of Khoisan leaders. Khoisan claims began to receive the attention of the government. In late 1995, GNC leader and Paramount Chief A. A. S. LeFleur II brought to the attention of President Nelson Mandela the issue of Sara Baartman and the importance of repatriating her remains. The GNC also formally appealed to the French embassy in Pretoria, invoking the United Nation's Declaration of Human Rights and the Draft Declaration on the Rights of Indigenous People. Mandela subsequently raised the issue with French president François Mitterrand.

Between late 1996 and early 1998, the South African and French governments held discussions in Pretoria and in Paris. The intervention of Nelson Mandela ultimately involved formal engagement of the South African government, specifically the Department of Arts and Culture (DAC) then headed by Ben Ngubane (a member of the opposition Inkatha Freedom Party) and Deputy Minister Bridgette Mabandla (ANC). In 1996, the deputy minister approached Professor Philip Tobias to enter into discussions with his French colleagues at the Museum of Man. South Africa's most esteemed scientist and professor emeritus of anatomy and human biology at the University of Witwatersrand, which houses a copy of Sara's skull, Tobias is one of the world's leading scientists working on hominid development. For more than four decades Tobias has been excavating the famous Sterkfontein sites, which have produced a veritable treasure trove of some of the world's oldest anthropoids. In popular parlance these fossils are often referred to as the relics of "ape men," the missing links separating modern *Homo sapiens* from their more primitive ancestors. There was a delicious irony here that was lost on participants at the time. Tobias spent much of his long career looking for a missing link. In the body of Sara Baartman, Cuvier thought he had found a living missing link connecting animals to humankind.[27]

Tobias seemed like the ideal person to initiate discussions with his French counterparts, particularly Professor Henry de Lumley, then director of the Musée de l'Homme and the Musée National d'Histoire Naturelle. Tobias knew Lumley. Moreover, Tobias's enormous prestige and gentlemanly demeanor might not only expedite discussions but, also, potentially de-politicize what might become a nasty international dispute. Tobias's efforts met with negligible results until 2001. The French, and particularly Lumley, strenuously opposed repatriation, insisting that nothing short of a new French law would be necessary to bring Baartman home to South Africa. Lumley feared (as did curators in England, the United States, and elsewhere) the politicization of human remains and that agreeing to South Africa's demands would open the floodgates to similar calls to repatriate the bones of colonized peoples. The Musée de l'Homme had hundreds, perhaps thousands, of human remains from across the globe. The French also bristled that the Baartman campaign was accusing one of their nation's most famous scientists—Georges Cuvier—of racism, colonialism, and, in his interests with Baartman's genitalia, a kind of sexual harassment.

In late December, French senator Nicolas About argued, "L'histoire de Saartjie Baartman est pathetiique"; moreover, "Il est stupéfiant de penser que cette sordide exhibition a duré en France justqu'en 1974."[28] It was, About argued, in France's interests, its honor, to return Sara Baartman to South Africa. The South Africans assured the international community that the case of Sara Baartman was sui generis and not part of a wider effort to repatriate the remains of people whose bones lay in so many public and private collections around the world. Because her identity was known, because part of her history could be reconstructed, and because of her unique presence in Western history, Sara Baartman stood alone as a symbol and as an icon, indeed as something of a sacral object.

In late February 2002, the National Assembly unanimously passed a bill for her return. The final law came into effect as "Loi no 2002-323 du 6 mars 2002 relative à la restitution par la France de la dépouille mortelle de Saartjie Baartman à l'Afrique du Sud." The legislation instructed the museum to repatriate Sara Baartman's remains within two months. Sara was coming home.

In early 2002, the Department of Arts and Cultures (DAC) created a Reference Group to oversee the return, burial, and memorialization of Sara Baartman, or what many now referred to as "Mama Saartjie," the maternal figure of the new South Africa. Tobias became the most illustrious member of the group. The other twelve representatives appointed by the minister included members of the government, academics, the deputy chairperson of the Human Rights Commission, a representative of the Commission on Gender Equality, representatives of the Khoisan community, and the poet and University of Western Cape academic Diana Ferrus, who had written the widely distributed poem about Sara Baartman, "I Have Come to Take You Home."[29]

DAC officials knew they were dealing with a potentially explosive issue, but also one that might serve multiple purposes in the "new" South Africa. An early project proposal noted that the "story of Ms Saartjie Baartman has become synonymous with the pain and suffering of a black woman of a colonised people," a prime example of the creation of the "Other." Returning her remains "has national as well as international significance." Officials concluded that Baartman's return might become an important moment for "nation-building and reconciliation."[30] South Africa would, in effect, speak for Sara Baartman, defend her human rights, and in doing so claim her as a citizen of the fledgling democracy. DAC proposed an eighteen-month time frame and a budget of 8,700,000 South African rands (R); a later budget estimate extended the figure to a total of R10,350,000. It is unlikely we will ever know the exact amount spent bringing Sara Baartman home.[31]

The Reference Group faced a number of pressing questions it had to answer within an exceptionally short period of time. The most obvious and immediate issue was Baartman's name. Should she be referred to as Saartjie, the formal diminutive Cape name for slaves and peons, or Sarah Baartman, the name located on her baptismal register? Or should there be some invented, "traditional" name to refer to this African woman? Where and when would Sara Baartman be buried, according to the calendar of national and international politics, or in sync with how people imagined Khoekhoe may have once organized the ebb and flow of time? Should she be buried in the Eastern Cape, where she was born, or in Cape Town, where she had lived and from which she had left Africa's shores? How would her life be mourned and celebrated: as a South African woman, as a woman, as a Khoekhoe person, as a member of the Gonaqua tribe? How, precisely, should Sara Baartman be buried? As a "traditional" Khoekhoe woman? Or as a Christian, given the fact that she had been baptized in Manchester a few years before her death? Or should there be some combination of Christian and indigenous burial practices? In what order do the living organize the many adjectives describing the dead? In the many publics created and sustained on and around Sara Baartman and the "Hottentot Venus," and now within the Reference Group, people re-created a life and a history so powerful that Baartman seemed to come alive again as if she were sitting around a table deciding her fate.

The Reference Group pursued its charges at an explosive moment in the always fraught politics of identity in South Africa. The 1990s had seen both an imagining of national citizenship and a proliferation of groups making claims to indigeneity. Chiefs and chieftainesses, kings and queens, soon populated South Africa's ethnoscape. In the Western Cape, a man named Joseph Little, who had been active, if bizarrely so, in some local struggles involving the homeless, proclaimed himself chief of the peninsular Khoekhoe—a group identified with the earliest years of Dutch settlement in the mid–seventeenth century. Eccentric, evanescent, something of a charlatan with a powerful attraction to women, Little positioned himself as chairperson of the National Khoisan Council, established in 1999 to ostensibly represent indigenous rights and claims. To solidify his authenticity Little began dressing himself in faux leopard skin. And in speaking for Sara Baartman, Little proclaimed the "need to be proud of our identity instead of hiding behind the classification of 'coloured' which was given to us by the racist apartheid regime."[32]

Other groups claiming indigeneity spoke for Sara Baartman and attempted to take possession of her remains. Koranna people living near Namibia announced that Sara Baartman belonged to them, despite their location in the north of the country far from either the Eastern or the Western Cape. They asserted that they were somehow more indigenous than anyone else and thus could most rightly claim lineage to Baartman.

Careers and significant sums of money were at stake. Indigeneity had become an important way by which some people clawed their way up the social and economic ladder, in South Africa and across large areas of the world. Substantial funds from the South African government and from nongovernmental organizations, including the World Bank, flowed to groups claiming indigenous status and who were reclaiming and protecting fragile cultures. As early as 1991, the World Bank had begun an initiative relating to indigenous peoples. A decade later, and as a direct result of their efforts to return Sara Baartman to South Africa, the Griqua National Conference received World Bank money for Ratelgat. According to the report, "The Griqua community of Southern Africa is undergoing a revival, spurred by the preservation of sacred sties on a farm called Ratelgat in the Western Cape. The people believe that these developments fulfill prophecies made by respected leaders now buried there. . . . Retelgat [sic] is not simply an infrastructure project, but is part of a larger effort to develop the Griqua community and the broader communities of South Africa."

Important economies emerged around the figure of Sara Baartman and the efforts to bring her home at a time when there was a burst of public culture throughout the country. These economies and the local, national, and international politics of indigeneity became an important if at times unspoken part of the Reference Group's work. These crosscurrents are well represented in the role of Henry Bredekamp, one member of the Reference Group. During the 1990s Bredekamp rode the wave of indigenous rights politics in South Africa. In addition to participating in the reassertion of tribal identities by adopting the ostensibly Khoekhoe name "Jatti," he had been chairperson of the Western Cape Business Opportunities Forum. In November 2002, Bredekamp would soon be appointed as the first black chief executive officer of Iziko Museums, a highly paid position of national, and indeed international, importance, since the CEO is in charge of all the country's national museums.

In late February 2002, Bredekamp wrote a confidential e-mail to a member of government. He wrote as patron of the National Khoi-San Consultative Conference, an organization formed in 2001 to represent Khoekhoe and San communities throughout South Africa to develop a sense of identity among a "people [who] are confused and have no sense of belonging" and to make claims to economic development in the country. Bredekamp wrote, with the voice of authority coming to the rescue:

> Allow me to note cautiously my concern about signals reaching legitimate Khoisan representatives and their structures who really started the process leading to last week's decision [to create the Reference Group] are now being ignored as in the Deputy Ministers [*sic*] statement of last week. Toned-down media responses to it might appear this week due to my timely intervention.
>
> There's general consensus outside government within Khoisan ranks that the National Khoisan Consultative Conference represents the legitimate voices on the issue. . . . Please attend to the matter urgently and with due sensitivity.[33]

For Bredekamp the issue centered on the proliferating claims to Sara Baartman, to her past, and to her bodily remains. Many indigenous rights groups had only just been formed; Bredekamp feared the politics around Sara Baartman might divide people as much as bring them together. But there is more here than meets the proverbial eye. A striking feature of these politics is the dominance of men, who seemed to lead the effort to claim Sara Baartman while relegating women to a largely consultative role. Possession of her body had become not simply a political but an economic good, a kind of hyperbolic version in which men continued to possess women and to control their reproduction. Sara Baartman had become a commodity in three senses: as a body to be held, as a woman owned by others, and as economic capital that could generate additional resources, indeed, give birth to new identities in a post-apartheid South Africa.

The politics of science was never very far away from the claims of indigeneity. The Khoisan were widely seen as the "original people" because they had occupied the Cape before the European settlement. The Khoisan had long been at the center of Western scientific investigation. Science continued to loom large in the many claims to Sara Baartman, in the rich imagining of her life by experts, artists, activists, and various national and international publics. Just how "indigenous" *was* Sara Baartman, after all? Two scientists sat on the Reference Group: Philip Tobias, the esteemed anatomist and paleontologist; and his colleague Trevor Jenkins, a geneticist. Both scientists hailed from the respected School of Anatomical Sciences at the University of the Witwatersrand. Deeply sympathetic to the tragedies of Sara Baartman's life and death, and to the many injustices perpetrated on South Africa's Khoisan community, the scientists wanted a DNA sampling of the remains. Sara hailed from an exceptionally diverse part of South Africa, where different communities—Khoisan, Bantu-speaking African, European, Asian—had interacted for hundreds of years, in the case of the Khoisan and Bantu-speaking communities for many centuries. Genetic information could cast important light on this complicated and rich history, as if biology might tell us who, in fact, Sara Baartman *was* and how she stood in relation to South Africa's complicated racial histories.

Genetic information also could have provided crucial information tying Sara Baartman to kin now living in South Africa. As Tobias wrote, "There are living Baartmans in South Africa who may belong to the same lineage."[34] People with the surname "Baartman" had begun making claims—to the government, within the Khoisan movement, and to the press—that they were related to Sara. Even a "white" Baartman had written to Yvette Abrahams asking if, perhaps, they might be somehow related to Sara. DNA testing would have been "extremely convenient" in addressing these claims, particularly as the Reference Group concluded that it seemed nearly impossible to trace Sara Baartman's descendants through the archival record.

The scientists, however, seemed unwilling to press the point. Some members of the group adopted the mantle of Sara Baartman's kin, in some instances figuratively became Baartman, representing the family's interests and concerns and speaking as if Baartman were alive and sitting at the table. Abrahams was adamant. The problem was not the indeterminacy of Baartman's life. Abrahams expressed outrage with the idea of yet another scientific intervention on Sara Baartman's body. The "problem" was putting one's "faith in the hands of science,"[35] of subjecting Baartman yet again to a predatory science. Perhaps more than any other group, the Khoisan had been the subject of science, the classic "primitive" frozen in time. Abrahams, who positioned herself as spokeswoman for Khoisan interests, would have none of this. For Abrahams, "hard science" would have ended up determining who "was" Khoekhoe or not, who was descended from Baartman, and so on, questions that were in her mind of a "social," not a "scientific" nature.

For Abrahams, science was not only psychologically and culturally "invasive" but also "neo-fascist." Performing any tests immediately violated a body some two centuries old, a body quite literally in pieces, and would "disrespect" Baartman yet again. The issues the Reference Group confronted were "not in the past." The desires of the French scientists to understand the minutiae of Sara Baartman's body, the centuries-old display of her body in a Paris museum, the seemingly infinite crimes of the West, this long, infamous history continued unbroken in the scientific claims to do DNA testing on the remains.

It was as if Sara Baartman was alive again before Cuvier. The scientific gaze in 2002, in Abrahams's view, brought the recently deceased woman before the scalpels of the racist, misogynist French scientists who wanted to touch, to probe the inner recesses of her body, to discover the biology of her sexuality. The arguments within the Reference Group concerning research into Baartman's remains became a "very similar battle" as that between contemporary activists and their critique of Cuvier and Saint-Hilaire, between the present and two long since dead scientists who stood accused of horrendous crimes. The past had never become history; Sara remained the living dead.

The position of some members of the Reference Group—particularly Yvette Abrahams—was profoundly antiscience. Even the two scientists Jenkins and Tobias failed to muster much of a defense of science. In fact Tobias, the world-famous professor of anatomy, would publicly condemn his intellectual fathers Georges Cuvier and Saint-Hilaire. For the Reference Group, Cuvier and Saint-Hilaire became the epitome of an unholy marriage of science and racism. Contemporary scientists—including Tobias, who had expended so much effort working for Baartman's return—remained indelibly stained by late eighteenth-century and early nineteenth-century science. Their wish to examine the body was, for Abrahams, the "last stab of post-Enlightenment science," the last chapter in a sordid history, another exercise of "gender-based violence."

Abrahams might concede that science sought, if it did not always practice, "knowledge in the service of humanity." However flawed Cuvier and
Saint-Hilaire might be, they were also extraordinarily brilliant scientists,
among the most important progenitors of what we now know as evolutionary biology and physical anthropology. This was a claim even Abrahams believed one "could not argue with on its merits." But Abrahams
invoked an additional set of arguments, ones that are quintessentially
Western in origin: human rights and the rights of the individual. These
arguments also, ironically, owed something to the very circumstances of
Sara Baartman's encounter with the abolitionists in London. Her treatment at the hands of others had elicited the attention of humanitarians.
The legal proceedings in London in 1810 helped establish a precedent
that has saved tens of thousands of people who have suffered abuse by the
more powerful.

For Abrahams the question was: "Would Sarah Baartman have wanted
to have her body researched?" What are Sara Baartman's "human rights"?
The Reference Group discussed the issue of whether dead people can have
human rights and sought legal opinion on the matter. Abrahams insisted
that Sara Baartman's "wishes" should be taken into account and respected.
Indeed, she felt herself obliged to "prove" that Sara Baartman would not
have wanted to be scientifically investigated. Abrahams produced a six-
page memorandum in which, speaking for Baartman, she concluded that
Sara would not consent to DNA testing. This final effort effectively ended
what had been the most volatile issue within the Reference Group.

And yet it was precisely in a language of biology—the language of biological descent—that Abrahams and others spoke for and made claim to
Sara Baartman. The violence of the past had created an unbridgeable
chasm separating the time before and after colonial violence and cultural
loss. What was left by that violence was a scattering of people—of the
bones—and the unbearable yearning for identity, for an authenticity after
apartheid, after "Colouredness," after the inflictions of history. Only by
claiming ancestry, by claiming descent through blood, could bones be
brought back together again. And through that blood connection Abrahams and others could speak for, indeed almost become, Sara Baartman.

But who "was" Sara Baartman? A skeleton, a plaster cast, and preserved
body parts became invested with complex histories and volatile politics
stretching across the globe. Baartman returned as a mother and symbol of

a new, democratic South Africa, part of the country's efforts at "nation-building" even as people also claimed her as an ethnic, not a national, subject. Sara's story became *the* story of what men (especially white men) do to women (especially black women), and thus part of the politics of global feminism. What happened to Baartman happened to women all the time, the world over. Men perpetrated violence on women's bodies, dispossessed their bodies through violent appropriations, worked out their fantasies though stories, songs, and scalpels. For good reason Sara Baartman's story became a history of human rights and their all-too-frequent violation, the body as a narrative of the ignominies of science, an eighteenth-century and early nineteenth-century woman a testament to the great and enduring disgraces of Western civilization.

The more iconic Sara Baartman became, the more she stood for a range of causes, the less complicated her past became. In life, death, and now in her resurrection as a person, Baartman remained desire's cipher. Many African cultures venerate ancestors. The attempts to bring Sara home helped join her to the pantheon of ancestors. Yet families allow their ancestors to fade away into the distant past through time. Ancestors, beloved and respected, are also allowed to finally die, to disappear from memory. Baartman remained too powerful, too linked with the present, to be able to be given back to the winds and the stars.[36]

The Reference Group was immediately confronted with how to bury Baartman. They knew that she had been baptized, so there was no way around incorporating Christianity into the burial. At the same time, they contracted a noted archaeologist to produce a description of "traditional" Khoekhoe burial practices, so that Baartman could be laid to rest recognizing her Christian faith but still buried as a Khoekhoe woman.

"Political pressure" became "enormous" as the time of the burial drew closer. Sara Baartman had become a symbol and icon the world over. She also had become a government figure, a symbol for the new South Africa. In 1999, a center for women and children in the rough Cape Flats was named after Baartman. The decision of the French government to repatriate her remains received international media attention. Papers such as the *New York Times* and the *Washington Post* covered the unfolding story. In South Africa, even local papers devoted long articles to Sara Baartman "coming home." The Reference Group, working with government and nongovernmental institutions, reached the decision to lay Sara Baartman to rest near the banks of the Gamtoos River on the outskirts of Hankey, a town about thirty-five kilometers from Port Elizabeth. (There had been some discussion about burying Baartman in Cape Town, or at least creating a monument to her in the port city.) One primary source had suggested that Baartman was indeed from this area, and so she would now be buried near where she had been born. Some also believed that Hankey had potential as a destination for tourists, and that memorializing Baartman there could have an important economic impact in a desperately poor region of the country.

The South African government decided that Sara Baartman would be laid to rest on 9 August 2002, to coincide with International Indigenous Peoples' Day and South Africa's Women's Day. The latter commemorated the famous 1956 march on Pretoria when nearly twenty thousand women protested the pass laws and the introduction of apartheid and where the famous saying "You have struck the women, you have struck a rock" was born. In choosing Women's Day, the government recognized the contribution of individual women as leaders of the group that campaigned for Baartman's return, and sought to acknowledge the broader suffering of women under colonialism and apartheid.

The government's decision was not without dissent. Chief Jean Burgess of the "Chonaqua" (Gonaqua) House and Chief Margaret Coetzee of the Inqua believed that burying Baartman on National Women's Day was "a great insult to us." Baartman "deserves," they continued, "a day that belongs to her alone and not a day that will be clouded across the country with Women's Day celebrations. She deserves a day that we will remember as the day that our Great Foremother has been buried."

Burgess and Coetzee invoked the Vermillion Accord on Human Remains that privileged local communities in the dispensation of remains. They insisted that Sara Baartman was first and foremost a "Khoisan . . . Icon, as she symbolized to us the abuse that our great foremothers were exposed to. . . . During her birth the blood that was shed was given to the earth and it is to the same earth that her remains need to be laid to rest. . . . Ms Baartman deserves the peace that was never given to her spirit."

Their protests were met with indifference. By now the government had spent considerable funds in its negotiations with the French government and in organizing the Reference Group, and a small fortune planning for the funeral. Officials had every intention of staging the burial as an international event. Sara Baartman would be repatriated not to a family but to a nation that, during her own lifetime, did not exist. "Media interest" had been "intense," coverage "huge," according to one internal document. "It would be difficult," the document continued,

> to over-rate both the national and international importance to South Africa of this event. It was a victory over colonialism, racism and sexism. It very visibly and publically restored the dignity of a South African woman exploited and humiliated in her lifetime. It brought together and united South Africans of all backgrounds in seeing justice done.

Internationally the return of Sara Baartman changed French political culture and "substantially contributed to the discussions and debates around the issue of human rights in French society," while also encouraging other countries "to pursue similar requests to have the remains of their nationals . . . repatriated."[37]

The government planned a small ceremony in Cape Town, where Baartman would first arrive back in South Africa from Paris. This celebration, the enrobement or Aantrek ceremony, titled Flowers for Sarah Bartmann, began on a Sunday afternoon on 4 August 2002. Mabandla, the deputy minister of arts, culture, science and technology, church members, Griqua National Conference leaders, and members and other representatives of the Khoisan community, as well as the Reference Group, attended the ceremony. Women figured prominently in the somber welcoming of Baartman's return, Abrahams performing a putatively "traditional" San dance. A few days later the remains were flown east to Port Elizabeth.

On 9 August, 2002, between seven and fifteen thousand people converged on the small village of Hankey to see and to participate in laying to rest the remains of Sara Baartman.[38] Foreign visitors, many of whom were women, flew to Hankey from the United States, Europe, and Asia. The South African Broadcasting Corporation provided full, uninterrupted coverage of the daylong funeral. The national and international importance of Baartman easily overwhelmed the concerns of the local Khoisan community, which had wanted to bury her at a time that coincided with the moon. Baartman had become a national symbol and a symbol for women everywhere, though the ceremonies largely entailed men speaking on behalf of women and their rights as South African citizens.

FIGURE 7.1. Mural of Sara Baartman. Hankey, South Africa. Photographer, Clifton Crais, 2005.

As Bredekamp said at the funeral, "We are laying to rest a national icon, not just a Khoikhoi symbol, and Sarah's return should be elevated to a national celebration." For Deputy Minister Mabandla, the funeral signified an "end of oppression to women," the funeral part of the rebirth of Africa "out of the shackles of colonialism." For Tobias, Baartman was "an icon . . . a symbol . . . a victim" of an era that should be cast into the dustbin of history. For the poet Ferrus, Baartman was "a human rights icon." For Raymond Mhlaba, the veteran political activist and then premier of the Eastern Cape, Sara Baartman's life "depicts the attitude of colonialism."

Mhlaba saw in the funeral nothing less than the arrival of a new historical consciousness. For too long South African history had been produced by white historians who spoke of the savagery of Africans and who had airbrushed, as it were, the many evils they had perpetrated. Baartman's funeral was an exercise in producing history from the other side, from the vantage of the poor and the oppressed.

Thabo Mbeki arrived in full presidential splendor, the helicopter arriving on the outskirts of the town, the motorcade winding its way up to the grave site. Following a "traditional" praise poem the president delivered a long speech that ranged from critiques of the Enlightenment, the history of American slavery, the legacies of colonialism and apartheid, the necessity of gender equality, to the poetry Langston Hughes. For Mbeki, it was crucial that Sara Baartman was being laid to rest on National Women's

Day. Her history reminded the world—and especially South Africans—of the long history of women's oppression. Mbeki spoke of the persistence of gender violence and of the necessity of gender equality to realizing a truly democratic South Africa. "We cannot undo the damage that was done to her," Mbeki said early in the speech.

> But at least we can summon the courage to speak the naked but healing truth that must comfort her wherever she may be. I speak of courage because there are many in our country who would urge constantly that we should not speak of the past. They pour scorn on those who speak about who we are and where we come from and why we are where we are today. They make bold to say the past is no longer, and all that remains is a future that will be. But, today, the gods would be angry with us if we did not, on the banks of the Gamtoos River, at the grave of Sarah Bartmann, call out for restoration of the dignity of Sarah Bartmann, of the Khoi-San, of the millions of Africans who have known centuries of wretchedness.

For the president, as for many others, Sara Baartman's story was the story of South Africa. It was, he said, the "story of the loss of our ancient freedoms . . . of the dispossession of our lands," and the reduction of once proud people into mere objects, a "people without a past." Reciting the history of Sara Baartman at her grave site formed part of a more widespread awakening of history in South Africa, a reclaiming of pasts too long denied. The "restoration" of the dignity of Sara Baartman was part and parcel of the restoration of the dignity of black South Africans, and especially of the Khoisan. "We need only start here, on the banks of the Gamtoos River, and advance to the rest of our country." The past is with us, Mbeki instructed the world, and because of this we have the burden of eradicating the legacies of colonialism and apartheid, of ensuring that Sara Baartman "did not suffer and die in vain."

Much of President Mbeki's speech took up the history of European colonialism, racism, and science. For the president, Europeans were the ones who were truly monstrous, the barbarism of people who considered themselves "men *par excellence*." Cuvier received the harshest words, the man most responsible for Sara Baartman being "sucked into the evil" of not simply Western science but the Enlightenment itself. From an indictment of Cuvier, Mbeki quickly expanded his condemnation to Montesquieu, Diderot, and Voltaire. These men were the barbarians, not the "defenseless" Sara Baartman who had been "ferried" to Europe.

Mbeki's attack on the West, especially Western science, was not simply an instance of presidential blather. Since coming to power in June 1999, the Mbeki government has regularly issued scathing denunciations of Western science as part of its denying the medical basis of the HIV/AIDS crisis in South Africa, where infection rates are among the highest anywhere in the world today. Sara Baartman already had been used to condemn science, in academic studies particularly as part of the rise of cultural studies, in artistic works, in the popular press, in public discussions across the world, and most immediately in the work of the Reference Group. Now the president of South Africa deployed Baartman and her history as part of a harangue against science and the West.

The president ended his speech announcing that Sara Baartman's resting place would become a designated National Heritage site. Mbeki also promised that a fitting monument would be erected in Cape Town, where she had left Africa's shores on her fateful voyage to Europe. It was now time to finally bury Sara. She was laid to rest recognizing her Christian faith but still buried as a pure Khoekhoe woman. The coffin containing her skeleton and remains was lowered into the ground with the due solemnity of a Christian burial. The top of the grave reproduced traditional Khoekhoe burial practices from the eighteenth century. A pile of stones marked her final resting place.

In the ensuing weeks and months people composed small messages or wrote their names on some of the stones, reminders of their visiting the grave, their allegiance to the dead. Within months, however, the grave site and memorial had fallen into disrepair. Graffiti marred the site, the cement boundaries had been chipped away, perhaps by those wanting relics. Some saw the state of the site as an "insult" to the Khoisan, as "totally degrading for Sarah and the Khoi-San people." Most seriously, the grave itself was vandalized. Although it is impossible to determine the motives of the culprits, it may have been that the powerful symbolic site offered ritual specialists powerful *muti* (medicine) to cause harm, to ensure benefits, or to ward off witchcraft.

In September 2003, a four-year-old child, Makhumandile "Trompies" Bantom, was abducted by two men outside a day care center. The child's father had died, and Trompies was heir to the R150,000 inheritance, a

FIGURE 7.2. Grave of Sara Baartman. Hankey, South Africa. Photographer,
Clifton Crais, 2005.

vast sum in South Africa's impoverished Eastern Cape. His body was later
found near Sara Baartman's grave; the child's throat had been slit, perhaps
on the order of his mother, who had contested the will.[39]

Originally red African soil surrounded Baartman's grave. A simple cement rectangle marked the grave, on top of which were placed stones
and the *boegoe* bush to purify her spirits, to reunite Baartman with the
earth. The vandals changed all this. Officials decided to cement the area
immediately around the grave. Tall green metal bars now surround the site
on the hilltop overlooking the Gamtoos River valley, the river Khoekhoe
had named as "wily as a lion" as it wound its way down to the Indian
Ocean. Returned to South Africa, Sara Baartman remains behind bars,
imprisoned still.

Most everyone in South Africa knows about Sara Baartman and her
history. Very few people voyage to this area to visit Sara Baartman's grave.
The memorial has not brought much income to the nearby town of
Hankey, which still relies mostly on orange cultivation controlled by the
Ferreira family, whose ancestors knew some of the original Baartmans.
The people of Hankey memorialized Sara in a huge mural, copying the
very drawings made under Cuvier's supervision. Those who do come to

the area do so to backpack and camp in the nearby Baviaans Kloof Mountains, not to visit "Mama" Sara. This is indeed a beautiful part of South Africa. Clouds race across brilliant blue skies. The winds whisper in the trees, just as they had centuries before when Gonaqua believed that the winds carried with them the spirits of the departed. Sometimes the clouds reach down close enough to embrace Sara Baartman's grave.

Epilogue: Family

S ara Baartman walked across the Cape Flats on her way to Cape Town in the closing years of the eighteenth century. Two centuries later, a shelter bears her name not too far from the path Sara traveled on her way to the great port city. Abused women and children come to the Saartjie Baartman Centre, open twenty-four hours a day, seeking accommodation, food, and, most of all, safety and a respite from the terrible violence of the Cape of Storms.

In the eighteenth century the Flats were but an expanse of empty sandy land whipped by wind and rain. Nowadays there is little in the Flats that has not been built over. Under South Africa's policies of segregation and apartheid, the government relegated people it defined as "Coloured" and "African" to the Flats. Over the course of many years suburbs emerged, each located farther away from the mother city.

There are no traces of Sara's life in Cape Town except for the bones of her young children in their lost makeshift graves. The memorial promised by President Mbeki has yet to appear. Anna and Hendrik's home is gone, too, as is Sara's *pondok* from which she labored up the mountain to wash clothes and to visit her Dutch lover. The Naval Hospital Sara frequented has disappeared as well. Railroad construction in the second half of the nineteenth century destroyed many old buildings and communities, pushing people into Woodstock and District Six.

What economic progress did not accomplish, racial gerrymandering did. Hugging Table Mountain, the destruction of District Six became the last insult in a long history of racial oppression. Residents spoke of Table Mountain as their grandfather, District Six his right foot. Apartheid severed these abiding connections, the deep sense of place, of family, of history, of the rough-and-tumble of District Six. In the 1970s, the government forced upwards of sixty thousand people from their homes, homes bulldozed by the state, the residents pushed out to the Cape Flats.

Other communities shared the same fate of District Six, though few carry the symbolic resonance and pain of Grandfather's missing right foot. These were after all people's homes and livelihoods. Across Cape Town people had labored all their life to carve a niche, however small, in an oppressive and racist society. They may have been able to purchase a small house, adorn its walls with the pictures of loved ones, send their children to decent schools, watch the waterfalls form off the mountain during the rainy season, smell jasmine blooming in the Cape spring. As late as the 1980s, real estate agents stood ready to pounce, to buy low from people forced out to the "Coloured" townships on the Flats, and to sell high to whites who moved into rigidly segregated neighborhoods.[1]

Mitchell's Plain, Bellville, Athlone, Grassy Park, Hanover Park, Lavender Hill—these are some of the outer suburbs that make up the Flats. Most of these areas are uniformly poor, many desperately so, in part because since 1994 the new black middle class has sought new abodes. The Flats are racked by violence and gangs. Nearly a million people live in Mitchell's Plain alone, where gangs armed with Uzis, AK-47s, and even hand grenades terrorize the community. The wind, as ever, still whips through the Flats. Dirt and trash swirl about in little twisters running up and down the streets. The ubiquitous flimsy blue plastic bags South Africans use to carry their purchases fill up with air. At a distance they seem like the balloons children let go of on their way home from birthday parties, little feet and hands running to catch the string before eyes swell with tears and the balloon drifts away.

In summer the Cape Flats become stiflingly hot. There are few trees to offer shade, and the wide horizontal landscape seems punished by the African sun. The wind blows the dust and sand everywhere, into every nook and cranny, even into the beds. People try to keep the sand and dirt at bay, constantly brooming the steps of their homes. In the winter the temperatures drop to near freezing; a light dusting of snow appears on the Hottentots Hollands Mountains, and even Grandfather from time to time turns gray. The rains can be torrential. On the Flats there is little place for the water to go. Flooding forces people from their homes, and the cheap kerosene heaters people use to chase away the cold daily bring fires and tragedy.

Many of the descendants of South Africa's slaves still largely live in the Western Cape, and most in the Cape Flats. The phone book still lists people with the last name of "September," "October," "November," or "December," a mark of slavery designating the month when one human being purchased another. In the disgrace of naming people according to the month of a commercial transaction, or as a cruel joke, lay powerful, enduring silences. "January" has nothing to do with the bonds of descent and affection around which people make their lives. The name marks a history of enslavement and racial oppression as it denies the particularities of history that are the stuff of human relationships. Slavery was all about the denial of family, the irrevocable renunciation of kinship even if people struggled and created affective ties, created lives in a world that denied them their humanity.

There are many people in the Cape Flats who bear the last name of "Caesar" and its various spellings, the name of the man who, with Alexander Dunlop, brought Sara Baartman to England and France. They too are the descendants of slaves. Naming chattel after great Roman emperors became increasingly common during the late eighteenth century as slavery expanded away from Cape Town into the farmlands of the Western Cape. A few live in rural communities like Worcester, Ceres, and Saron, but most live in the Cape Flats, a hundred or so people sharing the same last name.

The Cesarses of today are united by a shared history of slavery, but they are also profoundly, forever separated by that history. It is impossible to "join the dots" that might connect a living Caesar to the nearly two centuries of slavery that endured in South Africa between the seventeenth and nineteenth centuries. Hendrik Cesars's great-grandfather, owned as chattel by none other than Commander Simon van der Stel, was baptized as an adult in 1686, a mere three decades after the Dutch East India Company had founded the colony. In the eighteenth century, the family became Free Blacks, people who were no longer slaves but who could not become "burghers," citizens, white. In the nineteenth century, after the ending of slavery, they disappeared into the larger community of ex-slaves who had inherited the name of a Roman emperor.

The Cesarses living in the Western Cape are unable to trace their family histories much beyond about 1900. There are few extant records to help the historian or a descendent interested in family history. Slavery produced records, records of people kept as property. Emancipation liberated people from the confinement detailed also in the documents. The newly freed moved to other farms, to Cape Town, or to the small towns of the Cape. Some ventured far afield. People once listed as property disappear or spread into the archival record, into the paper shreds of the past. The poor leave few records, and when they do appear it is usually before the state for petty crimes.

Sara Baartman's utter dispossession permitted people, indeed entire communities, a nation even, to reconstruct her in an image of their own choosing. Appropriation is simple when the relatives are not around to claim the bones as their own, to reconstruct histories intimate and singular. Yet it is easier to trace the history of Sara Baartman's clan than the families (including Dunlop) of those who exploited her. The history of the Baartman clan continued in South Africa as Sara's life came to an end in Europe. In 1811, when Sara Baartman was being paraded in Piccadilly, Ruiter ("Rider") Baartman yet again argued with the farmer Cornelius Muller, the man who had sold Sara Baartman. Ruiter marched over to the Drosty in Uitenhage and laid a formal complaint against Muller for withholding cattle and a second complaint against a Christian Kok for owing him a year's wages.

Baartman had joined Muller in a raid commando into Xhosaland. Ruiter headed one of the wagons. For "having done something amiss," Muller flogged Ruiter "as an example to the rest of the Commando—and as a punishment for his wicked intention." Muller further commanded Ruiter to work for "one year without wages and placed him with C. Kok" near the Drosty building in Uitenhage. According to the official, the London Missionary Society missionary Reverend van der Kemp "urged" Baartman to bring his complaint forward. The reverend, "whose exertions in bringing forward complaints of this kind are very notorious," knew the Baartman clan well and had interceded on their behalf in the early years of the nineteenth century.[2]

Life was brutally hard for Khoekhoe throughout the Cape Colony and especially in the Eastern Cape. By 1810 they were landless people. One man remembered that he could see the "land, but he cannot possess it. Our fathers had abundance of cattle and sheep," but "they became weak and lost their property and were obliged to enter into the service of the Farmers." In 1809, a year before Sara went to London, the new British rulers enacted the infamous Caledon Code. The code brought labor relations under the state's purview. It also stipulated that workers were to be paid in wages and began to address the punishing debt peonage system that kept most workers in a state of near slavery. But the crucial feature of the code, the "pivot of the whole system," centered on the pass system, which greatly reduced people's movements.[3] Without passes, blacks were subject to arrest. The passes, moreover, required the signature of their master or official. In effect, the Caledon Code tied Khoekhoe ever more firmly to the yoke of the white farmer.

In 1828, however, Ordinance 50 abolished the Caledon Code. For the Khoekhoe the ordinance was their Emancipation Proclamation, the ending of their slavery. Now Khoekhoe could own land and, crucially, the pass system was done away with, though Ordinance 49 extended the pass system to Africans. When the "50th Ordinance came out then did we first taste freedom that other men eat so sweet," one man said a few years later. "We rejoiced at the very word freedom + Free Labour even before it was mingled with Water + Ground, and now that it is mingled with Water + Ground it is 20 times sweeter than forced labour."[4]

After 1828, Sara's kin moved to various areas in the Eastern Cape. The few who had made it to the mission stations of Bethelsdorp and Theopolis headed north along the wagon trails that led first to Grahamstown and then to Fort Beaufort along the colony's edge with Xhosaland. Here they settled on the rich lands of the Kat River settlement. By 1829, some 144 families had left the mission stations for Kat River. There they cleared the ground, built houses, laid out gardens, constructed an elaborate irrigation system, began schools, and built beautiful churches with elaborate ceilings warm with the glow yellowwood. On Sundays three or four hundred people assembled to hear the Word, dressed in their best clothes. To one missionary it all "appeared more like a dream than a reality."[5] The sons and daughters of parents who could not write read from the Bible signed the names of their fathers and mothers.

Sara's male relatives who moved to the Kat River settlement faithfully served the British in their wars with the neighboring Xhosa. Their small farms became "blood ground," the land they received in exchange for their service, the land they made rich with wheat and barley. In the 1830s and 1840s, however, avaricious white farmers eyed the sweet land of the Kat River farmers. Conflict and competition increased. With the outbreak of war with the Xhosa in 1851, the peasant farmers of Kat River rebelled against the British and joined forces with Africans in what was one of the most brutal wars anywhere in Africa in the nineteenth century. The Baartman rebels lost their plots and joined the region's laboring poor. There are still Baartmans in the area around Kat River, distant relatives of the famous "Hottentot Venus." People now living in Kat River made the journey to Hankey, to attend Baartman's funeral. Some returned home with a T-shirt marking the event.

While some Baartmans remained in Uitenhage or settled in Kat River, others left for Graaff Reinet, a town about two hundred kilometers north along the main wagon road. They were not alone. After Ordinance 50 of 1828 many other Khoekhoe from the area ventured north, including relatives of the Khoekhoe leader Stuurman, who had tried to defend his people in the closing years of the eighteenth century. The journey took a solid week as families and their animals lumbered up and over the nearby mountains and through the valleys and finally into the great plains of the Camdeboo. The older Baartmans may have been familiar with this route, especially Ruiter, for their journey to Graaff Reinet brought them near to their old home, Baartman's Fonteyn. But there was no returning to the land they lost in the eighteenth century when they had tended their flocks along the edge of the Green Valley.

They arrived in Graaff Reinet by 1830. That year a jury of white farmers convicted Ruiter, by then an old man, and sentenced him to a year in jail with hard labor. It was Ruiter's bad luck that the brother of Cornelius Muller presided over the case.[6]

Following his arrest and sentence for theft, Ruiter Baartman disappears from the archival record. By the end of the decade at least a half dozen Baartmans lived in the Graaff Reinet area. None owned land. Most labored on nearby white farms. In 1837, Cobus Baartman contracted himself to a blacksmith in Graaff Reinet town. The following year Jager Baartman agreed to serve a colonist on a trading journey across the Orange River. The others, like Present Baartman, worked on the farms for few shillings, food, and clothing in exchange for six month's labor.

By the 1850s and 1860s the number of Baartmans in the Graaff Reinet area had doubled. In the early part of the 1850s five Baartmans found themselves before the magistrate. They had been charged with "squatting within the limits of the Municipality." The officials fined and reprimanded the landless and destitute people and chased them from the town. The

FIGURE E.1. Ms. Baartman (maiden name), husband, and grandson. Graaff Reinet, South Africa. Photographer, Clifton Crais, 2005.

same year two other Baartmans fell foul of the law. The white court convicted Hans Baartman, who also went by the name of "Storm," for stealing a sheep and for assault with intent. The court sentenced Hans to three years in prison with hard labor and twenty-five lashes. Gert Baartman had received an advance from one white master but turned around and hired himself to another; for his crime Gert received fourteen days hard labor.

The Baartmans lived in a world increasingly dictated by the fears of whites who ensured that blacks would remain landless and kept in order by the local police. The Kat River Rebellion had shaken white farmers to the core. Throughout the 1850s and into the 1860s, they feared another "Hottentot" rebellion, that their servants might one night slit their throats. In 1866, a young Hendrik Baartman came before the court on a charge of theft. A boy of just twelve or fourteen at the time, Hendrik took a horse, saddle, and bridle from the blacksmith's shop on the farm Adendorp. Hendrik was asked why he stole the horse: he answered that "he wanted to visit his relations on Beaufort West" about 150 kilometers away. He was sentenced to three years in prison. The same year Klaas Baartman, who had contracted himself to a white farmer in 1837, was tried for theft. Klaas had killed a goat, kindled a fire, and roasted the meat to fill his belly.[7]

By the 1860s the Baartman clan had spread out in a region stretching from Beaufort West to the Kat River, and from Graaff Reinet to Uitenhage. A few had ventured farther, across the Orange River into South Africa's interior. One Baartman living in Willowmore district near the Baviaans-kloof Mountains prepared a will in 1876, though he himself could only affix an "X" to mark his name. But the great majority remained in the Eastern Cape, as they do this day. And most remained very poor and landless, working on the white man's farms tending his sheep and the womenfolk laboring as domestic servants.

In 1865, the state charged Jephta Baartman, Jan Baartman, and Jan Boesack with housebreaking with the intent to steal. The prisoners immediately confessed to the crimes. Jan received the harshest sentence: six months in prison with hard labor. Jan was again a free man by the winter of 1866. Just six months later, however, Jan was again in trouble with the law. And this time it was serious, the murder of a young child, a toddler, whom he killed accidentally. "Boy, I've done mischief," he told one man, "and if I am caught, I'll be in for it; it will turn to gaol matters." Jan subsequently pleaded guilty to culpable homicide and received a sentence of three years with hard labor.[8]

Jan left jail in 1870 and tried to begin his life again. He was now about twenty-seven and had spent close to four years of his life behind bars doing hard labor. His first marriage fell apart. Over the next decades Jan Baartman settled down with a second wife, Hannie, and had a number of sons and daughters. By the 1890s the number of Baartmans had increased still further. Most still lived as laborers on white farms, but a few moved into Graaff Reinet proper. On 8 May 1890 Jan's wife gave birth to a son, probably their last child. They named him Abel Johannes Baartman, after the peaceful, good shepherd of the Old Testament. Abel, the second son of Adam and Eve, tended his sheep and loved God. He was the consummate herdsman, the kind of person Khoekhoe men yearned to be. And because God loved him, Abel's jealous brother Cain murdered him. In the Bible, and for Christians the world over, Abel is the epitome of good, the peaceful shepherd.

Neither Jan nor any of the other Baartmans owned land in the Graaff Reinet area. In the early part of the twentieth century some settled in the town, where they took up jobs in the businesses that sprang up to serve the nearby farmers, some of whom prospered from raising mohair goats. Abel likely was born on a farm but later moved to the town of Graaff

Reinet, where he would spend his entire life. His father, Jan, passed away in his seventies or eighties. Abel was a self-made man. One of his daughters described him as "an ordinary laborer" who also made additional money selling firewood. He worked for "rich people," the Lukhoffs, who owned a store in the town on Caledon Street.[9]

When Abel was in his twenties, he married a local woman from the Arries clan, the eldest daughter of her family and six years his junior. Over many years the couple had eleven children, and by all accounts they had a stable and deeply felt marriage. By the early decades of the twentieth century there were dozens of Baartmans living in the Eastern Cape. Many still worked on white farms. Others took up jobs in the small towns of the region: a postman in Graaff Reinet, another working on the railways. At least one Baartman served in the Great War.

Abel and Hannie named their eldest after Abel's father, Jan. They were a devout family, attending the Dutch Reformed Church on Church Street. Abel became active in church affairs and in the local politics of the town. He served on the church council. In the early part of the century people defined as "Coloured" lived in the town. The Dutch Reformed Church on Church Street was their house of worship. They walked to the church, prayed, were baptized and married in the chapel, and were buried on its grounds. Abel, his wife, and their first four children lived on Somerset Street right in the middle of the town. From their house they could walk to church and to work. Theirs was not an easy life, but it was in its own way a rich one.

"They loved us very much," a daughter remembers. We "never went hungry." Four children had been born on Somerset Street. The rest were born during the 1930s and 1940s in a house Abel built in the location created to house the "Coloured" community. Segregation and racial intolerance increased in South Africa especially from the late 1920s, and families that had once lived in the town found themselves forced out into the "Coloured" location. Where their church had once been just around the corner, now it was a long walk down from the township into the increasingly "white" Graaff Reinet. Despite being forced from the town, Abel Baartman loved the house he had built by the sweat of his brow. Still active in the church, Abel also served on the municipal council, where he represented the concerns of his community to the white local officials.

In 1950, the apartheid government passed the infamous Group Areas Act, which organized urban areas according to race. The Group Areas Act destroyed the lives of many people in South Africa. Communities became designated as so many black spots subject to forced removal, spots made white by the racial madness of apartheid's rulers. In Cape Town far to the west, the Cesarses found themselves pushed out to the Cape Flats. In Graaff Reinet the Abel Baartman family would lose their home.

The Group Areas Act made it difficult, and in many cases impossible, for people to maintain a sense of community, to participate in shared histories, to talk of the past, to have a sense of place they really valued. The "Coloured" community of Graaff Reinet already had been forced out of the town to the township designated for them. Their dead had been buried on the church grounds. In the late 1960s or the 1970s they lost their church and suffered a further indignity. The authorities destroyed the graveyard. They "made it flat," obliterated the names etched on tombstones, destroyed the possibility of people paying respect to their dead.

In the 1960s the authorities founded a new township for the "Coloured" community, Kroonvale, located yet farther from the center of Graaff Reinet across the Sundays River. The old location was now designated for the black population, for the Africans. The people of the old location were "forced to move" to Kroonvale. But Abel would have none of this. He had built his house with his bare hands. Hannie had given birth to seven children. They had raised their children as best they could in a world where the color of one's skin determined where one lived, whom one married, what sorts of lives people could live. Each Sunday the family had trekked into town to worship the Lord. Abel was a church elder, a man of importance in the community, a voice of reason and of tolerance. But moving was intolerable. Abel dug in his heels, "said he won't move until he died."

Abel passed away in 1965, at age seventy-five. Hannie followed him to the grave seven years later. Abel was laid to rest on the ground of the old church he had served so well. Little did he know that within a few years the cross that bore his name would be destroyed. The church is now a museum, part of the rejuvenation of the town in the 1970s by the multimillionaire Anton Rupert. The older residents of Graaff Reinet know that the museum was once a church for the "Coloured" community, but for the visitor it is impossible to learn of this prior history. History here, as in so much of South Africa, quite literally has been obliterated.

Hannie is buried in Kroonvale, separated some miles from her husband of nearly a half century. There are no Baartmans left in the old location. Apartheid successfully displaced the family from one locale to another. But the memory of Abel Baartman lives on. The people of Kroonvale remember him for his faith and for representing them in the dark years of apartheid. He was the consummate elder, now a true ancestor. Across the street from the old house was once an empty block of land. Following the old man's death people named it Baartman Square, after the good man Abel. An elementary school now stands on the square, the children in their dusty uniforms bustling here and there, the commotion and excitement of schoolchildren everywhere. Most of the residents know nothing of Abel Baartman or of the Baartmans before him, though everyone knows something of Sara Baartman.

The Baartmans themselves remember their family going back only to 1890, the year of Abel's birth. There is a silence, a void, separating the world of Abel Baartman from the Baartmans who once walked the Camdeboo, the Green Valley, the Baartmans that trekked north from Uitenhage in the years after the emancipation of 1828. There are no discussions around the dinner table recounting Rider Baartman's argument with Cornelius Muller, or Sara Baartman leaving her homeland on a wagon heading for Cape Town, or the people of Baartman's Fonteyn, and certainly not of an even more distant past before so much violence and pain. But there is a patch of land in an old town in the Eastern Cape, Baartman Square, named after the good man Abel. People remember Abel. And now the many members of the Baartman clan wonder about their past and wonder about those tender threads of history that may connect them to Sara and the Green Valley.

ACKNOWLEDGMENTS

This book has taken us to many different continents and archives and has led to conversations we never anticipated. We could not have navigated the terrain or the languages without help from many people. In particular, we would like to thank Dominique Tessier, who pointed us to documents held in the Hampshire Record Office and the Suffolk Record Office. In Leiden, Marianne van der Wal, Franca Pont, Betty Rijpma, Jan Bart Gewald, and Robert Ross were most helpful. In Paris, Adrien Mattatia of the Musée de l'Homme extended great kindness to us. The staff at the Chetham Library, Manchester, were exceedingly helpful. Sandra de Wet, Kathy Brooks, and Jonathan Frost at Museum Africa in Johannesburg helped us locate images; we also thank Cecil Cortje and Lalou Meltzer of Iziko Museums in Cape Town for their help. The archivists at the National Archives in Cape Town have shared their expertise with us over many years. Thanks to Rina Brink for doing follow-up research in Cape Town, and to Andrew Fleming, who tracked down a few sources. Ashley Brenner helped with preparation of the final manuscript.

We thank our friends and colleagues at Emory University, who have been unfailingly helpful and supportive. A number of colleagues on different continents and in different disciplines kindly helped us with our research and commented on chapters. We would like to acknowledge the help and insights of Angelika Bammer, Stephane Crochet, Max Cullinan, Jeanette Deacon, Nadja Durbach, Elizabeth Elbourne, Katherine Elks, Richard Elphick, David Eltis, Natasha Erlandk, Carla Freeman, Mervyn and Lola Frost, Elizabeth Gallu, Patricia Hayes, Jennifer Heuer, Jane Hooper, Mitchell House, Esther Jones, Ivan Karp, Bruce Knauft, Lisa Knisely, Cory Kratz, Premesh Lalu, Isaac Land, Chris Lee, Lisa Lindsay,

Julie Livingston, Kristin Mann, Thomas McClendon, Cynthia McCreery, Kirsten McKenzie, Helen Moffett, Susan Newton-King, Sue Peabody, Nigel Penn, Ciraj Rassool, Philippe Rosenberg, Robert Ross, Meg Samuelson, Michael Sibalis, Michelle Strange, Michael Twyman, Dror Wahrman, Kerry Ward, Kathleen Wilson, Angela Woollacott, and Nigel Worden. Rosemarie Garland-Thomson has been that most excellent of colleagues, sharing insights and commenting on the entire manuscript.

We have been inspired by our students both at Kenyon and Denison University and at Emory. For comments on the first draft of the manuscript, we are particularly grateful to the graduate students who participated in the course Heterographies at Emory University in fall 2006.

The work benefited from comments from audiences at presentations given at Duke University, Emory University, Indiana University, McGill University, New York University, Rice University, Rutgers University, Southwestern University, the University of Cape Town, and the University of the Western Cape. The July 2006 "Transnational Biography" conference at the Australian National University in Canberra allowed us to rethink a number of issues relating to writing biography.

Grants from the National Endowment for the Humanities, Kenyon College, Denison University, and Emory University funded the research. Our new institutional home, Emory University, has been unflagging in its support. We owe special thanks to Robert Paul, the Dean of the College, and Lisa Tedesco, the Dean of the Graduate School, for their help.

We are grateful to our agent, Tim Seldes, and our editor, Brigitta van Rheinberg, as well as Ellen Foos and Susan Ecklund, for their help in shepherding the book through production. This book was conceived in Ohio and written in our new home in Atlanta. Family and friends have been supportive throughout. Benjamin and Christine endured many, we are sure too many, dinner conversations where we discussed one issue or another relating to Sara Baartman. They have been a constant source of amazement and joy.

NOTES

INTRODUCTION

1. Academic writings on the Hottentot Venus are vast. See, for example, Badou, *L'énigme de la Vénus Hottentote*; Abrahams, "Images of Sara Bartman"; Abrahams, "Disempowered to Consent"; Fausto-Sterling, "Gender, Race, and Nation"; Magubane, "Which Bodies Matter?"; Qureshi, "Displaying Sara Baartman"; Strother, "Display of the Body Hottentot."

2. Literary references mentioned in the text were obtained by data-mining www.freelibrary.com/literature.aspx, which contains many literary classics in electronic format. Gobineau, *Inequality of the Human Races*.

3. Knox, *Races of Man*; Gilman, *Difference and Pathology*. Today the situation is reversed. Labial surgery (labiaplasty) is an increasingly sought-after form of cosmetic surgery, not to control sexuality but to seek its enhancement.

4. This is true even of the latest book by Holmes, *African Queen*.

5. For more than three years we have been engaged in a struggle using the Promotion of Access to Information Act (2000) to get the South African government to release records relating to Sara Baartman's return. The government has not released the records we have requested, while the few pages of documents it has supplied are largely of marginal importance. In Paris, one archivist refused to allow us to examine a nearly two-hundred-year-old document on the basis that it might cause a "diplomatic incident." We surreptitiously photographed records that were not intended for inquisitive eyes, let alone ours. We became enmeshed in the intrigues and complexities of the academic and publishing worlds. As of writing, an important document has disappeared from one of the archives. In this book we have confined our sleuthing and discussion of some of the mysteries largely to the notes.

6. Ricoeur, *Time and Narrative*, 1:75.

7. Hughes, quoted in Israel, *Names and Stories*, 17.

8. The issue of the self is notoriously vexing. We have found the following works particularly helpful: Taylor, *Sources of the Self*; Carrithers, Collins, and Lukes, *Category of the Person*; Sorabji, *Self*; Metzinger, *Being No One*; Seigel, *Idea*

of the Self; and Ermath, "Agency in the Discursive Condition." See also Wahrman, *Making of the Modern Self.* We have explored this conundrum elsewhere employing the concept of "heterography" to refer to ways of writing about the lives and interactions of people who had different conceptions of being and who inhabited contingent, provisional worlds undergoing rapid historical change. See Crais, "Heterographies"; Scully, "Peripheral Visions"; Scully and Crais, "Race and Erasure." We are indebted to our graduate class Heterographies, which we taught in the fall 2006 semester.

CHAPTER 1
WINDS OF THE CAMDEBOO

1. We know that Sara died in Paris at the very end of 1815. The challenge is to work backward from this certainty to childhood and birth. George Cuvier wrote that "she believed that she was about twenty-six years old," in which case Sara was born in 1789 and traveled to London when she was twenty-one. This is the conventional wisdom, repeated everywhere and, most recently, in Holmes, *African Queen.* Interestingly, the label on Case Number 33 in the Museum of Man in Paris said that she died at the age of thirty-eight, in which case Sara would have been born in 1777, not 1789, and moved to London when she was thirty-three. Kirby, "Hottentot Venus" (1949), 61. We shall see later that Pieter Cesars, who brought Sara westward, served a man who died in 1799, and for whom Sara worked as a servant; therefore, Sara had to be in Cape Town before the man's death, that is, in or before 1799. Pieter Cesar was away from his Cape Town home around 1797, almost certainly in the eastern part of the Cape Colony. (CA) J 443, List of Free Blacks, 1797; compare to list in the same file for 1800, though here spelled "Peterus." Pieter was also on the frontier in the spring of 1793. (CA) 1/SWM 3/17, statement of Cesars, 17 Oct. 1793. Sara likely traveled to Cape Town around 1796–97. We know as well that Sara came to Cape Town as a woman, not a child, for she became pregnant either during the trip west or soon after arriving in the port city. (CA) ZI 1/25 2431/12/1: Cape Papers. Khoekhoe women reached menarche usually in their late teens, on the basis of comparative ethnographic data probably around sixteen and seventeen. See, for example, Shostak, *Nisa*, and original sources cited below. With this information Sara would have been born no later than 1780 and, more likely, around the mid-1770s. She therefore died not at the young age of twenty-six but in her midthirties to early forties. At the time, the life expectancy of working-class Parisians was scarcely much better. We will present the concrete evidence as the story unfolds. Suffice it to say at this very early juncture that many of the most basic features of the standard narrative are incorrect; this in and of itself is of interest in solving the puzzle and mystery of Sara Baartman and the Hottentot Venus.

2. A classic introduction to the region is still Palmer, *Plains of the Camdeboo.* Additional descriptions of the Camdeboo can be found in the reports of ex-

plorers such as Thunberg, Sparrman, and Le Vaillant. Each of these sources is discussed below.

3. For introductions to the Khoekhoe and to the early colonial period, including the Gonaqua, see Elphick and Giliomee, *Shaping of South African Society*; Newton-King, *Masters and Servants*; Elbourne, *Blood Ground*. The best early published original sources on the Khoekhoe are Kolbe, *Present State of the Cape of Good Hope*; Schapera, *Early Cape Hottentots*. Some of the earliest descriptions of the Gonaqua can be found in "Relaas van Adriaan Janz. . . . " and "Journaal gehouden door Adsistend Carel Albregt Haupt," in Molsbergen, *Reizen in Zuid-Afrika*, vol. 3. There is a considerable debate among scholars concerning both the relationship between Khoekhoe and hunter-gatherers as well as that between the Gonaqua and the Xhosa, especially with regard to culture and consciousness. Some have argued for a pliable relationship between pastoralists and hunter-gatherers, while others have asserted that pastoralists saw the world in fundamentally different ways than peoples living by hunting and gathering. See above and Smith, "Keeping People on the Periphery." However one conceives of the economic and political differences separating herders and hunters, culturally they had much in common, for instance, the same creation myths and a belief in the ineluctable relationship between animals and people. See below and Schapera, *Khoisan Peoples*; Barnard, *Hunters and Herders of Southern Africa*.

4. Who Sara Baartman *really was* became an issue of debate in her time and in some respects continues today. Throughout the nineteenth and twentieth centuries the debate has centered on race, most often whether or not Baartman was a "Bushman" or a "Hottentot." Handwritten comments in 1950 on skeletal measurements noted "Very good Bush measurements," reproducing discussions more than a century earlier (Kirby, "Hottentot Venus of the Musée de l'Homme"). Phillip Tobias, who as we shall see played a crucial role in returning Baartman's remains to South Africa, discussed the racial origins of "Hottentots" in 1955. Tobias, "Physical Anthropology and the Somatic Origins of the Hottentots." Evidence suggests that herders marginalized hunters. However, while they did not participate in rock painting (as did most hunter-gatherers), their material and cultural lives nonetheless maintained many similarities. Could Baartman have been of recent Sonaqua origin? Possibly. However, there were few hunter-gatherers in this valley area. More important, early records referencing "Baartman," and particularly a "king," points to the existence of a clan, whereas Sonaqua were typically incorporated into colonial households on an individual basis and as captive laborers.

5. "Baartman" is not an uncommon name; a Dutch telephone directory will list many people with this surname. The surname is less widespread in South Africa. There were a number of European men who moved to the Cape named "Baartman," and in the eighteenth century it was relatively common for Khoekhoe being incorporated into colonial households to adopt their master's name. However, a comprehensive analysis of 8,809 farms granted to Europeans

throughout the Dutch period reveals not a single person with the surname "Baartman." Leonard Guelke, EXCEL files EDLFI.WKE and EDLFII.WKE, in authors' possession. There are, however, two farms with the name: "Baartmans thuin" and Baartman's Fonteyn. The former is located in the Western Cape. The second, however, is located precisely in Gonaqua country. The deed ("remitted to graze") granted to David Fourie describes the farm as on the "Riet" or "Reed" River, of which there are many throughout the Cape. (CA) RLR 17/2, Licences: Loan Farms, 4 Mar. 1763. (The archival card catalogue indicates that the deed is located in RLR 17/1.) In the 1770s Fourie was serving under Charles Marais when he was mortally wounded. A brief description of the 1779 commando when Fourie was wounded can be found in Moodie, *The Record*, pt. iii, 81, and (CA) VC 884. This section of *The Record* provides data on the wars of the period. Other data can be found in (CA) VC 882–888. See also Newton-King, *Masters and Servants*. We discuss this attack later in the chapter. Marais lived at the foot of the Snow Mountains in the Camdeboo. The same report mentions Tjaart van der Walt, who lived north of Graaff Reinet. Using these data, along with material such as historical maps, GDS maps, and Google Earth, allows us to identify the farm along the far eastern edge of the Camdeboo, and not the Gamtoos River valley.

6. Reconstructing Khoekhoe culture and society is notoriously vexing. This and the paragraphs below are based on a variety of sources. There has been a long-standing discussion among historians and archaeologists on the relationship between southern African pastoralists and hunter-gatherer communities. For somewhat dated but still useful introductions, see Elphick and Giliomee, *Shaping of South African Society*; Elphick, *Khoikhoi*. Bennun, *Broken String*, has useful information on the cosmology of related hunter-gatherer communities. See also the classic Bleek and L. Lloyd, *Specimens of Bushman Folklore*. For a dictionary, see Haacke and Eiseb, *Khoekhoegowab*. For a recent discussion of the wind within Khoisan culture, see Low, "Khoisan Wind."

7. See illustrations in chapter 3.

8. Thunberg, *Travels*, 236–37. Thunberg was one of the first scientists to introduce Europe to the Eastern Cape's natural world. The Cape became known throughout Europe for its fossil record and for its biodiversity, leading scientists to think that its ancient and living records held important clues to the history of the world. Sara Baartman's life would become an important part of this scientific inquisitiveness.

9. Sparrman, *Voyage*, 2:16–17.

10. Le Vaillant, *Travels into the Interior Parts of Africa*, 2:380–81, 14–15, 21.

11. Mentzel, *Life at the Cape*, 92. *Palangbangers*, named after a southeast Sumatra kingdom famous in the pepper trade, were used throughout the Dutch Indian Ocean world.

12. Le Vaillant, *Travels from the Cape of Good-Hope*, 2:111.

13. Sparrman, *Voyage*, 2:281–82.

14. Thunberg, *Travels*, 222–23. Into the early 1800s a few of the last "captains" hoped the government would somehow come to their rescue. See, for example, (CA) CO 2559: Petition Hottentot Capt. Klaas Kees, 22 July 1806: "Having inherited a place from his Father called the Seven Fountains situated behind the Kozmans Cloof. . . . at which place he is much injured by William Van Wyk and John Roux, by their continually oppressing him + making use of his best water."

15. Quoted in Elphick and Giliomee, *Shaping of South African Society*, 427.

16. Information gleaned from tax rolls and from estate records allows us to reconstruct histories of the Fourie clan. See, for example, (CA) J 316, Swellendam, c. 1752; J 317, Swellendam, 1762, 1765, 1788. (CA) MOOC 13/1/23 contains details of the estate of Louisa Erasmus, widow of David Fourie, 1800, as does (CA) J 109, tax roll for Graaff-Reinet for 1790. Additional information located in the Swellendam district archives, for example, (CA) 1/SWM 3/10, sworn statements, and other documents in this series, helped us reconstruct the frontier during this period. The Dutch East India Company VOC only established the district of Graaff-Reinet in 1786.

17. Moodie, *The Record*, pt. iii, 44–45. See also (CA) VC 882–86.

18. (CA) VC 884, report of 4 June 1779.

19. (CA) 1/GR 15/43: Contracts, 1786. The location of these contracts provides further evidence that the Baartman clan was not originally located in the Gamtoos Valley.

20. Holmes suggests that Hillegert (also spelled Hillegard) Muller had dispossessed Sara's people in 1778 during a "murderous landgrab." Holmes, *African Queen*, 11, though, provides no citation. At this time, however, Hillegert lived in Graaff-Reinet, where, for a while, he became a powerful local official. Nor was Hillegert granted a loan farm in 1778. Since he had relatives in the Gamtoos area, however, Hillegert, did frequently visit there. Moodie, *The Record*, pt. iii, 48; Guelke, EXCEL file EDLFII.WKE. The Muller and Fourie families intermixed.

21. Thunberg, *Travels*, 97.

22. Boer families were famously large. Women married by twenty, men by twenty-five, few children succumbed to disease, and Boers lived long lives, typically well into their fifties.

23. (CA) J 316: Swellendam 1752, here misspelled as "Mulder."

24. For Muller's property, see (CA) 1/SWM 12/67: Tax roll, 1793.

25. (CA) 1/SWM 12/67: Tax roll, 1793.

26. Barrow, *Account*, 94–95

27. LMS 2, 3 (D), Alberti, 21 Dec. 1803; see also 29 Dec. 1803 and 7 Jan. 1804 in same.

28. We discuss this history in the final chapter, where we provide additional evidence. For the moment, see, for example, (CA) CSC 1/2/1/6: Trial dated 28 Sept. 1830; J 405: Tax rolls for Bethelsdorp and Theopolis, 1822; (CA) LG 588: List of occupants at Fullers Hoek, Dec. 1843.

CHAPTER 2
CAPE OF STORMS

1. Barrow, *Account*, 228. Barrow's account roundly condemned the Boers while he heaped praise on the British, the Cape's new rulers.

2. See below, note 8. In (PRO) KB 1/36/4: "Examination of the Hottentot Venus," 27 Nov. 1810, Sara said she had two brothers and four sisters but did not specify their locations. (CA) J 442: Summary, District of Stellenbosch, 1806–24, shows Khoi in the Western Cape.

3. Elzer, also discussed below, is mentioned as a butcher in Schutte, *Briefwisseling van Hendrik Swellengrebel*, 226. In 1786, Elzer purchased part of the old hospital grounds for 23,850 guilders, then a very considerable sum. See Leibbrandt, *Precis of the Archives of the Cape of Good Hope*, esp. 1:130–31, 138–39, 211–20.

4. Pieter Hendrik Ferreira. The location of Ferreira farms can be found in EXCEL files EDLFI.WKE and EDLFII.WKE. See also Schutte, *Briefwisseling van Hendrik* Swellengrebel, 119; Thunberg, *Travels*, 96–97; Sparrman, *Voyage*, 1:281. In September 2004, Crais traveled to Hankey and stayed at a bed-and-breakfast owned by the Ferreira family.

5. (PRO) KB 1/36/4: "Examination of the Hottentot Venus," 27 Nov. 1810.

6. Thunberg, *Travels*, 94. Reconstruction of the trip westward is based on the reports of travelers, for example, Barrow, *Account*; Sparrman, *Voyage*; Thunberg, *Travels*; Lichtenstein, *Travels*; Steedman, *Wanderings*. Maps such as (CA) M 4/50 (1800) were also helpful.

7. Mentzel, *Description*, 3:49–50.

8. (PRO) KB 1/36/4: "Examination of the Hottentot Venus," 27 Nov. 1810.

9. (CL) MMS: Baptisms, Romana Bartman, child of Adonis and Elisabeth. On contracts, see (CA) 1/STB 18/198: Hire and Apprentice contracts, 1833–39, which lists: "Platje Johannes Baartman" (1834); "Jan Baartman" (1836); "Jan Baartman" (1837); "Hendrik Baartman" (1837); and "Klaas Baartman" (1838). These are typical names of colonized Khoekhoe. In (CA) MMS: Baptisms there is another Bartman in the same record, Arend Bartman, who was born c. 1791 in Mozambique. The earliest record we have in the Western Cape with the name "Baartman" is 1803, located in Paarl and certainly of German descent. See (CA) MOOC 6/2. It is possible the Khoekhoe noted above picked the name up from this settler, or they were, in fact, related to the Baartman clan in the Eastern Cape. Nearly a decade later, the name Baartman enters into the records of mission station inhabitants, composed entirely of Khoekhoe and former slaves, in this case regarding men who volunteered to fight against the Xhosa in one of the many frontier wars. On the Zuurbrak mission station lived a Baartman man with his wife, Delia, at Genadendal a Rachel Baartman, and at Elim an Adonis Baartman, his wife and three children. (CA) CO 2838: List of persons belonging to Zuurbrak, 28 May 1847, Genadendal, 28 May 1847, and Elim, 28 May 1847. Clearly, then, there

were people scattered across the Western Cape with the surname Baartman and, while we cannot be certain, there is a high probability that Pieter Cesars brought westward more than one member of the Baartman clan.

10. In July 1796, Elzer and his wife, Cornelia, prepared a will, which listed a "Saartjie of the Cape" as one of their slaves. (CA) MOOC 7/1/44, ref. 22, will of Elzer and Theron, 18 July 1796, though clearly this must remain speculative given the widespread use of the name "Saartjie." For material on Elzer, see above and (CA) CJ 2624: No. 5, Elzer and Theron, 6 Mar. 1770; (CA) CJ 2912: No. 68, contract, 24 Jan. 1786; (CA) CJ 2639, codicil, 12 Sept. 1785.

11. For descriptions of Cape Town, see, for example, Lenta and le Cordeur, *Cape Diaries of Lady Anne Barnard*; Thunberg, *Travels*, 24–52. Lady Ann Barnard was living in the city at the same time as Sara. See also Worden, Van Heyningen, and Bickford-Smith, *Cape Town*. An excellent primary source is Mentzel, *Description*.

12. On Cape washerwomen, see Jordan, " 'Unrelenting Toil.' "

13. Some of the best depictions of prostitution can be found in Mentzel, *Description*, 3:99: "If you have no money, I have no cunt," slave women said to men coming to the lodge, "Kammene kas, kammene Kunte." See also Shell, "Lodge Women."

14. Staal deposition in (CA) ZI 1/25 2431/12/1: Cape Papers, mentions Sara's first pregnancy.

15. See the Staal deposition in (CA) ZI 1/25 2431/12/1: Cape Papers.

16. A discussion of demography in Cape Town can be found in Elphick and Giliomee, *Shaping of South African Society*.

17. Jonker, "Excavating the Legal Subject."

18. Elzer (also spelled Elser) died on 27 Feb. 1799; he had married Cornelia Theron on 19 Mar. 1769. See www.familysearch.org, accessed 16 Feb. 2007; (CA) MOOC 7/1/44, will of Elzer and Theron, 26 Mar. 1796, and above.

19. The following paragraphs are based on a variety of sources. We know that Sara worked for Hendrik Cesars and for Pieter Cesars, based on her own testimony in London. (PRO) KB 1/36/4: "Examination of the Hottentot Venus," 27 Nov. 1810. The Staal deposition in (CA) ZI 1/25 2431/12/1: Cape Papers, tells us that Sara worked for Elzer and for Hendrik and Staal. Staal stated that Sara "lived with said Elzer + with others, whom I however don't know." Interestingly, Staal does not mention Sara working for Pieter, her brother-in-law. Staal's mother likely was Elizabeth of the Cape, and her brother Hermanus Staal, who in 1791 married a woman of the Barends clan. The *African Court Calender for the Year 1812* mentions a "Widow Hermanus" who kept a shop at 72 Long Street. The Frenchman Charles Villet, who we discuss at the end of the chapter, lived at 71 Long Street. In the records of the legal proceedings in London, Sara is described as serving Hendrik Cesars as a "Nursery maid." (PRO) KB 1/36/4, "Examination of the Hottentot Venus," 27 Nov. 1810; Gaselee, in (CA) ZI 1/25 2431/12/1: Cape Papers. For additional materials on the Cesars clan and their relations, see below

and GISA Microfilm, Christian baptism in the years 1788–91, 1793, 1796–98, and 1800, and weddings, 1787; the tax rolls (CA) J 39, 41, 46, 55, 57, 443, which contain census material; and wills and estates in (CA) MOOC 7/1/16, 7/1/61, 7/1/85, 7/1/201, 7/1/269. Additional information on Free Blacks can be obtained in the records of the Burgher Council, especially BRD 5/1/7/3 and BRD 5/1/7/5. See also Mansell, "From the Venus Sickness"; Heese, *Groep Sonder Grense*, 77, 82; Heese, "Die Inwoners van Kaapstaad," 48, 52. We very much appreciate Dr. Heese and Mr. Upham for speaking and/or corresponding with us. The Elser family had connections through marriage with the Free Black community, while one member of the Cesars clan appears to have married a prominent British naval officer. See J 39.

20. The 1797 tax roll, (CA) J 443 listed 162 men, 240 women, 149 sons, and 149 daughters. The community owned a total of 140 slaves. The classic work on Free Blacks is still Boeseken, *Slaves and Free Blacks at the Cape*. See also Ross, *Status and Respectability*, and his *Beyond the Pale*.

21. See (CA) J 443. On burgher households, see Elphick and Giliomee, *Shaping of South African Society*, 283–323. In 1731, free burgher women had on average 2.41 children, compared with 1.5 children for Free Black women. Worden, Van Heyningen, and Bickford-Smith, *Cape Town*, 50.

22. For baptismal lists, see (DRC) 1/1: Kerken-boek van de Caap de Goede Hoop.

23. Free Blacks tended to marry late. If, for the sake of argument, one assumed that Hendrik married in 1787 at age twenty, then he would have been born in 1767. Hendrik thus left Cape Town in his forties. It is likely that Hendrik married in his late twenties or in his thirties. This would mean that he was born c. 1757, his father c. 1732 (± 15), his grandfather c. 1702 (± 15), and Hendrik's great-grandfather c. 1677 (± 15). These must remain the crudest of estimates in the absence of consistent baptismal and marriage data.

There were of course other slaves named Caesar. See, for example, Worden and Groenewald, *Trials of Slavery*, 445. However, we were unable to locate additional manumitted slaves with the name "Caesar" (however spelled) whose life intersected with what we definitively knew about Hendrik. Cape manumission rates were relatively low, roughly four thousand over the course of nearly two centuries. The highest manumission rate fell in the years roughly from about 1677 through the 1690s. Discounting these years, manumission rates would have been below those for the very low rates for the American South. Shell, *Children of Bondage*, 383. There were two types of manumission, the first of which granted the former slave the status of a free citizen. The second form of manumission granted the slave his or her liberty but denied the status of citizen. Free Blacks had their origin in this second pattern of gaining freedom. This had important implications, as we shall see. Shell, *Children of Bondage*, 374. Also see Upham, "From the Venus Sickness," for other investigations into the Cesar name.

24. Free Black was a status category, not a racial one. Hendrik would have been largely indistinguishable from Europeans at the Cape, which explains why some Londoners saw him as a colonial settler. On Free Blacks and increasing prejudice, see Ross, *Status and* Respectability.

25. This is based on the tax rolls (CA) J 443, 39, 41.

26. The will is located at (CA) MOOC 7/1/61: will of Cesars and Staal, 29 Mar. 1810. The will does not mention Sara or the other servants.

27. One of the tax rolls in (CA) J 443 was completed in April 1800

28. See tax rolls in (CA) J 443 and 39, and wills in (CA) MOOC 7/1/16 and 7/1/269.

29. For a discussion of the war, see Newton-King, *Masters and Servants*, and (CA) J 39 for the number of Khoekhoe in Papendorp.

30. Because it seems most likely that the Khoekhoe moving into the Western Cape came from the eastern frontier, these newcomers would have been able to communicate. At worst there may have been a few issues of local dialect. However, the war had been confined to a quite specific area of the frontier.

31. We know that Cesars was already in debt to Vos by August 1808. Vos, in (CA) ZI 1/25 2431/12/1: Cape Papers. The property, virtually all of it in human beings, increased after 1800. Cesars likely began falling into substantial debt around 1803.

32. Ibid.

33. (PRO) KB 1/36/4, "Examination of the Hottentot Venus," 27 Nov. 1810; Staal deposition in (CA) ZI 1/25 2431/12/1: Cape Papers.

34. (PRO) KB 1/36/4, "Examination of the Hottentot Venus," 27 Nov. 1810; Staal deposition in (CA) ZI 1/25 2431/12/1: Cape Papers.

35. Robinson, *Letters of Lady Anne Barnard*, 59.

36. As recorded in (CA) J 39 and J 41.

37. See below and *RCC* 3:297; 4:158–59; 5:367; 2:323–28, for material on the Concordia Club, discussed below. Vos's property is recorded in (CA) J 37. For further information on Vos, see (CA) MOOC 7/1/04: No. 133, will 1805. See also Elbourne, *Blood Ground*,114.

38. Leibbrandt, *Precis of the Archives of the Cape of Good Hope*, 2:879.

39. Mentzel, *Geographical and Topographical*, 75.

40. The site has been renamed Heritage Square in recognition of its eighteenth-century architecture. The original theater still stands. At one point it became a church; now a sculptor has a shop in the basement and sells his ironware on the sidewalk.

41. *African Court Calender for the Year 1812.*

42. For a discussion of the theater and Baartman, see Upham, "From the Venus Sickness," 16–18. For more on the African Theater's founding, see Laidler, *Annals of the Cape Stage*; *Dictionary of South African Biography*, vols. 1, 3. On the controversy about the diorama, see Skotnes, *Miscast*.

43. Upham, "From the Venus Sickness," 17.

44. *List of All the Officers*, 557.

45. The following paragraphs on Dunlop's plans and Hendrik's predicaments leading up to their departure with Sara Baartman are based on (CA) ZI 1/25 2431/12/1: Cape Papers, especially depositions by Staal and Vos; (CA) CO 3875, Memorial of Dunlop, 16 June 1809; (CA) CO 22, Grey to Caledon, 26 Jan. 1810; Hussey to Forster, 25 Jan. 1810; Hussey to van Ryneveld, 1 Mar. 1810; Dunlop to Alexander, 7 Mar. 1810; No. 29, 16 Mar. 180. The proposed closing of the Slave Lodge is detailed in (CA) GH 23/1, Lord Caledon to Lord Viscount, 23 July 1807.

46. (CA) CO 3871, Memorial of Dunlop, 7 Feb. 1809. See also Upham, "Venus Sickness," 10.

47. On the Caledon Code, see, for example, Ross, *Beyond the Pale*.

48. On 12 Nov. 1810, "H. Cezar & a free Black Saar from the Cape" received permission to leave the colony. On 20 March they again received permission to leave, this time on the HMS *Raisonable*. (CA) CO 6067, Permission to leave. Cesars and Sara were set to sail on the HMS *Raisonable*, which departed on 2 Apr. 1810; it appears they ended up on the HMS *Diadem* instead. (PRO) ADM 37/1973: Muster-Table; (PRO) ADM 51/2751: Logbook of HMS *Raisonable*.

CHAPTER 3

LONDON CALLING

1. Reconstruction of the voyage is based on (PRO) ADM 37/1973, (PRO) ADM 51/2284, and (PRO) ADM 51/2751.

2. David Eltis kindly provided information on naval ship customs. See also Lyon, *Sailing Navy List*, which contains descriptions of the vessels and their history.

3. For a useful description of Saint Helena, see Cook, *Cook's Voyages*.

4. (PRO) ADM 37/1973, (PRO) ADM 51/2284, and (PRO) ADM 51/2751.

5. On Chatham, see Oldfield, *An Entire and Complete History*. Historical images of Chatham can be seen at http://www.imagesonline.bl.uk/britishlibrary, searching "Chatham."

6. On London in this period, see Davies, *Map of London*. Tobias Smollet, quoted in Davies, *Map of London*, 67.

7. Microfilm 74777, vol. 3, *Liverpool Mercury*, 20 Aug. 1813, 63.

8. Margetson, *Regency London*, 3. For this and following descriptions of London in this era, see Porter, *London*; Ogborn, *Spaces of Modernity*; Rendell, *Pursuit of Pleasure*, 70.

9. "Piccadilly, South Side," testimony of Macaulay in his deposition. This is verified by Jacob Guitard, notary, who said he translated a contract from Dutch to English for Dunlop, who lived at "Duke Street." (PRO) KB 1/36/4: Statement of Jacob Guitard, 27 Nov. 1810, and Testimony of John George Moojen, 27 Nov. 1810, who says he examined Sara at her home in Duke Street.

10. Davies, *Map of London*, 27.

11. Altick, *Shows*, 235.

12. Richardson, *Annals*, 229.

13. James Newland, theft: housebreaking, 6 June 1810, The Proceedings of the Old Bailey Ref: t18100606–36; Malachi Murray, theft: simple grand larceny, 14 July 1813, The Proceedings of the Old Bailey, Ref: t18130714–18. http://www.oldbaileyonline.org/html_units/1810s/t18100606–36.html.

14. Schwarz, "London," 663, 666; Louis Simond quoted in Margetson, *Regency London*, 114.

15. Rendell, *Pursuit of Pleasure*, 70. Bury Street and Duke Street housed "ever-crowded nests of bachelor's lodgings." Hare, *Walks in London*, 68.

16. In 1772 a party of some two hundred gentlemen, "and their Ladies, had an Entertainment at a Public house in Westminster, to celebrate the Triumph which their Brother Somerset had obtained. . . . Lord Mansfield's health was echoed round the Room, and the Evening was concluded with a ball." *Public Advertiser*, 27 June 1772, cited in Grant, "William Brown and Other Women," 53.

17. Land, "Bread and Arsenic."

18. The scholarship on black London concentrates on either the eighteenth century or the Victorian era. On the history of black Londoners in this period, and the difficulty of doing research and estimating numbers for this particular period, see Myers, *Reconstructing the Black Past*, 77, 57. Also Myers, "Black Presence"; Wedderburn, *Horrors of Slavery*. Also see Edwards, "Unreconciled Strivings," 24–48, for a discussion of the gaps in the historiography. On this period in particular, see Duffield, "Skilled Workers or Marginalized Poor?" 49–87; Killingray, "Africans in the United Kingdom," 2–27. Important works on black British history include Fryer, *Staying Power*; Gerzina, *Black London*; Lorimer, *Colour, Class and the Victorians*; Shyllon, *Blacks in Britain*; Grant, "William Brown and Other Women."

19. On the clubs of the area, see Margetson, *Regency London*.

20. Altick, *Shows*, 235–39; Chancellor, *Life in Regency*, 101. A year after Sara arrived in London, Bullock began building his famous Egyptian Hall at 170–171 Piccadilly. That museum, housing some fifteen thousand artifacts, opened in 1812; among its most successful exhibits was Napoleon's carriage. The building was completed in 1812 and demolished in 1905. Richardson, *Annals*, 235, 239.

21. (PRO) KB 1/36/4: Testimony of William Bullock, 21 Nov. 1810.

22. Ibid.

23. See chapter 2 for material on Dunlop's career in Cape Town. In addition, see RCS. "Company of Surgeons Examination Book"; Drew, *Commissioned Officers in the Medical Services of the British Army*, which summarizes Dunlop's career, including his death in Portsmouth, 18 July 1812. For an early record relating to his naval career, see (PRO) ADM 106/989: Dunlop to ?, 10 Jan. 17 [illeg.].

24. On various Khoekhoe visitors to London, see Elbourne, "The Savage and the Saved."

25. Kicherer described in purple prose the great alteration in the "Hottentots'" manners: "Before they were naked. . . . before dirty, vile. . . . before they lived in huts . . .now in houses, before they eat like Animals . . . now like man." Kicherer, *Extract*, 32–35, 43. See Elbourne, "The Savage and the Saved," for an excellent examination of this visit.

26. McCreery, *Satirical Gaze.*

27. Altick, *Shows*, 2–3.

28. See Altick, *Shows*, 35–36. However, one author says the fair moved to September in the eighteenth century because of the change of the calendar. Cavendish, "London's Last Bartholomew Fair."

29. Information on Bartholomew Fair is from Morley, *Memoirs*. On the boy, Edwards and Walvin, *Black Personalities*, 155–56. Altick, *Shows*, chap. 13, discusses Richardson. See also Youngquist, *Monstrosities.*

30. Letter from Hend. Cezar, *Morning Post*, 23 Oct. 1810, 4. Hendrik Cesars was illiterate. It is highly likely that Dunlop wrote the letter.

31. Altick, *Shows*, 38. The freak show tended to render an individual odd, in part through overt comparison with others or through focusing on one feature to the exclusion of knowledge about the whole person. Thus, a promoter might display a large man next to an excessively thin person, and would have literature focusing on a person's nose, height, or weight. For fascinating analyses of freak shows in the nineteenth century, with an emphasis on the United States, see Garland-Thomson, *Freakery,* especially the chapter by Bogdan, "The Social Construction of Freaks," 23–37.

32. It is unclear why Cesars was the showman rather than Dunlop, although perhaps Dunlop would have seen such a role as demeaning. Cesars's presence as showman might also have heightened the show's allusion to the exoticism of the Cape. Perhaps Sara Baartman refused to do the exhibit without Cesars, as she had earlier refused to go to London unless accompanied by him.

33. Altick, *Shows*, 38.

34. We are grateful to Rosemarie Garland-Thomson for helping us think through these issues.

35. McCreery, *Satirical Gaze*, 19, 25.

36. For information on Lewis and on aquatint, see especially Twyman, *Printing*, chaps. 6, 88.

37. The first copyright act of 1735 responded to the complaints of Hogarth and other caricaturists that people copied their works for profit. The 1735 act was quite limited in its intent: protecting only artists, such as Hogarth, who also published their own work. They had copyright for fourteen years. The Act of 1767 extended copyright for twenty-eight years, and copyright referred now to all prints reproduced from an original painting, sculpture, drawing, and so on. The original plate contained the date of the original and the name of the holder of copyright. Copyright could be transferred by selling the original plate. For

information on copyright and printing, see Clayton, *English Print*, esp. 198. Also Rickards, "Ephemera"; Lambert, *Image Multiplied*, 101.

38. (BL) c.103.k, Lysons, "Collectanea," 1, 102. For a published version, see Edwards and Walvin, *Black Personalities*, 171. Early nineteenth-century London offered new ways for men to socialize and observe one another, but elite women had fewer opportunities apart from salons. It is perhaps for this reason that advertisement of the Hottentot Venus particularly targeted "the ladies." The letter justifying the exhibit is ostensibly from Cesars, but he was illiterate. *Morning Post*, 23 Oct. 1810, 4.

39. One of the few complaints that Baartman made about London was that it was cold. (PRO) KB 1/36/4: "Hottentot Venus Statement of Messrs Solly and Moojen . . .," 27 Nov. 1810. For an innovative treatment of the relationship between starer and staree, see Rosemarie Garland-Thomson, *Staring: How We Look*.

40. (PRO) KB 1/36/4: Testimony of William Bullock, 21 Nov. 1810. Macaulay and others described the show. See (PRO) KB 1/36/4: Statement by Zachary Macaulay, Thomas Gisborne Babington, and Peter Van Wageninge, 17 Oct. 1810.

41. Information on the carriage rides is taken from Baartman's statement to Solly and Moojen in (PRO) KB 1/36/4.

CHAPTER 4
BEFORE THE LAW

1. (PRO) KB 1/36/4: Statement of Macaulay, 17 Oct. 1810.

2. Ibid.

3. Knutsford, *Life and Letters of Zachary Macaulay*, 7–8.

4. Booth, *Zachary Macaulay*, 20. Macaulay would name his son, Thomas Babington Macaulay, in Babington's honor. Thomas went on to become the famous Whig historian, author of the five-volume *History of England* and of the famous "Minute on Education in India of 1835."

5. See Turner, " Limits of Abolition," 322.

6. Wesley "Neglected Period," 162.

7. Turner, "Limits of Abolition," 331.

8. T. P. Thompson, letter dated 3 Aug. 1809, recipient unknown; quoted in Turner, "Limits of Abolition," 345–46.

9. (UCL) MS 797, I/5622: Booth Correspondence, Macaulay to Colin Macaulay, 6 Apr. 1810.

10. The discussion below is derived from Turner, "Limits of Abolition."

11. Turner, "Limits of Abolition," 340, 343, 350; Knutsford, *Life and Letters of Zachary Macaulay*, 287.

12. See Magubane, "Which Bodies Matter?"

13. Another man claimed the boys as his own. The conflict ended up in the courts, Macaulay winning the judgment; the boys remained in Clapham under the tutelage of a local rector. Raising Sara's plight might dig up this episode. Had they traveled to England of their own free will? The subject was open to nasty speculation. Ultimately the children Macaulay sponsored lived in Clapham under the tutelage of Rector John Venn. Knutsford, *Life and Letters of Zachary Macaulay*, 220–21, 237.

14. Letter from an Englishman, *Morning Chronicle*, 12 Oct. 1810.

15. (CA) MOOC 7/6/61: Will of Cesars and Staal, 29 Mar. 1810, filed 16 May 1811. Humanitas, writing a letter that appeared on 24 October 1810, also had his doubts about authorship of Cesars's letters, saying "*by whomsoever written.*"

16. The statement "both our families" echoes powerfully but is difficult to resolve. As far as we know, Sara had no children; she did not live in an independent family formation. Dunlop writing as Cesars either meant that proceeds from the show would benefit his and Cesars's families, and here he collapsed Sara into Cesars's family using the noun as a synonym for household. Alternatively, Dunlop implicitly meant that the arrangement would benefit Cesars/Dunlop as one family, and Sara as part of another. If the latter is the case, it suggests closer connections with her extended family, brother, and sisters, nieces and nephews, than the record permits us to see. Letter from an Englishman, *Morning Chronicle*, 12 Oct. 1810.

17. Letter from Hendric [*sic*] Cezar, *Morning Chronicle*, 13 Oct. 1810, 3.

18. (PRO) KB 1/36/4: Statement by Zachary Macaulay, Thomas Gisborne Babington, and Peter Van Wageninge, 17 Oct. 1810.

19. Letter from White Man, *Morning Post*, 29 Oct. 1810, in Lysons, "Collectanea." Also letter from "A Man and a Christian," *Morning Post*, 18 Oct. 1810, 3.

20. Signed Hend. Casar [*sic*], *Morning Chronicle*, 22 Oct. 1810.

21. Letter from White Man, *Morning Post*, 29 Oct. 1810, in Lysons, "Collectanea."

22. Barrow, *Account*.

23. Signed Hend. Casar [*sic*], *Morning Chronicle*, 22 Oct. 1810.

24. Law Intelligence; Court of the King's Bench, 28 Nov., "Hottentot Venus," *Morning Chronicle*, 29 Nov. 1810, 3.

25. Letter from Humanitas, *Morning Chronicle*, 24 Oct. 1810, 3; Letter from White Man, *Morning Post*, 29 Oct. 1810, in Lysons, "Collectanea." On Cesars, see Scully and Crais, "Race and Erasure."

26. Altick, *Shows*, 270.

27. (HRO) DDGR 43/30/48: Henry Grimston to Thomas Grimston, 23 Nov. 1810.

28. "The Three Graces," 13 Nov. 1810, shown in Strother, "Display of the Body Hottentot," 30.

29. *Morning Herald*, 23 Nov. 1810, 3. On the Duke, see Robinson, *Old Q.*

30. Charles Williams, "Neptune's Last Resource or the Fortune Hunter Foiled, a Sketch from Heathen Mythology," collected in George, *Catalogue*, 9, 11748, 38–39. For a discussion of cartoons regarding Baartman, see Lindfors, "Hottentot, Bushmen, Kaffir."

31. East, "Case of the Hottentot Venus."

32. On the link between antislavery and Britain's identity in the aftermath of the American Revolution, see Brown, *Moral Capital*.

33. (CA) ZI 1/25 2431/12/1: Cape Papers, "Copy from Mr Guerney's Short Hand Notes of the Proceedings in the Court of King's Bench, 24 November 1810."

34. (CA) ZI 1/25 2431/12/1: Cape Papers, "Mr Guerney," 24 Nov. 1810. Statement of Zachary Macaulay, 3.

35. "Rule on the person who at present had the custody of the female in question, to admit some person or persons, who spoke the language which she alone understood, to converse with her, out of the presence of her keeper." See comments of Lord Ellenborough and the Attorney General in Law Intelligence, Court of the King's Bench, Saturday, 24 Nov, 1810, as recorded in "The Hottentot Venus," *Morning Chronicle*, 26 Nov. 1810, 3. Also see (CA) ZI 1/25 2431/12/1: Cape Papers, "Mr Guerney," 24 Nov. 1810.

36. Kirby, "More," 125, says the original in Paris is drawn up in Dutch. But see (PRO) KB 1/36/4: Statement regarding testimony of the Hottentot Venus, 27 Nov. 1810, signed affadavit of A. J. Guitard, who says he translated it into Dutch from English for Sara Baartman. It is this translation that Baartman took with her to Paris.

37. Hottentot Venus, *Morning Chronicle*, 29 Nov. 1810, 3.

38. Two subsequent apparent interviews in Paris seem to have been cobbled together by authors rather than being genuine interviews.

39. The following is recorded in (PRO) KB 1/36/4: "Hottentot Venus Statement of Messrs Solly and Moojen . . .," 27 Nov. 1810, and also "Hottentot Venus," *Morning Chronicle*, 29 Nov. 1810, 3.

40. Note the *Morning Post*'s summary of Gaselee's statement to the King's Bench said that she said she had "a black boy and girl to wait upon her." *Morning Post*, 29 Nov. 1810.

41. (PRO) KB 1/36/4: Statement of A. J. Guitard, 27 Nov. 1810.

42. (PRO) KB 1/36/4: "Hottentot Venus Statement of Messrs Solly and Moojen . . .," 27 Nov. 1810. For a helpful published copy, see Strother, "Display of the Body Hottentot," Appendix 1, 41.

43. In contrast, Yvette Abrahams sees Baartman as wholly a victim in this context. See Abrahams, "Disempowered to Consent."

44. The role of Lord Caledon, governor of the Cape, in allowing Sara Baartman, as a Khoekhoe person, to leave the Cape, was subsequently investigated at the Cape. Caledon said he had been unaware of her leave-taking. Cesars seems to have identified Sara as Free Black, not Khoekhoe. Free Black status posed no legal

problem in leaving the colony. The matter was dropped. (CA) ZI 1/25 2431/12/1, Cape Papers: Letter permitting departure of H. Cezar and "the freeblack Zaar," signed by Henry Alexander, secretary, 20 Mar. 1810; Statement by Caledon, 27 Feb. 1811.

45. On habeas corpus and third-party applications and the Hottentot Venus, see Sharpe, *Habeas Corpus*, 222. For a recent citation to the case of the Hottentot Venus, see U.S. District Court, for the District of Columbia, *Hamdan v. Rumsfeld*, 13 Dec. 2006. This was an appeal of the Supreme Court ruling in favor of Hamdan, on 29 June 2006. Hamdan was Osama Bin Laden's driver and bodyguard, born in Yemen, captured by the Americans in Afghanistan, and taken to Guantánamo. The Supreme Court ruled that military tribunals were illegal under U.S. law and the Geneva Convention without the approval of Congress. We take up this issue in the last chapter.

46. On the ballad, see "A Ballad" (London: Collophon, James Gillet printer, n.d. (1810), collected in Toole-Stott, *Circus and Allied Arts*, 336. The court case and publicity in London is the part of Baartman's life that has received the most scholarly attention. See especially Kirby, "The 'Hottentot Venus' of the Musée de l'Homme," 55–61; Kirby "More"; Lindfors, "The Afterlife."

CHAPTER 5
LOST, AND FOUND

1. Bodleian Library, online, Ballads Catalogue: Harding B 25 (863), "The Hottentot Venus," C. Berry, printer, Norwich. The dates given for the printing are 1757 to 1807. This cannot be correct, as the Hottentot Venus was displayed only from 1810, and Bullock's museum is also mentioned, which postdated 1807.

2. *Morning Post*, 12 Dec. 1811.

3. Advertisement, "The Hottentot Venus Takes Her Final Departure," *Morning Post*, 30 Apr. 1811, 1.

4. Hampshire Record Office, Herbert Family Correspondence, 75m91/c5/25, 7 Jan. 1811.

5. See Macaulay's letter to this effect. University of London, MS 797 I/5622, Booth Correspondence, 1 5629 (i), Macaulay to nephew Kenneth Macaulay, ? May 1812.

6. See Unknown, "The Humours of Bartlemy Fair," in Cruikshank and Cruikshank, *The Universal Songster*, 118–19.

7. Dunlop signed the copy of Sara Baartman's baptismal certificate. For a copy of the certificate, and Dunlop's signature, see Kirby, "More," 129.

8. William, *Annals of Manchester* (1812), 143.

9. Microfilm 7477, *Liverpool Mercury*, 25 Mar. 1814, 510.

10. The African Institution and other organizations also continued their lobbying on behalf of Africans in Europe, again primarily with the intention of sending individuals back to Africa. Microfilm 7477, "African Slave Trade," *Liv-*

erpool Mecury, 30 Dec. 1814, 214; and "Destitute Africans," 3 Feb. 1815, 255; 17 Feb. 1815, 272.

11. On Brookes, see Chetham Library, Phelps Collection, Manchester Cathedral: Clergy, newspaper cutting, Swindells, "Joshua Brookes."

12. Microfilm 7477, *Liverpool Mercury,* 20 Dec. 1811, 198, col. 3.

13. The details of Brookes's correspondence with the bishop of Chester have been lost; note of this correspondence scribbled at the top of Baartman's baptismal certificate and in the cathedral baptismal book. Nor do we have any records of Sara's conversation with the reverend. Chetham Library, Records of Baptisms: Manchester Cathedral, no. 2689, 1 Dec. 1811. We are grateful to individuals at Chetham and the cathedral for their help in interpreting this baptism and what would have been entailed.

14. Elizabeth Elbourne makes a similar point regarding connections to the Cape in her excellent paper "The Savage and the Saved."

15. In its obituary, the *Manchester Mercury* mentioned Sara's baptism, adding that, "at the same time, [Sara] entered into the holy state of matrimony." *Manchester Mercury,* 16 Jan. 1816. No record of the marriage exists in the cathedral or relevant archives in Manchester.

16. This would not have been out of bounds—Julia Pestrana was married to the showman in charge of her enfreakment. In Paris, newspapers claimed that Sara was married to the man who exhibited her there. On Pestrana and Sara Baartman, see Garland-Thomson, *Extraordinary Bodies,* chaps. 2 and 3.

17. The copy of the baptism, signed by Brookes, is dated 7 December 1811. On the labor contract and the copy of the baptism (and for an image of the latter), both originally held at the Museum of Man in Paris, see Kirby, "More."

18. Lenihan, *Limerick,* 416.

19. The phrase is in Lindfors, "The Afterlife," 299.

20. *Universal Songster,* 119. *Historical Account of Bartholomew Fair,* 29, shows a few lines of an earlier version of the song, which had no reference to the Hottentot Venus.

21. "Suffolk," Gazetteer of Markets and Fairs in England and Wales to 1516. http://www.british-history.ac.uk/report.asp?compid=40435&strquery=Bury%20 St%20Edmunds%20Fair (accessed 5 Jan. 2006). On the Bury Fair, see also *Suffolk Chronicle,* 28 Sept. 1812; "Norfolk Circuit," *Times of London,* online, 31 July 1835, col. D, 4.

22. Suffolk Record Office, Bury St. Edmunds, 1783/91: Printed notice— "Hottentot Venus at Mr. Crask's, Angel Hill, Bury St. Edmunds," n.d., but October 1812 is written in hand on the document.

23. Cited in Malcomson, *Popular Recreation,* 21.

24. We are grateful to Kerry Ward for this insight. A showing happened at Colchester, probably in the same year, as it is close to Bury. The Colchester and Bury pamphlets are very similar. See Jay, *Extraordinary Exhibitions,* 69.

25. Review of Percy Bysshe Shelley and Mary Shelley's *History*, quoted in Colbert, "Bibliography of British Travel Writing," 6.

26. "Relative Value of Sums of Money." http://privatewww.essex.ac.uk/~alan/family/N-Money.html. Still, in 1830 the entire voyage cost more than four pounds, nearly a half year's wages for a skilled craftsman.

27. See Herbert, *An Actual Survey and Itinerary of the Road from Calais to Paris.*

CHAPTER 6

PARIS, CITY OF LIGHT

1. On her arrival, see "Notice," *Manchester Mercury and Harrops General Advertiser*, 13 Sept. 1814; "Paris: Le Venus Hottentote," *Affiches, Annonces et Avis Divers ou Journal General de France* (hereafter *JGF*), 18 Sept. 1814, 15.

2. *JGF*, 22 Sept. 1814, 3.

3. Scully and Crais, "Race and Erasure."

4. For an examination of this history, see Fauvelle-Aymar and François-Xavier, *L'invention du Hottentot.*

5. The literature on women's rights and the French Revolution is vast. For an introduction, see Landes, *Women and the Public Sphere*; Scott, *Only Paradoxes to Offer.*

6. Quoted in Horne, *Seven Ages of Paris*, 184.

7. Rutland, *Journal of a Trip to Paris*, 17. On Napoleon and on Paris during these years, see Horne, *Seven Ages of Paris*, 196.

8. The following paragraphs describing the Palais-Royal are based on *Galignani's Picture of Paris* from 1818, which includes selected menus; Jerdan, *Six Weeks in Paris*, based on 1815 information; Rutland, *Journal of a Trip to Paris*; Fellowes, *Paris during the Interesting Month of July*; Mercier, *New Picture of Paris*; *Journal de Paris* (hereafter *JP*), 18 Sept. 1814; *Gazette de France*, 24 Oct. 1814; Stéphane, *Dictionnaire des nom de rues*. For a history of the palace, see Champier, *Le Palais Royal.*

9. *Galignani's Picture of Paris*, 184. "All that is holy is profaned, and man is at last compelled to face with sober senses his real condition of life and his relations with his kind." The quotation is from Karl Marx commenting on the nature of modernity under capitalism; *The Communist Manifesto*, 70. See also Benjamin, *Arcades Project.*

10. *Galignani's Picture of Paris.*

11. Henry Redhead Yorke, quoted in Sibalis, "Palais-Royal," 118.

12. *Galignani's Picture of Paris*, 187,

13. Fellowes, *Paris*, 16.

14. Quoted in Sibalis, "Palais-Royal," 118.

15. This paragraph is derived from Jennifer Heuer, who kindly shared her unpublished work "The One Drop Rule in Reverse?" Analysis of black experiences in France in this period is only beginning. For work on race in France, see Peabody,

There Are No Slaves in France; Aubert, "'The Blood of France'"; Peabody and Stovall, *Color of Liberty.*

16. *JP*, 18 Sept. 1814. See also *Gazette de France*, 24 Oct. 1814.

17. Badou, *L'enigme de la Venus Hottentote*, 101–2.

18. Quoted in Strother, "Display of the Body Hottentot," 33.

19. Ibid.

20. "La Venus Hottentote arrivee de Londres. L'affiche annonce qu'elle a des manieres tres engagentes. Come les idees de la beaute vareint suivent les climats, les amateurs ne doivent point s'attendre a' trouver dans la VH, les formes de la Venus de Medicis." *JP*, 22 Sept. 1814, 2.

21. Kirby provides information on the prints. Kirby, "More," 130.

22. *JGF*, 22 Sept. 1814, 3. Zoe Strother notes also that in Paris, Baartman was displayed as an ethnographic subject rather than within the traditions of the freak show. Strother, "Display of the Body Hottentot," 33.

23. See Racinet, *Le costume historique*, 40.

24. Badou, *L'enigme de la Venus Hottentote*, 11; *Galignani's Picture of Paris*, 586. On the play, see Sharpley-Whiting, *Black Venus*; McCormick, *Popular Theatres*, 14. Napoleon had reshaped the theatrical world of which Sara and renditions of her became a part. In the 1780s, street shows, puppet shows, and theaters filled the area around the Palais-Royal. In 1807 Napoleon issued a decree limiting the number of theaters to four official ones and four secondary theaters. Controlling the avenues for the expression of popular culture, Napoleon allowed the Gaite, the Ambique-Comique, the Varietes, and finally the Vaudeville to continue as sites for popular drama.

25. *La Quotidienne*, 24 Nov. 1814, 4; see also *Journal des Dames et des Modes*, 25 Nov. 1814, 65.

26. *Annales, Politiques, Morales et Literaires*, 3 Jan. 1816, 2; *Journal des Debats Politique et Literaires*, 21 Nov. 1814, 3–4.

27. An 1803 decree banned marriages between blacks and whites but allowed marriages between people considered mulatto and whites. For analysis of this decree and its implications, see Heuer, "The One Drop Rule in Reverse?"

28. Kirby, "Further Note."

29. *La Quotidienne*, 15 Jan. 1815, 3.

30. "La Venus Hottentote," *JGF*, 25 Jan. 1815.

31. Ibid. He ended his piece by imagining the fate of a French woman, a Parisian Venus, captured by "Arabs." Of all the many writings on Sara and the Hottentot Venus, this man alone joined Sara with the plight of other women taken by men, if men made awful to the French by being "Arab."

32. "La Venus Hottentote," *JGF*, 25 Jan. 1815; Badou, *L'enigme de la Venus Hottentote*, 120. As Badou has pointed out, the account of Sara's life here contradicts some of her statements in London; she details more voyages and does not talk of her mother's death or of her father's work as a cattle driver. Perhaps, as Badou suggests, Sara embellished her life for an audience. More likely, as Badou

also muses, the journalist sought to recast a hypothetical story of Sara's life to generate sympathy from his readership.

33. *JGF,* 4 Jan. 1815; 7 Jan. 1815.

34. On Cuvier, see Appel, *Cuvier-Geoffroy Debate;* Smith, *Georges Cuvier.* On Saint-Hilaire, see Hervé Le Guyader, *Étienne Geoffroy Saint-Hilaire: Visionary Naturalist.*

35. Appel, *Cuvier-Geoffroy Debate,* 36. For a contemporary description of the Jardin des Plantes, see also *Galignani's Picture of Paris,* 398–416; and Rousseau and Lemonnier, *Promenades au Jardin des Plantes.*

36. Strother, "Display of the Body Hottentote," 12.

37. Kirby, "Further Note," 165–66.

38. Cuvier, "Extrait," 259–74; Kirby, "Hottentot Venus," 60.

39. De Blainville, "Sur une Femme de la Race Hottentote," 185.

40. On this examination, see also Strother, "Display of the Body Hottentot"; Schiebinger, *Nature's Body.*

41. Fellowes, *Paris,* 15, 30–31.

42. "Paris: La Venus Hottentote," *La Quotidienne,* 11 Sept. 1815, 3–4.

43. Kirby, "Hottentot Venus," 60; *JGF,* 31 Dec. 1815.

44. See Parsons, "El Negro"; Davies, *Return of El Negro;* Qureshi, "Displaying"; Fausto-Sterling, "Gender, Race and Nation."

45. *Annales Politiques, Morales and Literaires,* 3 Jan. 1816.

46. Darwin, *Descent of Man.*

47. Cuvier, "Extrait." This was reprinted numerous times. See Chandler Smith, *Georges Cuvier,* 157, for details.

CHAPTER 7
GHOSTS OF SARA BAARTMAN

1. See below and Sharpe, *Habeas Corpus,* 222. See also Hunt, *Inventing Human Rights;* Sontag, *Regarding the Pain of Others.*

2. U.S. Supreme Court, *Rasul v. George W. Bush* (2004), 13.

3. U.S. District Court for the District of Columbia, *Hamdan v. Rumsfeld* (2006), 19. For other cases, see, for example, U.S. Supreme Court, *Hamdan v. Rumsfeld* (2005); United States Court of Appeals, *Boumediene et al. v. George W. Bush* (2007); and *Khalid v. George W. Bush* (2006).

4. See Darwin, *Narrative of the Surveying Voyages;* Darwin, *Descent of Man.* On the history of dissection, see MacDonald, *Human Remains.*

5. See, for example, Friedlander, *Origins of Nazi Genocide;* Muller-Hill, *Murderous Science.* See also Sòrgoni, " 'Defending the Race' "; Gewald, *Towards Redemption;* Wildenthal, *German Women for Empire.*

6. NaziLauck NSDAP/AO, http://www.nazi-lauck-nsdapao.com. See also the short article by Lindfors, "The Afterlife."

7. Literary references were obtained by data-mining www.freelibrary.com/literature.aspx.

8. Coetzee, *Dusklands*; Pynchon, *Mason and Dixon*.

9. Quoted in Gordon, "Natural Rhythm," 632. See also Corbin, *Filles de Noce*; Torgovnick, *Gone Primitive*; and especially Sharpley-Whiting, *Black Venus*.

10. The literature on Picasso is vast, but see, for example, Madeline and Martin, *Picassoand Africa*; Kleinfelder, *The Artist*; Glimcher and Glimcher, *Sketchbooks*; Clair, *Picasso*.

11. Gordon, "Natural Rhythm, 619.

12. Quoted in Stuart, *Showgirls*, 79. See also Gale and Stokes, *Cambridge Companion to the Actress*.

13. Lindfors, "The Afterlife," 299–300; Schiller, *Paul Broca*, 162. See also Schiebinger, *Nature's Body*. On race in France, see Peabody and Stovall, *Color of Liberty*.

14. Freud visited the Jardin des Plantes and was well informed of Cuvier's work. Freud, *Complete Psychological Works of Sigmund Freud*, vol. 3.

15. See especially Freud, *A Case of Hysteria*. For standard biographies of Freud, see Gay, *Freud*; Clark, *Freud*. Charcot was an avid art collector, as was Freud himself. Charcot and Richer, *Les Demoniaques*; Burke, *Sphinx on the Table*.

16. Gilman, *Difference and Pathology*; Showalter, *Female Malady*.

17. Queen, "Fat Bottomed Girls" (1978). Esther Jones kindly provided us with various popular culture references.

18. Campbell, "Myths about Female Black Sexuality."

19. Generations of anthropology and archaeology students had vague glimpses of the Hottentot Venus, largely through the writings of Cuvier and the history of modern comparative anatomy. Some even had viewed the plaster cast in the Museum of Man. They had no need to learn about Sara.

20. Alexander, "The Venus Hottentot."

21. Brantley, "Of an Erotic Freak Show," *New York Times*, 3 May 1996.

22. Young, "The Re-objectification and Re-commodification of Saartjie Baartman in Suzan-Lori Parks's 'Venus.'"

23. Maseko, *Life and Times of Sara Baartman*. In July 2000 the artist Willie Bester unveiled his sculpture *Sara Bartmann*.

24. The politics of history and identity is taken up brilliantly in Wicomb, *David's Story*. See also the controversies that swirled about the exhibition by Pippa Skotnes, "Miscast" discussed in Skotnes, *Miscast*. See also Samuelson, "Sarah Bartmann."

25. Material on the Griqua movement can be found at www.toekncoin.com.lefleur.htm.

26. We thank Mr. Upham for responding to our written questions.

27. Professor Tobias refused our request for an oral interview. Tobias recently published the first volume of his memoir, *Into the Past*.

28. French Senate, http://www.senat.fr/leg/ppl01–114.html.

29. Diana Ferrus has a Web site at http://dianaferrus.blogspot.com.

30. Department of Arts and Culture, "Project Proposal." The final report pointed out the request to repatriate the remains "was made within a post-1994 cultural/historic/democratic context, aimed at restoring, within the framework of nation building, the dignity and human rights of Saartjie Baartman and her people, while acknowledging the contributions made by the Khoi and San peoples to South Africa." Toward the end the report noted, "It is would [*sic*] be difficult to over-rate both the national and international importance to South Africa of this event." Department of Arts and Culture, "Final Report."

31. Department of Arts and Culture, "Minister's Briefing Document."

32. "Return of Hottentot Venus Unites Bushmen," http://news.bbc.co.uk/2/hi/africa/1971103.stm.

33. This material was located in the personal papers of Jeanette Deacon, who kindly shared her materials with us.

34. Tobias, "Saartje Baartman," 109.

35. This and other material is taken from Clifton Crais's interview with Abrahams.

36. We owe this point to Julie Livingstone.

37. Department of Arts and Culture, "Final Report."

38. The following is based on the SABC broadcast of the Baartman funeral.

39. "Trompie's Murder," *Port Elizabeth Herald,* 13 Nov. 2003.

EPILOGUE
FAMILY

1. Yunus, *Grandfather.*

2. (CA) 1/UIT 15/1: Jacob Cuyler to Truter, n.d. [1811]. See also (SOAS) LMS 2, 3 (D), Alberti, 21 Dec. 1803; see also 29 Dec. 1803 and 7 Jan. 1804 in same, for example, (CA) CSC 1/2/1/6: trial dated 28 Sept. 1830; (CA) J 405: tax rolls for Bethelsdorp and Theopolis, 1822; (CA) LG 588: list of occupants at Fullers Hoek, Dec. 1843.

3. Macmillan, *Cape Colour Question,* 161.

4. (CA) ACC 50: Report of a meeting held at Philipton. See also Elbourne, *Blood Ground.*

5. (CA) CO 4447: Documents accompanying the tabular view of the missions in South Africa belonging to the London Missionary Society.

6. (CA) CSC 1/2/1/6: plea of Ruiter Baartman, 28 Sept. 1830. See also labor contracts in (CA) 1/GR 15/43 and (CA) 1/GR 15/61–64.

7. (CA) 1/GR 2/84: *Queen v. Baartman,* 4 and 12 June 1866; *Graaff Reinet Herald,* 20 Oct. 1866.

8. For court cases concerning the Baartmans discussed in this chapter, see above and *Graaff Reinet Herald,* 20 Oct. 1866, 23 Jan. 1867, 26 Jan. 1867, 6 Feb. 1867, 9 Feb. 1867; (CA) 1/GR 2/85: records of proceedings, Baartman and Windvogel for murder, 18 Jan. 1867.

9. We are very grateful for conversations with Baartman clan members held in the Uitenhage and Graaff Reinet areas during the Cape winter, 2005.

SELECT BIBLIOGRAPHY

PRIMARY SOURCES

Unpublished Sources

ENGLAND

British Library, London (BL)
c. 103.k. Lysons, Daniel. "Collectanea; or a Collection of Advertisements and Paragraphs from the Newspapers, Relating to Various Subjects." Vol. 2. Scrapbook.
Chetham Library, Manchester
Record of Baptisms, 1812.
Hampshire Record Office (HRO)
DDGR 43/30/48, Herbert Family Correspondence.
Public Records Office, Kew (PRO)
Admiralty (ADM)
ADM 51/2284: Captains's Logs, 1810–15.
ADM 51/2751: Captain's Logs, 1810–15.
ADM 106/989: Navy Board Records, 1743.
ADM 37/1973: Ships' Musters, 1810.
ADM 1/1941: Correspondence and Papers, 1810.
King's Bench (KB)
KB 1/36/4 Records Regarding the Hottentot Venus, 21–28 Nov. 1810.
Royal College of Surgeons, London (RCS)
Company of Surgeons Examination Book with Index, 1745–1800.
School of Oriental and African Studies, London (SOAS)
London Missionary Society (LMS)
LMS 2, 3: 1803.
University College, London (UCL)
MS 797, I/5622, Booth Correspondence

SOUTH AFRICA

Cape Archives (CA), Cape Town
Accessions (ACC)
ACC 50 Report of a Meeting Held at Philipton, 1834.

Burgher Council (BRD)
5/1/7/3, 5/1/7/5, Burgher Roll . . . Free Blacks and Their Widows, 1799, 1802.

Cape Supreme Court (CSC)
CSC 1/2/1/6: Criminal Cases: Circuit Court. Records of Proceedings. Western and Eastern: 2nd Circuit, 1830.

Colonial Office (CO)
CO 22: Letters Received: Sundry Military Officials and Private Individuals, 1810.
CO 3871: Memorials Received, vol. 1, nos. 1–116, 1809.
CO 3875: Memorials Received, vol. 1, nos. 1–90, 1810.
CO 4447: Letters and Papers Received: On Specified Subjects: Sir R. S. Donkin's Collection of Missionary Complaints, 1820–27.

Council of Justice (CJ)
CJ 2624: Wills and Codicils, 1770.
CJ 2639: Wills and Codicils, 1785.
CJ 2838: Powers of Attorney in Respect of Salaries, 1784.
CJ 2912: Contracts, 1780–85.

Government House (GH)
GH 23/1: General Despatches, 1–46, 8 Mar. 1806–20 May 1808.

Lieutenant Governor (LG)
LG 588: Papers Concerning Allocation of Land at Fullershoek, Old School, and Blinkwater, Jan. 1844–Dec. 1854; Papers Relative to Erven in Katriver Settlement, Dec. 1844–Sept. 1859; Papers re: Arrear Claims for Land in Eastern Districts, Oct. 1847–Jan. 1848; Forests for Reference, ca. 1837; Mr. Southey's Claims for Land, May 1847–Oct. 1847; Rough Drafts of Land Reports of Various Districts, Jan. 1848.

Magistrate of Graaff Reinet (1/GR)
1/GR 15/43: Contracts of Service: Hottentots or Free Persons of Colour, 1786–1882.
1/GR 15/61: Contracts of Service: Hottentots or Free Persons of Colour, 1836–39.
1/GR 15/62: Contracts of Service: Hottentots or Free Persons of Colour, 1837.
1/GR 15/63: Contracts of Service: Hottentots or Free Persons of Colour, 1838–39.
1/GR 15/64: Contracts of Service: Hottentots or Free Persons of Colour, 1840–41.
1/GR 2/84: Records of Proceedings in Criminal Cases, Oct.–Dec. 1866.
1/GR 2/85: Records of Proceedings in Criminal Cases, Jan.–June 1867.

Magistrate of Stellenbosch (1/STB)
1/STB 18/198: Register of Wage and Indenture Contracts, Aug. 1828–Sept. 1840.

Magistrate of Swellendam (1/SWM)
1/SWM 3/10: Diverse and Criminal Records: Sworn Statements, Sept. 1746–Oct. 1758.
1/SWM 3/17: Sworn Statements, 1793–95.
1/SWM 12/67: Census Returns, 1793; 1818.

Magistrate of Uitenhage (1/UIT)
1/UIT 15/1: Letters Despatched by Landdrost, 1806–13.

Master's Office and Orphan Chamber (MOOC)
MOOC 6/2: Death Register, vol. 1, 1797–1803; vol. 2, 1804–21.
MOOC 7/1/42: Wills, 1798.

MOOC 7/1/44: Wills, 1799.
MOOC 7/1/61: Wills, 1811.
MOOC 7/1/81: Wills, 1820.
MOOC 13/1/23: L. & D. Accounts, 1800.

Microfilm (Z)

ZI 1/25 2431/12/1: Cape Papers: Correspondence, Reports and Legal Papers Concerning the Female Saartje's Departure to and Exhibition in England, 1810–11. Microfilm of records located in the Public Records Office of Northern Ireland, PRO, Northern Ireland.

Notarial Protocols, Western Cape Districts (NCD)

NCD 1/14/1167: Minutes of Powers of Attorney and Powers of Attorney re: Salaries and Deeds of Assumption and Substitution: Notary Johan Jacob Frederik Wägener, nos. 1120–1375, Jan. 1800–Dec. 1800.

Opgaafrolle [Tax Rolls] (J)

J 37: Cape Town, 1800.
J 39: Cape District, 1805.
J 41: Cape Town and Cape District, 1807.
J 46: Cape District, 1815.
J 48: Cape District, 1818.
J 109: Graaff Reinet, 1790 .
J 113: Graaff Reinet, 1796.
J 316: Swellendam, c. 1752.
J 317: Swellendam, 1762, 1765, c. 1788.
J 405: Uitenhage, 1822.
J 443: Cape District, c. 1752, 1797; Cape Town, 1800.

Receiver of Land Revenue (RLR)

RLR 17/1–17/2: Licences: Loan Farms, Feb.–Aug 1762.

Verbatim Copies (VC)

VC 882: Reports of Veldwagtmeesters re Stolen Cattle, Journals of Commandos against Robbers, Memorials Submitted to Landdrost, Extracts from Documents of Landdrost and Heemraden, Graaff Reinet, 1786–95.

VC 883: Proceedings of Landdrost and Heemraden and Records of the Military Court, Graaff Reinet, 1786–1836; Memorials and Letters of Veldwagtmeesters, Graaff Reinet, 1790–98; Correspondence between Government and Landdrost, Graaff Reinet and Commissioner of Enquiry, 1795–1830; Memorials of 267 Farmers, Bruynshoogte to Sluysken, 16 Apr. 1795; Resolutions, Proclamations, 1770–1788; Mss Notes of D Moodie re His Researches, n.d.

VC 884: Letters of Veldwagtmeesters and others to Landdrost of Graaff Reinet and Swellendam, Correspondence between Landdrost and Government, 1767–1809.

VC 885: Letter of J. van Riebeeck to the Lords XVII, May 1661; Letter of Commissioners of the Cape to the Heemraden at Graaff Reinet and Swellendam, Aug. 1795; Memo re Conditions at the Cape, 10 Sept. 1795; Letter to Col. Scott, Commander of the Troops on the Frontier, Apr. 1822; Report of the Protector of Slaves, c. 1807.

VC 886: Official documents of the Civil Commissioner Graaff Reinet re Relations between Government and the Bushman, Hottentots, Including Letters and Reports of Field Cornets and Records of Military Court, 1782–95.
VC 887: Moodie's Manuscript Notes, n.d.
VC 888: Official Documents of the Civil Commissioner, Graaff Reinet re Relations between Government and the Bushman Hottentots, Including Letters and Reports of the Field Cornets and Records of the Military Court, 1780–96.

Cory Library, Grahamstown
Methodist Missionary Society, Baptismal Records.

Dutch Reformed Church (DRC), Stellenbosch
1/1: Kerken-boek van de Caap de Goede Hoop.

Genealogical Institute of South Africa (GISA), Stellenbosch
Microfilm, Christian baptisms in the years 1788–91, 1793, 1796–98, 1800, and weddings, 1787.

Johannesburg Public Library
Kirby, Percival R. "The 'Hottentot Venus' of the Musée de l'Homme, Paris."

Oral Interviews

Yvette Abrahams, interview with the author, 10 May 2005.
Abel Baartman, interview with the author, 17 May 2005.
Hannie Baartman, interview with the author, 18 May 2005.
Jatti Bredekamp, interview with the author, 21 May 2005.
Jean Burgess, interview with the author, 19 May 2005.
Jeanette Deacon, interview with the author, 12 May 2005.
Rosie Esau, interview with the author, 25 May 2005.
Martin Hall, interview with the author, 11 May 2005.
Steven Robins, interview with the author, 24 May 2005.

Printed Sources

ENGLAND

The British Library (BL)
Playbills for theatrical productions, 1812–14.
Bristol Gazette and Public Advertiser, 1811–12.
General Advertiser or Limerick Gazette, 1812.
Ipswich Journal, 1811–12.
Manchester Mercury and Harrops General Advertiser, 1814.
Morning Chronicle (London), 1810–11.
Morning Herald (London), 1810–11.
Morning Post (London), 1810–14.
Suffolk Chronicle or Ipswitch Advertiser, 1812.

Suffolk Record Office
Bury St. Edmunds 1783/91 Printed notice, "Hottentot Venus at Mr. Crask's, Angel Hill, Bury St. Edmunds."

FRANCE

The Library of the City of Paris
Affiches, Annonces et Avis Divers ou Journal General de France (Paris), 1814–15.
Gazette de France, 1814–15.
Journal de Paris (Paris), 1814–15.
Journal des Debats Politique et Literaires (Paris), 1814.
La Quotidienne (Paris), 1814–15.

THE NETHERLANDS

Leiden University
Journal des Dames et des Modes (Paris), 25 Nov. 1814; 25 Jan. 1815.
Journal General de France, 1814–15.

SOUTH AFRICA

Cape Archives (CA), Cape Town
African Court Calendar for the Year 1812.
The National Library, Cape Town
Smith, A. B., and R. H. Pfeiffer, eds. *The Khoikhoi at the Cape of Good Hope: Seventeenth-Century Drawing in the South African Library.* Cape Town: South African Library, 1993.

General

ARTICLES, BOOKS, AND FILMS

Alexander, Elizabeth. *The Venus Hottentot.* Charlottesville: University Press of Virginia, 1990.
Alison, Archibald, Sir. *Travels in France during the Years 1814–15.* Vol. 1. Edinburgh: London: Black, Parry, and Co., 1816.
Allen, W. Gore. *King William IV.* London: Cresset Press, 1960.
Aspinall, A., ed. *The Correspondence of George, Prince of Wales 1770–1812.* Vol. 3. New York: Oxford University Press, 1970.
Barrow, Sir John. *An Account of Travels into the Interior of Southern Africa in the Years 1797 and 1798.* London: Printed by A. Strahan for T. Cadell Jun. and W. Davies, 1801–4.
Bleek, W. H. I., and L. Lloyd. *Specimens of Bushman Folklore.* London: G. Allen and Co., 1911.
Brantley, Ben. "Of an Erotic Freak Show and the Lesson Therein." *New York Times,* 3 May 1996.
Campbell, Bebe Moore. "Myths about Female Black Sexuality." *Essence,* Apr. 1989.
Chambers, R., ed. *The Book of Days: A Miscellany of Popular Antiquities in Connection with the Calendar Including Anecdote, Biography, and History, Curiosities of Literature and Oddities of Human life and Character.* Vol. 11. Edinburgh: W. & R. Chambers, 1864.

Chase-Riboud, Barbara. *Hottentot Venus.* New York: Doubleday, 2003.

Cook, James. *Cook's Voyages round the World, for Making Discoveries towards the North and South Poles. With an Appendix.* Manchester: Printed by Sowler and Russell, 1799.

Corry, John. *A Satirical View of London; Comprehending a Sketch of the Manners of the Age.* 2nd ed. London: J. Morton, 1803.

Cullinan, Patrick. "Robert Jacob Gordon and Denis Diderot: The Hague 1774." *Quarterly Bulletin of the South African Library* 43, no. 4 (June 1989): 146–52.

Cuvier, Georges. "Femme de race boschismanne" in Étienne Geoffroy Saint-Hilaire and Frédéric Cuvier, *Histoire naturelle des mammifères.*, 2 vols. Paris, 1824.

——. "Discourse sur les révolutions de la surface du globe." In *L'Angleterre avant les hommes le quinzième déluge discours sur les révolutions du globe mémoire sur la Vénus Hottentote,* edited by G. Cuvier, A. Esquiros, P. Ch. Joubert, and F. L. Passard. Reissue. Same as 4th edition of the Discourse, but without the section on the Venus Hottentote, 1–222. Paris: Passard, 1864.

——. "Extrait d'observations faites sur le cadavre d'une femme connue a Paris et à Londres sous le nom de Vénus Hottentote." *Mémoires (Paris), Muséum d'Histoire Naturelle* 3 (1817): 259–74.

——. "Rapport . . . sur le Mémoire de M. Duvernoy, sur l'Hymen." *Académie des Sciences. Procès verbaux, 1804–1807* 3 (1913): 244–45.

Dallas, Alexander. *The Pleasure Fair.* London, 1843.

Darwin, Charles. *The Descent of Man, and Selection in Relation to Sex.* New York: Modern Library, 1990.

——. *Narrative of the Surveying Voyages of His Majesty's Ships Adventure and Beagle.* London: H. Colburn, 1839.

De Blainville, Henri. "Sur une Femme de la Race Hottentote." *Bulletin des Sciences par la Société Philomatique de Paris* (1816), 183–90.

De Lambet, Théaulon. *The Hottentot Venus; or the Hatred of Frenchwomen.* Paris: Martinet, 1814.

Drew, Sir Robert. *Commissioned Officers in the British Army, 1660–1960.* Vol. 1. London: Wellcome Historical Medical Library, 1968.

East, Edward Hyde. "The Case of the Hottentot Venus." *Reports of Cases Argued and Determined in the Court of King's Bench.* Amended by Thomas Day. Vol. 13, 195–96 . . . Hartford, Conn.: Hudson and Goodwin, 1816.

Fellowes, W. D. *Paris: During the Interesting Month of July, 1815.* London: Gale and Fenner, 1815.

Ferrus, Diana. "A Poem for Sara Baartman." V gallery, 2007. *http://www.vgallery.co.za/2000article28/vzine.htm.*

Freud, Sigmund. *A Case of Hysteria: Three Essays on Sexuality and Other Works.* London: Hogarth Press and the Institute of Psycho-analysis, 1953.

——. *The Standard Edition of the Complete Psychological Works of Sigmund Freud.* Vol. 3. London: Hogarth Press and the Institute of Psycho-analysis, 1960.

Galignani's Picture of Paris: Being a Complete Guide to All the Public Buildings, Places of Amusement, and Curiosities in That Metropolis: and Containing a Full and Correct Description of the Environs. Paris: The Firm, 1818.

Gobineau, Arthur de. *The Inequality of the Human Races.* London: William Heinemann, 1915.

Griffith, Edward. "The Animal Kingdom." In *The Animal Kingdom Arranged in Conformity with Its Organization,* by Baron Georges Cuvier, Edward Griffith, Charles Hamilton Smith, Edward Pidgeon, John Edward Gray, and George Robert Gray. London: Geo. B. Whittaker, 1827.

Hare, Augustus J. C. *Walks in London.* New York: G. Routledge and Sons, 1878.

Herbert, L., and G. Dupont. *An Actual Survey and Itinerary of the Road from Calais to Paris.* London: Longman, Hurst, Rees, Orme and Brown, 1814.

Hindley, Charles. *Curiosities of Street Literature.* London, 1930.

An Historical Account of Bartholomew Fair. London: John Arliss, 1810.

Jerdan, William. *Six Weeks in Paris; or, A Cure for the Gallomania. By a Late Visitant.* Vol. 1. London: J. Johnston, 1817.

Kicherer, Johannes Jacobus. *An Extract From the Rev. Mr. Kicherer's Narrative of His Mission in South Africa Together with a Sketch of the Public Conference with the Hottentots.* Wiscasset, Maine: Babson and Rust, 1805.

Knox, Robert. *The Races of Man: A Fragment.* Philadelphia: Lea and Blanchard, 1850.

Knutsford, Margaret, Viscountess. *Life and Letters of Zachary Macaulay.* London: E. Arnold, 1900.

Kolb, Peter. *Naaukeurige en Uitvoerige Beschryving van Kaap Goede Hoop.* Amsterdam: B. Lakeman, 1727.

Kolbe, Pieter. *The Present State of the Cape of Good Hope, or a Particular Account of the Several Nations of the Hottentots with a Short Account of the Dutch Settlement at the Cape.* London, 1731.

Le Vaillant, François. *New Travels into the Interior Parts of Africa by Way of the Cape of Good Hope, in the Years 1783, 1784 and 1785.* 3 vols. London: G. G. and J. Robinson, 1796.

——. *Travels from the Cape of Good-Hope into the Interior Parts of Africa, Including Many Interesting Anecdotes.* 2 vols. London: W. Lane, 1790.

Lee, Mrs. R. *Memoirs of Baron Cuvier.* New York: J. & J. Harper, 1833.

Leibbrandt, H. C. V., ed. *Precis of the Archives of the Cape of Good Hope: Requesten or Memorials.* 5 vols. Cape Town: W. A. Richards and Sons, 1905.

Lenihan, Maurice. *Limerick; Its History and Antiquities, Ecclesiastical, Civil, and Military, from the Earliest Ages, with Copious Historical, Archeological, Topographical and Genealogical Notes.* Dublin: Hodges, Smith, 1866.

Lenta, Margaret, and Basil le Cordeur, eds. *The Cape Diaries of Lady Anne Barnard.* 2 vols. Cape Town: Van Riebeeck Society, 1999.

Lichtenstein, Henry. *Travels in Southern Africa.* Translated by Anne Plumptre. London: Henry Colburn, 1812.

A List of All the Officers of the Army and Royal Marines on Full and Half-Pay; with an Index; and a Succession of Colonels. London: War Office, 8 Feb. 1812.

Lyon, David. *The Sailing Navy List: All the Ships of the Royal Navy. Built, Purchased and Captured, 1688–1860.* London: Conway Maritime Press, 1993.

Macaulay, Thomas Babington. *The History of England from the Accession of James II.* 5 vols. New York: Harper, 1849–61.

Macdonald, R. *A Peep at Bartholomew's Fair.* London, 1837.

Marshall, Julian, ed. *The Life and Letters of Mary Wollestonecraft Shelley.* New York: Haskell House, 1970.

Marx, Karl. *The Communist Manifesto.* New York: Penguin Classics, 2002.

Mathews, Mrs. Charles. *Memoirs of Charles Mathews.* London: R. Bentley, 1839.

Mentzel, O. F. *A Geographical and Topographical Description of the Cape of Good Hope.* 3 vols. Cape Town: Van Riebeeck Society, 1944.

———. *Life at the Cape in the Mid–Eighteenth Century.* Cape Town: Van Riebeeck Society, 1919.

Mercier, Louis-Sébastien. *New Picture of Paris.* London: Printed by C. Whittingham, for H. D. Symonds, 1800.

Molsbergen, E. C. Godee. *Reizen in Zuid-Afrika in de Hollandse Tijd.* Vol. 3. Gravenhage: Martinus Nijhoff, 1922.

Moodie, Donald. *The Record.* Cape Town: A. A. Balkema, 1960.

Morley, Henry. *Memoirs of Bartholomew's Fair.* London: Frederick Warne and Co., 1859.

Oldfield, T. H. B. *An Entire and Complete History, Political and Personal, of the Boroughs of Great Britain; To Which Is Prefixed, an Original Sketch of Constitutional Rights.* London: Printed for G. Riley et al., 1792.

Owen, William. *An Authentic Account of All Fairs in England and Wales.* London: W. Owen, 1756.

Parks, Suzan Lori. *Venus: A Play.* New York: Theatre Communications Group, 1997.

Ploss, Hermann Heinrich, Max Bartels, and Paul Bartels. *Woman: An Historical Gynaecological and Anthropological Compendium* (1885). Edited by Eric John Dingwall. London: William Heinemann, 1935.

Racinet, M. A. "Afrique: Familles Austro-Africaines-Hottentots, Cafres et Betchouanas." In *Le costume historique,* edited by M. A. Racinet. Vol. 2. Paris: Librairie de Firmin-Didot et Cie, 1888.

———. "Afrique: Hottentot, Cafres et Betchouanas." In *Le costume historique,* edited by A. Racinet. Vol. 1, 139–40 . . . Paris: Librairie de Firmin-Didot et Cie, 1888.

Robinson, A. M. Lewin, ed. *The Letters of Lady Anne Barnard to Henry Dundas.* Cape Town: A. A. Balkema, 1973.

Rousseau, L., and C. Lemonnier. *Promenades au Jardin des Plantes: Comprenant la Description 1 de la Menagerie, 2 du Cabinet d'Anatomie Comparée; 3 des Galeries de Zoologie, de Botanique, de Minéralogie et de Géologie; 4 de l'École de Botanique; 5 des Serres et du Jardin de Naturalisation et des Semis; 6 de la Bibliothèque, etc.* Paris: Chez J. B. Baillière et al., 1837.

Rutland, Duke and Duchess. *Journal of a Trip to Paris.* London: T. Bensley, 1814.

Schapera, Isaac. *The Early Cape Hottentots Described in the Writings of Olfert Dapper (1668), Willem Ten Rhyene (1686) and Johannes Grevenbroek (1695).* Cape Town: Van Riebeeck Society, 1933.

Schutte, H. J., ed. *Briefwisseling van Hendrik Swellengrebel Jr. Oor Kaapse Sake, 1778–1792.* Cape Town: Van Riebeeck-Vereniging, 1982.

Sparrman, Anders. *A Voyage to the Cape of Good Hope from the Year 1772–1776.* 2 vols. Edited by V. S. Forbes. Cape Town: Van Riebeeck Society, 1975–77.

Steedman, Andrew. *Wanderings and Adventures in the Interior of Southern Africa.* 2 vols. Cape Town: C. Struik, 1966.

Thunberg, Carl Peter. *Travels at the Cape of Good Hope 1772–1775.* Cape Town: Van Riebeeck Society, 1986.

Tobias, Philip V. "Physical Anthropology and the Somatic Origins of the Hottentots." *African Studies* 14, no. 1 (1955): 1–15.

Unknown. "The Humours of Bartlemy Fair." In *The Universal Songster, Or Museum of Mirth*, by George Cruikshank and Robert Cruikshank, 118–19. London: Printed for John Fairburn et al., 1825.

Unknown. *The Pleasure Fair.* London: J. Nisbet and Co., 1843.

Wedderburn, Robert. *Horrors of Slavery and Other Writings.* Edited by Ian McCalman. New York: Marcus Weiner, 1991.

William, Axon. E. A. *The Annals of Manchester: A Chronological Record from Earliest Times to the End of 1885.* Manchester: London: J. Heywood, Deansgate and Ridgefield, 1886.

MICROFILM

Graaff Reinet Herald (Graaff Reinet, South Africa), 1853–70, MF 311.

Liverpool Mercury, or Commercial, Literary and Political Herald (Liverpool), 1813–14, MF 7477.

La Quotidienne (Paris), MF 7981, reel 1.

ONLINE

The Bodleian Library Broadside Ballads. http://www.bodley.ox.ac.uk/ballads/ballads.htm.

British Library. http://www.imagesonline.bl.uk/britishlibrary.

FamilySearch.org. The Church of Jesus Christ of Latter-Day Saints. http://www.familysearch.org.

Ferrus, Diana. "Diana Ferrus, Poetry, Art & Literature." *Blog.* http://dianaferrus.blogspot.com.

www.freelibrary.com/literature.aspx (discontinued).

French Senate. Session Ordinaire de 2001–2. Annexe au procès-verbal de la séance du 4 décembre 2001, Proposition de Loi. "Autorisant la restitution par la France de la dépouille mortelle de Saartjie Baartman, dite 'Vénus hottentote,' à l'Afrique du Sud." http://www.senat.fr/leg/pp101–114.html.

"The Modern Griquas' Story." www.tokencoin.com.lefleur.htm.

"Piccadilly, South Side." *Survey of London.* Vols. 29 and 30, *St James Westminster*, pt. 1 (1960), 251–70. http://www.british-history.ac.uk/report.asp?compid=40571.

"Return of Hottentot Venus Unites Bushmen." *BBC News*, 6 May 2002. http://news.bbc.co.uk/2/hi/africa/1971103.stm.

Times of London, 1810–16, 1835. *http://www.timesonline.co.uk.*

"Trompie's Murder: Stepmum Refused Bail." *Port Elizabeth Herald*, 13 Nov. 2003. http://www.theherald.co.za/herald/2003/11/13/news/n41_13112003.htm.

PAPERS IN AUTHORS' POSSESSION

Department of Arts and Culture. "Project Proposal: Return and Internment of the Remains of Ms Saartjie Baartman." N.d. Copy in author's possession.

———. "Final Report." N.d. Copy in author's possession.

Papers relating to Sara Baartman. Originals held by Dr. Jeanette Deacon.

———. "Final Report on the Repatriation of the Remains of Saartjie Baartman from France to South Africa." N.d. Copy in author's possession.

———. "Minister's Briefing Document: Return and Internment of Saartjie Baartman's Remains." N.d. Copy in author's possession.

U.S. GOVERNMENT CASES

Boumediene et al. v. George W. Bush (2007). U.S. Court of Appeals, No. 05–5062.

Hamdan v. Rumsfeld (2005). U.S. Supreme Court, No. 04–702.

Hamdan v. Rumsfeld (2006). U.S. District Court for the District of Columbia, No. 04–1519.

Hamdan v. Rumsfeld (2006). U.S. Supreme Court, No. 05–184.

Khalid v. George W. Bush (2006). U.S. Court of Appeals, No. 05–5063.

Rasul v. George W. Bush (2004). U.S. Supreme Court, Nos. 03–334 and 03–335.

SECONDARY SOURCES

Abrahams, Yvette. "Colonialism and Disjuncture: The Historiography of Sarah Bartmann." Ph.D. diss., University of Cape Town, 2000.

———. "Disempowered to Consent: Sara Bartman and Khoisan Slavery in the Nineteenth-Century Cape Colony and Britain." *South African Historical Journal* 35 (1996): 89–114.

———. "Images of Sara Bartman: Sexuality, Race, and Gender in Early-Nineteenth-Century Britain." In *Nation, Empire, Colony: Historicizing Gender and Race*, edited by Ruth Roach Pierson and Nupur Chaudhuri, 220–36. Bloomington: Indiana University Press, 1998.

Agosin, Marjorie. *Women, Gender and Human Rights: A Global Perspective.* New Brunswick, N.J.: Rutgers University Press, 2001.

Alexander, Elizabeth. "The Venus Hottentot (1825)." *Callaloo* 39 (Spring 1989): 688–91.

Alexander, Sally. *St Giles's Fair, 1830–1914: Popular Culture and the Industrial Revolution in 19th Century Oxford.* Oxford: History Workshop, 1970.

Alpern, Sara. *The Challenge of Feminist Biography.* Urbana: University of Illinois Press, 1992.

Altick, Richard D. *The Shows of London.* Cambridge, Mass.: Harvard University Press, 1978.

Anon. "Crown Jewel for Bury St. Edmunds." *British Heritage* 27, no. 1 (Mar. 2006): 12. http://proquest.umi.com/pdlink?did=94343306 (accessed 6 Jan. 2006).

———. *An Historical Account of Bartholomew Fair.* London: John Arliss, 1810.

———. *A Peep at Bartholomew Fair.* London: R. Macdonald, 1837.

Appel, Toby A. *The Cuvier-Geoffroy Debate: French Biology in the Decades before Darwin.* Edited by Richard Burian and Richard Burkhardt Jr. New York: Oxford University Press, 1987.

Armitage, David, and Michael Braddick. *The British Atlantic World, 1500–1800.* Houndmills: Palgrave, 2002.

Aubert, Guillaum. " 'The Blood of France': Race and Purity of Blood in the French Atlantic World." *William and Mary Quarterly* 61, no. 3 (2004): 439–78.

Badou. Gérard. *L'énigme de la Vénus Hottentote.* Paris: Petite Bibliotheque Payot, 2002.

Bailyn, Bernard, and Philip Morgan. *Strangers within the Realm: Cultural Margins of the First British Empire.* Chapel Hill: University of North Carolina Press, 1991.

Barnard, Alan. *Hunters and Herders of Southern Africa: A Comparative Ethnography of the Khoisan Peoples.* New York: Cambridge University Press, 1992.

Bassani, E., and L. Tedeschi. "The Image of the Hottentot in the 17th and 18th Century. An Iconographic Investigation." *Journal of the History of Collections* 2 (1990): 157–86.

Benjamin, Walter. *The Arcades Project.* Translated by Howard Eiland and Kevin McLaughlin. Cambridge, Mass.: Belknap Press of Harvard University Press, 1999.

Bennun, Neil. *The Broken String: The Last Worlds of an Extinct People.* New York: Viking, 2004.

Block, Sharon, and Kathleen M. Brown. "Clio in Search of Eros: Redefining Sexualities in Early America." Special issue of *William and Mary Quarterly* 60, no. 1 (Jan. 2003).

Boeseken, A. J. *Slaves and Free Blacks at the Cape: 1658–1700.* Cape Town: Tafelberg, 1977.

Bogdan, Robert. *Freak Show: Presenting Human Oddities for Amusement and Profit.* Chicago: University of Chicago Press, 1988.

———. "The Social Construction of Freaks." In *Freakery,* edited by Rosemarie Garland-Thomson, 23–37. New York: New York University Press, 1996.

Booth, Charles. *Zachary Macaulay: An Appreciation by Charles Booth.* London: Longmans, Green and Co., 1934.

Brantlinger, Patrick. *Dark Vanishings: Discourse on the Extinction of Primitive Races, 1800–1903.* Ithaca, N.Y.: Cornell University Press, 2003.

Brown, Christopher Leslie. *Moral Capital: Foundations of British Abolitionism.* Chapel Hill: Published for the Omohundro Institute of Early American History and Culture, Williamsburg Virginia, by the University of North Carolina Press, 2006.

Brown, Elsa Barkley. " 'What Has Happened Here': The Politics of Women's History and Feminist Politics." In *"We Specialize in the Wholly Impossible": A Reader in Black Women's History,* edited by Darlene Clark Hine and Wilma King, 39–56. Brooklyn, N.Y.: Carlson, 1995.

Burke, Janine. *The Sphinx on the Table: Sigmund Freud's Art Collection and the Development of Psychoanalysis.* New York: Walker and Company, 2006.

Butler, Judith. "Performative Acts and Gender Constitution: An Essay in Phenomenology and Feminist Theory." *Theatre Journal* 40, no. 4 (Dec. 1988): 519–31.

Cavendish, Richard. "London's Last Bartholomew Fair." *History Today* 55 (Sept. 2005): 52.

Champier, Victor. *Le Palais Royal: D'apres des documents inedits (1629–1900)*. Paris: H. Veyrier, 1991.

Chancellor, E. Beresford. *Life in Regency and Early Victorian Times: An Account of the Days of Brummell and D'Orsay 1800 to 1850*. London: B. T. Batsford, 1933.

Charcot, J. M., and Paul Richer. *Les Demoniaques dans l'Art*. Paris: Macula, 1984.

Clair, Jean, ed. *Picasso: Erotique*. New York: Prestel, 2001.

Clark, Ronald W. *Freud: The Man and the Cause*. New York: Random House, 1980.

Clayton, Timothy. *The English Print 1688–1802*. New Haven, Conn.: Yale University Press, 1997.

Coetzee, J. M. *Dusklands*. Johannesburg: Ravan Press, 1974.

Colbert, Benjamin. "Bibliography of British Travel Writing, 1789–1840: The European Tour, 1814–1818 (Excluding Britain and Ireland)." *Cardiff Corvey: Reading the Romantic Text* 13 (Winter 2004): 5–44.

Comaroff, John, and Jean Comaroff. *Of Revelation and Revolution: Christianity, Colonialism, and Consciousness in South Africa*. Chicago: University of Chicago Press, 1991.

Cooley, Thomas. *The Ivory Leg in the Ebony Cabinet: Madness, Race, and Gender in Victorian America*. Amherst: University of Massachusetts Press, 2001.

Corbin, Alain. *Les Filles de Noce: Misère Sexuelle et Prostitution: 19e et 20e Siècles*. Paris: Aubier Montaigne, 1978.

Crais, Clifton. "Heterographies: Writing the Self after the Linguistic Turn." Distinguished History Lecture delivered at Southwestern University, Georgetown, Texas, 26 Oct., 2006.

Davies, Andrew. *The Map of London: From 1746 to the Present Day*. London: B. T. Batsford, 1987.

Davies, Caitlin. *The Return of El Negro: The Compelling Story of Africa's Unknown Soldier*. London: Penguin, Viking, 2003.

Dictionary of South African Biography. 3 vols. Pretoria: Human Sciences Research Council, 1968–87.

Donald, Diana. *Age of Caricature: Satirical Prints in the Reign of George III*. New Haven, Conn.: Yale University Press, 1996.

Dresser, Madge. *Slavery Obscured: The Social History of the Slave Trade in an English Provincial Port*. London: Continuum, 2001.

Duffield, Ian. "Skilled Workers or Marginalized Poor? The African Population of the United Kingdom, 1812–1815." In *Africans in Britain*, edited by David Killingray, 49–87. Ilford, Essex: Frank Cass and Company, 1994.

Durbach, Nadja. "Exhibiting the Cannibal King: Irishmen and Africans in the Victorian Freakshow." Paper presented at panel "Spectacular Men," North American Conference on British Studies, Denver, Colorado, Oct. 2005.

Edwards, Paul. "Unreconciled Strivings and Ironic Strategies: Three Afro-British Authors of the Late Georgian Period (Sancho, Equiano, Wedderburn)." In *Africans in Britain*, edited by David Killingray, 28–48. Portland, Ore.: Frank Cass and Company, 1994.

Edwards, Paul, and James Walvin. *Black Personalities in the Era of the Slave Trade.* Baton Rouge: Louisiana State University Press, 1983.

Elbourne, Elizabeth. *Blood Ground: Colonialism, Missions, and the Contest for Christianity in the Cape Colony and Britain, 1799–1853.* Montreal: McGill University Press, 2002.

———. "The Savage and the Saved: Early Nineteenth-Century Khoikhoi Visitors to London and the Ambiguities of Colonialism." Unpublished paper.

Elphick, Richard. *Khoikhoi and the Founding of White South Africa.* Johannesburg: Ravan Press, 1985.

Elphick, Richard, and Hermann Giliomee, eds. *The Shaping of South African Society, 1652–1840.* Middletown, Conn.: Wesleyan University Press, 1988.

Ermath, Elizabeth. "Agency in the Discursive Condition." In *Practicing History: New Directions in Historical Writing after the Linguistic Turn,* edited by Gabrielle Spiegel. New York: Routledge, 2005.

Fabian, Johannes. *Time and the Other: How Anthropology Makes Its Object.* New York: Columbia University Press, 1983.

Fausto-Sterling, Anne. "Gender, Race, and Nation: The Comparative Anatomy of Hottentot Women in Europe, 1815–1817." In *Deviant Bodies: Critical Perspectives of Difference in Science and Popular Culture,* edited by Jennifer Terry and Jacqueline Urla, 19–48. Bloomington: Indiana University Press, 1995.

Fauvelle-Aymar, François-Xavier. *L'Invention du Hottentot: Histoire du Regard Occidental sur les Khoisan, XVe–XIXe Siècle.* Paris: Publications de la Sorbonne, 2002.

Fiedler, Leslie. *Freaks: Myths and Images of the Secret Self.* New York: Simon and Schuster, 1978.

François le Vaillant, Traveller in South Africa, and His Collection of 165 Water-colour Paintings, 1781–1784. Edited by A. M. Lewin Robinson. Cape Town: Library of Parliament, 1973.

Friedlander, Henry. *The Origins of Nazi Genocide: From Euthanasia to the Final Solution.* Chapel Hill: University of North Carolina Press, 1997.

Fryer, Peter. *Staying Power: The History of Black People in Britain.* London: Pluto Press, 1984.

Gale, Maggie B., and John Stokes. *The Cambridge Companion to the Actress.* Cambridge: Cambridge University Press, 2007.

Garland-Thomson, Rosemarie, ed. *Extraordinary Bodies: Figuring Disability in American Culture and Literature.* New York: Columbia University Press, 1996.

———. *Freakery.* New York: New York University Press, 1996.

———. *Staring: How We Look.* New York: Oxford University Press, forthcoming.

Gay, Peter. *Freud: A Life for Our Time.* New York: Norton, 1988.

George, Dorothy. *Catalogue of Political and Personal Satires in the Department of Prints and Drawings in the British Museum.* Vol. 9. London: British Museum, 1978.

Gerzina, Gretchen. *Black London: Life before Emancipation.* New Brunswick, N.J.: Rutgers University Press, 1995.

Gewald, Jan Bart. *Towards Redemption: A Socio-political History of the Herero of Namibia between 1890 and 1923.* Leiden: Research School CNWS, School of Asian, African, and Amerindian Studies, 1996.

Gilman, Sander. "Black Bodies, White Bodies: Toward an Iconography of Female Sexuality in Late Nineteenth Century Art, Medicine, and Literature." *Critical Inquiry* 12, no. 1 (1985): 204–42.

———. *Difference and Pathology: Stereotypes of Sexuality, Race and Madness.* Ithaca, N.Y.: Cornell University Press, 1985.

Gilroy, Paul. *The Black Atlantic: Modernity and Double Consciousness.* Cambridge, Mass.: Harvard University Press, 1993.

Glimcher, Arnold, and March Glimcher, eds. *Je Suis le Cahier: The Sketchbooks of Picasso.* Boston: Atlantic Monthly Press, 1986.

Gordon, Rae-Beth. "Natural Rhythm: La Parisienne Dances with Darwin: 1875–1910." *Modernism/Modernity* 10, no. 4 (2003): 617–56.

Gordon, Robert. "The Venal Hottentot Venus and the Great Chain of Being." *African Affairs* 15, no. 1 (1992): 185–202.

Gould, Stephen Jay. *The Flamingo's Smile: Reflections in Natural History.* New York: Norton, 1985.

———. *The Mismeasure of Man.* New York: Norton, 1996.

Grant, Joan. "William Brown and Other Women: Black Women in London c. 1740–1840." *Women, Migration, Empire,* edited by Joan Grant, 51–72. Stoke-on-Trent: Trentham Books, 1996.

Guy-Sheftall, Beverly. "The Body Politic: Black Female Sexuality and the Nineteenth-Century Euro-American Imagination." In *Skin Deep, Spirit Strong,* edited by Kimberly Wallace-Sanders, 13–35. Ann Arbor: University of Michigan Press, 2002.

Haacke, Wilfrid H. G., and Elphas Eiseb. *Khoekhoegowab Dictionary.* Windhoek, Namibia: Gamsberg MacMillan, 2002.

Heese, H. F. *Groep Sonder Grense: Die Rol en Status van die Gemengde Bevolking aan die Kaap, 1652–1795.* Bellville: Wes-Kaaplandse Instituut vir Historiese Navorsing, Universiteit van Wes-Kaapland, 1984.

———. "Die Inwoners van Kaapstad in 1800." *Kronos* 7 (1983): 42–61.

Henderson, Tony. *Disorderly Women in Eighteenth-Century London: Prostitution and Control in the Metropolis 1730–1830.* London: Longman, 1999.

Herzog, Don. *Happy Slaves: A Critique of Consent Theory.* Chicago: University of Chicago Press, 1989.

Heuer, Jennifer. "The One Drop Rule in Reverse? Interracial Marriages in Napoleonic and Restoration France." Unpublished paper.

Hevey, David. *The Creatures That Time Forgot: Photography and Disability Imagery.* London: Routledge, 1992.

Hine, Darlene Clark, and Jacqueline Macleod. *Crossing Boundaries: Comparative History of Black People in Diaspora.* Bloomington: Indiana University Press, 1999.

Hobson, Janell. *Venus in the Dark: Blackness and Beauty in Popular Culture.* New York: Routledge, 2005.

Holmes, Colin. *John Bull's Island: Immigration and British Society, 1871–1971.* London: Macmillan, 1988.

Holmes, Rachel. *African Queen: The Real Story of the Hottentot Venus.* New York: Random House, 2007.

Horne, Alistair. *Seven Ages of Paris.* New York: Knopf, 2002.

Hunt, Lynn. *Inventing Human Rights: A History.* New York: Norton, 2007.

ibn LoBagola, Bata Kindai Amgoza. *An African Savage's Own Story.* New York: Knopf, 1930.

Israel, Kali. *Names and Stories: Emilia Dilke and Victorian Culture.* New York: Oxford University Press, 1999.

Jarry, Paul. *Le Quartier du Palais-Royal.* Paris: F. Contet, 1926.

Jay, Ricky. *Extraordinary Exhibitions: The Wonderful Remains of an Enormous Head, the Whimsiphusicon, & Death to the Savage Unitarians.* New York: Quantuck Lane Press, 2005.

Jonker, Julian. "Excavating the Legal Subject: The Un-named Dead of Prestwich Place, Cape Town." *Griffith Law Review* 14, no. 2 (2006): 187–212.

Jordan, Elizabeth. " 'Unrelenting Toil: Expanding Archeological Interpretations of Female Slave Experience." *Slavery and Abolition* 26, no. 2 (Aug. 2005): 217–32.

Kerseboom, Simone. " 'Burying Sara Baartman': Commemoration, Memory and the Ethics of Heritage." Paper presented at the South African Historical Society Conference, University of Johannesburg, 26 June 2007.

Killingray, David. "Africans in the United Kingdom: An Introduction." In *Africans in Britain,* edited by David Killingray, 2–27. Portland, Ore.: Frank Cass and Company, 1994.

Kirby, Percival R. "A Further Note on the Hottentot Venus." *Africana Notes and News* 11, no. 5 (Dec. 1954): 165–66.

———. "The Hottentot Venus." *Africana Notes and News* 6, no. 3 (June 1949): 55–61.

———. "The 'Hottentot Venus' of the Musee de L'Homme, Paris." *South African Journal of Science* 50, no. 12 (July 1954): 319–22.

———. "More about the Hottentot Venus." *Africana Notes and News* 10, no. 4 (Sept. 1953): 124–33.

———. "La Venus Hottentote en Angleterre." *Aesculape* 33, no. 1 (Jan. 1952): 14–21.

Kleinfelder, Karen L. *The Artist, His Model, Her Image, His Gaze: Picasso's Pursuit of the Model.* Chicago: University of Chicago Press, 1993.

Kushner, Tony. "Selling Racism: History, Heritage, Gender and the (Re)production of Prejudice." *Patterns of Prejudice* 33, no. 4 (Oct. 1999): 67–86.

Laidler, P. W. *The Annals of the Cape Stage.* Edinburgh: William Bryce, 1926.

Lambert, Susan. *The Image Multiplied: Five Centuries of Printed Reproductions of Paintings and Drawings.* New York: Arabis Books, 1987.

Land, Isaac. "Bread and Arsenic: Citizenship from the Bottom Up in Georgian London." *Journal of Social History* 39, no. 1 (Sept. 2005): 89–110.

Landes, Joan. *Women and the Public Sphere in the Age of the French Revolution.* Ithaca, N.Y.: Cornell University Press, 1988.

Laqueur, Thomas. *The Making of the Modern Body.* Berkeley: University of California Press, 1987.

———. *Making Sex.* Cambridge, Mass.: Harvard University Press, 1990.

Le Guyader, Hervé. "Visionary Naturalist." In *Étienne Geoffroy Saint-Hilaire 1772–1844: A Visionary Naturalist,* by Hervé Le Guyader, translated by Marjorie Grene, 302. Chicago: University of Chicago Press, 2004.

Lightfoot, Cynthia. "Fantastic Self: A Study of Adolescents' Fictional Narratives, and Aesthetic Activity as Identity Work." In *Narrative Analysis: Studying the Development of Individuals in Society,* edited by Colette Daiute and Cynthia Lightfoot, 21–37. Thousand Oaks, Calif.: Sage, 2004.

Lindfors, Bernth, ed. *Africans on Stage: Studies in Ethnological Showbusiness.* Bloomington: Indiana University Press, 1999.

———. "The Afterlife of the Hottentot Venus." *Neohelicon* 18, no. 2 (1989): 293–301.

———. "The Bottom Line: African Caricature in Georgian England." *World Literature Written in English* 24, no. 1 (1984): 43–51.

———. "Courting the Hottentot Venus." *Africa* (Rome), 40 (1985): 133–48.

———. "Ethnological Show Business: Footlighting the Dark Continent." In *Freakery,* edited by Rosemarie Garland-Thomson, 207–33. New York: New York University Press, 1996.

———. "Hottentot, Bushmen, Kaffir: Taxonomic Tendencies in Nineteenth-Century Racial Iconography." *Nordic Journal of African Studies* 5, no. 2 (1996): 1–28.

Linebaugh, Peter, and Marcus Rediker. *The Many-Headed Hydra: Sailors, Slaves, Commoners and the Hidden History of the Revolutionary Atlantic.* Boston: Beacon Press, 2000.

Little, Kenneth. *Negroes in Britain.* London: K. Paul, Trench, Trubner, 1948.

Lorde, Audre. " 'The Master's Tools Will Never Dismantle the Master's House.' " In *Feminist Postcolonial Theory,* edited by Reina Lewis and Sara Mills, 25–28. New York: Routledge, 2003.

Lorimer, Douglas. "Black Slaves and English Liberty: A Re-examination of Racial Slavery in England." *Immigrants and Minorities* 3 (1984): 121–50.

———. *Colour, Class and the Victorians: English Attitudes to the Negro in the Mid-nineteenth Century.* New York: Holmes and Meier, 1978.

Low, Chris. "Khoisan Wind: Hunting and Healing." *Journal of the Royal Anthropological Institute* 13, no. 1 (April 2007): 71–90.

Macdonald, Helen. *Human Remains.* New Haven, Conn.: Yale University Press, 2005.

Macmillan, William M. *The Cape Colour Question.* London: Faber and Gwyer, 1927.

Madeline, Laurence, and Marilyn Martin, eds. *Picasso and Africa.* Cape Town: Bell Roberts Publishing, 2006.

Magubane, Zine. "Which Bodies Matter? Feminist Post-structuralism, Race, and the Curious Theoretical Odyssey of the Hottentot Venus." *Gender and Society* 15, no. 6 (Dec. 2001): 816–34.

Malcomson, Robert W. *Popular Recreation in English Society 1700–1850.* Cambridge: Cambridge University Press, 1973.

Malherbe, Vertrees. "Illegitimacy and Family Formation in Colonial Cape Town." *Journal of Social History* 39, no. 4 (Summer 2006): 1153–76.

Margetson, Stella. *Regency London*. New York: Praeger, 1971.

Maseko, Zola. Director. *The Life and Times of Sara Baartman*. New York: First Run/Icarus Films, 1998.

———. *The Return of Sara Baartman*. New York: First Run/Icarus Films, 2003.

McCormick, John. *Popular Theatres of Nineteenth Century France*. London: Routledge, 1993.

McCreery, Cindy. *The Satirical Gaze: Prints of Women in Late Eighteenth-Century England*. Oxford: Clarendon Press, 2004.

Metzinger, Thomas. *Being No One: The Self-Model Theory of Subjectivity*. Cambridge, Mass.: MIT Press, 2003.

Moon, Michael, and Cathy N. Davidson. *Subjects and Citizens: Nation, Race and Gender from Oroonoko to Anita Hill*. Durham, N.C.: Duke University Press, 1995.

Moore, Doris Langley. *Gallery of Fashion 1790–1822*. London: B. T. Batsford, 1949.

Morgan, Jennifer L. " 'Some Could Suckle over Their Shoulder': Male Travelers, Female Bodies, and the Gendering of Racial Ideology, 1500–1770." *William and Mary Quarterly* 54, no. 1 (Jan. 1997): 167–92.

Mort, Frank, and Miles Ogborn. "Transforming Metropolitan London, 1750–1960." *Journal of British Studies* 43 (Jan. 2003): 1–14.

Muller-Hill, Benno. *Murderous Science: Elimination by Scientific Selection of Jews, Gypsies, and Others, Germany: 1933–1945*. Translated by George R. Fraser. Oxford: Oxford University Press, 1988.

Myers, Norma. "The Black Presence through Criminal Records." *Immigrants and Minorities* 7, no. 3 (1988): 292–307.

———. *Reconstructing the Black Past: Blacks in Britain 1780–1830*. London: Frank Cass and Co., 1996.

Netto, Priscilla. "Reclaiming the Body of the 'Hottentot': The Vision and Visuality of the Body Speaking with Vengeance in Venus Hottentot 2000." *European Journal of Women's Studies* 12, no. 2 (2005): 149–63.

Newton-King, Susan. *Masters and Servants on the Cape Eastern Frontier, 1760–1803*. Cambridge: Cambridge University Press, 1999.

Ogborn, Miles. *Spaces of Modernity: London's Geographies, 1670–1780*. New York: Guilford, 1998.

Outram, Dorinda. *Georges Cuvier: Vocation, Science, and Authority in Post-revolutionary France*. Manchester: Manchester University Press, 1984.

———. *The Letters of Georges Cuvier: A Summary Calendar of Manuscript and Printed Materials Preserved in Europe, the United States of America, and Australasia*. Chalfont St. Giles: British Society for the History of Science, 1980.

Palmer, Eve. *The Plains of the Camdeboo*. New York: Viking, 1967.

Parsons, Neil. "El Negro/El Negre of Banyoles: Bushman from Bechuanaland, or Bechuana from Bushmanland?" Paper presented at the University of Botswana History and Archaeology Research Seminar, 30 Mar. 2000. http://ubh.tripod.com/news/banyol3.htm.

Peabody, Sue. *There Are No Slaves in France: The Political Culture of Race and Slavery in the Old Regime.* New York: Oxford University Press, 1996.

Peabody, Sue, and Tyler Stovall. *The Color of Liberty: Histories of Race in France.* Durham, N.C.: Duke University Press, 2003.

Porter, Roy. *London: A Social History.* Cambridge, Mass: Harvard University Press, 1995.

Pynchon, Thomas. *Mason & Dixon.* New York: Henry Holt, 1997.

Qureshi, Sadiah. "Displaying Sara Baartman, the 'Hottentot Venus.' " *History of Science* 42 (2004): 233–57.

Racinet, M. A. *Le costume historique.* Paris: Librairie de Firmin-Didot et Cie., 1888.

Rawley, James A. *London, Metropolis of the Slave Trade.* Foreword by David Eltis. Columbia: University of Missouri Press, 2003.

Reinharz, Shulamith. "Feminist Biography: The Pains, the Joys, the Dilemmas." In *Exploring Identity and Gender.* Vol. 2. of *The Narrative Study of Lives,* edited by Amia Lieblich and Ruthellen Josselson, 37–82. Thousand Oaks, Calif.: Sage, 1994.

Reiss, Benjamin. *The Showman and the Slave: Race, Death and Memory in Barnum's America.* Cambridge, Mass.: Harvard University Press, 2001.

Rendell, Jane. *The Pursuit of Pleasure: Gender, Space, and Architecture in Regency London.* New Brunswick, N.J.: Rutgers University Press, 2002.

Richardson, Joanna. *George the Magnificent: A Portrait of George IV.* New York: Harcourt Brace and World, 1966.

Richardson, John. *The Annals of London: A Year-by-Year Record of a Thousand Years of History.* Berkeley: University of California Press, 2000.

Ricoeur, Paul. *Time and Narrative.* 3 vols. Chicago: University of Chicago Press, 1984–88.

Rios, Theodore, and Kathleen Mullen Sands. *Telling a Good One: The Process of a Native American Collaborative Biography.* Lincoln: University of Nebraska Press, 2000.

Robinson, John Robert. *Old Q: A Memoir of William Douglas, Fourth Duke of Queensberry.* 1895. Reprint, Boston: Adamant Media Corporation, 2001.

Ross, Robert. *Beyond the Pale: Essays on the History of Colonial South Africa.* Hanover, N.H: Wesleyan University Press, 1993.

———. "The Occupation of Slaves in Eighteenth Century Cape Town." *Studies in the History of Cape Town* 2 (1980): 1–14.

———. *Status and Respectability in the Cape Colony: 1750–1870.* Cambridge: Cambridge University Press, 1999.

Rothfels, Nigel. "Aztecs, Aborigines, and Ape-People: Science and Freaks in Germany, 1850–1900." In *Freakery,* edited by Rosemarie Garland-Thomson, 158–72. New York: New York University Press, 1996.

Rubin, Gayle. "The Traffic in Women: Notes on the 'Political Economy' of Sex." In *Feminism and History,* edited by Joan Scott, 157–210. New York: Oxford University Press, 1996.

Samuelson, Meg. "Sarah Bartmann: Re-cast and Re-covered." In *Remembering the Nation, Dismembering Women? Stories of the South African Transition,* edited by Meg Samuelson, 85–118. Pietermaritzburg: University KwaZulu-Natal Press, 2007.

Scammell, Geoffrey V. *The First Imperial Age: European Overseas Expansion, 1400–1715.* London: Routledge, 1989.

Schapera, Isaac. *The Khoisan Peoples of South Africa.* London: Routledge, 1930.

Schiebinger, Londa. *Nature's Body: Gender in the Making of Modern Science.* Boston: Beacon Press, 1993.

Schiller, Francis. *Paul Broca: Founder of French Anthropology, Explorer of the Brain.* Berkeley: University of California Press, 1979.

Schwarz, Leonard. "London 1700–1840." In *The Cambridge Urban History of Britain,* edited by Peter Clark, 641–71. Cambridge: Cambridge University Press, 2000.

Scobie, Edward. *Black Britannia: A History of Blacks in Britain.* Chicago: Johnson, 1972.

Scott, Joan Wallach. *Only Paradoxes to Offer: French Feminists and the Rights of Man.* Cambridge, Mass.: Harvard University Press, 1996.

Scully, Pamela. *Liberating the Family? Gender and British Slave Emancipation in the Rural Western Cape, South Africa, 1823–1853.* Portsmouth, N.H.: Heinemann, 1997.

———. "Peripheral Visions: Heterography and Writing the Transnational Life of Sara Baartman." In *Transnational Lives,* edited by Desley Deacon, Penny Russell, and Angela Woollacott. Durham, N.C.: submitted to Duke University Press.

Scully, Pamela, and Clifton Crais. "Race and Erasure: Sara Baartman and Hendrik Cesars in Cape Town and London." *Journal of British Studies* 47 (Apr. 2008): 301–23.

Seigel, Jerrold. *The Idea of the Self: Thought and Experience in Western Europe since the Seventeenth Century.* New York: Cambridge University Press, 2005.

Sharpe, R. J. *The Law of Habeas Corpus.* Oxford: Clarendon Press, 1989.

Sharpley-Whiting, T. Denean. *Black Venus: Sexualized Savages, Primal Fears and Primitive Narratives in French.* Durham, N.C.: Duke University Press, 1999.

———. "The Dawning of Racial-Sexual Science: A One Woman Showing, a One Man Telling." In *Ethnography in French Literature,* edited by Buford Norman, 115–28. Amsterdam: Rodopi, 1996.

Shell, Robert. *Children of Bondage: A Social History of the Slave Society at the Cape of Good Hope, 1652–1838.* Hanover: University Press of New England, for Wesleyan University Press, 1994.

———. "The Lodge Women of Cape Town, 1671–1790." Paper presented to the conference "Slavery and Forces Labour." University of d'Avignon, 26–28 Oct. 2002.

Shostak, Marjorie. *Nisa: The Life and Words of a !Kung Woman.* Cambridge, Mass.: Harvard University Press, 1981.

Showalter, Elaine. *The Female Malady.* New York: Pantheon Books, 1985.

Shyllon, Folarin. *Blacks in Britain.* London: Oxford University Press, 1974.

Sibalis, Michael. "The Palais-Royal and the Homosexual Subculture of Nineteenth-Century Paris." In *Homosexuality and French History and Culture,* edited by Jeffrey Merrick and Michael Sibalis, 117–30. San Francisco: Harrington Park Press, 2001.

Skotnes, Pippa. *Miscast: Negotiating the Presence of the Bushmen.* Cape Town: University of Cape Town Press, 1996.

Smith, Andrew. "Keeping People on the Periphery: The Ideology of Social Hierarchies between Hunters and Herders." *Journal of Anthropological Archaeology* 17, no. 2 (June 1998): 201–15.

Smith, Jean Chandler. *Georges Cuvier: An Annotated Bibliography of His Published Works.* Washington, D.C.: Smithsonian Institution Press, 1993.

Smith, Sidonie, and Julia Watson, eds. *De/Colonizing the Subject: The Politics of Gender in Women's Autobiography.* Minneapolis: University of Minnesota Press, 1992.

Sontag, Susan. *Regarding the Pain of Others.* New York: Farrar, Straus and Giroux, 2003.

Sorabji, Richard. *Self: Ancient and Modern Insights about Individuality, Life, and Death.* New York: Oxford University Press, 2006.

Sòrgoni, Barbara. " 'Defending the Race': The Italian Reinvention of the Hottentot Venus during Fascism." *Journal of Modern Italian Studies* 8, no. 3 (2003): 411–24.

Stéphane, Bernard. *Dictionnaire des nom de rues.* Paris: Société des Editions Mènges, 2005.

Street, G. S. *Ghosts of Piccadilly.* London: Archibald Constable and Company, 1907.

Strother, Zoe. "Display of the Body Hottentot." In *Africans on Stage: Studies in Ethnological Showbusiness,* edited by Bernth Lindfors, 1–61. Bloomington: Indiana University Press, 1999.

Stuart, Andrea. *Showgirls.* London: J. Cape, 1996.

Taylor, Charles. *Sources of the Self: The Making of Modern Identity.* Cambridge, Mass.: Harvard University Press, 1989.

Tedlock, Barbara. *The Beautiful and the Dangerous: Encounters with the Zuni Indians.* New York: Viking, 1992.

———. "From Participant Observation to the Observation of Participation: The Emergence of Narrative Ethnography." *Journal of Anthropological Research* 47, no. 1 (1991): 69–94.

Thompson, Grace E. *The Patriot King: The Life of William IV.* New York: Dutton, 1933.

Thornton, John K. *Africa and Africans in the Making of the Atlantic World.* New York: Cambridge University Press, 1998.

Tobias, Philip. *Into the Past: A Memoir.* Johannesburg: Picador Africa and Wits University Press, 2006.

———. "Saartje Baartman: Her Life, Her Remains, and the Negotiations for Their Repatriation from France to South Africa." *South African Journal of Science* 98, nos. 3/4 (Mar./Apr. 2002), 107–10.

Tomlinson, Edward Murray. *A History of the Minories, London.* London: Smith, Elder and Co., 1907.

Toole-Stott, R. *Circus and Allied Arts: A World Bibliography.* Vol. 3. Derby, England: Harpur and Sons, 1962.

Torgovnick, Marianna. *Gone Primitive: Savage Intellects, Modern Lives.* Chicago: University of Chicago Press, 1990.

Townsend, Camilla. *Pocahontas and the Powhatan Dilemma.* New York: Hill and Wang, 2004.

Turner, Michael. J. "The Limits of Abolition: Government, Saints and the 'African Question,' c. 1780–1820." *English Historical Review* 112, no. 446 (Apr. 1997): 319–57.

Twyman, Michael. *Printing 1770–1970: An Illustrated History of Its Development and Uses in England.* London: Eyre and Spottiswoode, 1970.

Twyman, Michael, ed., with the assistance of Sally de Beaumont and Amoret Tanner. *The Encyclopedia of Ephemera: A Guide to the Fragmentary Documents of Everyday Life for the Collector, Curator, and Historian.* New York: Routledge, 2000.

Upham, Mansell. "From the Venus Sickness to the Hottentot Venus. Saartje Baartman and the Three Men in Her Life: Alexander Dunlop, Hendrik Caesar and Jean Riaux." *Quarterly Bulletin of the National Library of South Africa* 62, no. 1 (Jan.–Mar. 2007): 9–21.

Wagner-Martin, Linda. *Telling Women's Lives: The New Biography.* New Brunswick, N.J.: Rutgers University Press, 1994.

Wahrman, Dror. *The Making of the Modern Self.* New Haven, Conn.: Yale University Press, 2004.

Wallace-Sanders, Kimberly, ed. *Skin Deep, Spirit Strong: The Black Female Body in American Culture.* Ann Arbor: University of Michigan Press, 2002.

Watson, Julia, and Sidonie Smith. "Introduction: De/Colonization and the Politics of Discourse in Women's Autobiographical Practices." In *De/Colonizing the Subject: The Politics of Gender in Women's Autobiography,* edited by Sidonie Smith and Julia Watson, xiii–xxi. Minneapolis: University of Minnesota Press, 1992.

Wellcome Institute of the History of Medicine. *Commissioned Officers in the Medical Services of the British Army, 1660–1960.* 2 vols. London: Wellcome Historical Medical Library, 1968.

Wells, Julia. "Eva's Men: Gender and Power in the Establishment of the Cape of Good Hope, 1652–74." *Journal of African History* 39, no. 3 (1998): 417–37.

Wesley, Charles H. "The Neglected Period of Emancipation in Great Britain 1807–1823." *Journal of Negro History* 17, no. 2. (Apr. 1932): 156–79.

Wicomb, Zoë. *David's Story.* New York: Feminist Press at the City University of New York, 2001.

Wildenthal, Lora. *German Women for Empire.* Durham, N.C.: Duke University Press, 2001.

Wilson, Kathleen. *The Island Race: Englishness, Empire and Gender in the Eighteenth Century.* London: Routledge, 2003.

Worden, Nigel, and Gerald Groenewald. *Trials of Slavery: Selected Documents Concerning Slaves from the Criminal Records of the Council of Justice at the Cape of Good Hope, 1705–1794.* Cape Town: Van Riebeeck Society, 2005.

Worden, Nigel, Elizabeth van Heyningen, and Vivian Bickford-Smith. *Cape Town: The Making of a City.* Cape Town: David Philip, 1998.

Young, Jean. "The Re-objectification and Re-commodification of Saartjie Baartman in Suzan-Lori Parks's 'Venus.' " *African American Review* 31, no. 4 (1997): 699–708.

Youngquist, Paul. *Monstrosities: Bodies in British Romanticism.* Minneapolis: University of Minnesota Press, 2003.

Yunus, Ahmed. *Grandfather, Your Right Foot Is Missing.* Cape Town: Ahmed Productions, 1984.

Ziegler, Philip. *King William IV.* New York: Harper and Row, 1973.

INDEX